A GUIDE TO THE END
OF THE WORLD

Garland Reference Library of the Humanities, Vol. 1713

Religious Information Systems Series, Vol. 12

Religious Information Systems
J. Gordon Melton
General Editor

A GUIDE TO THE END OF THE WORLD:
POPULAR ESCHATOLOGY IN AMERICA

by
Jon R. Stone

RELIGIOUS INFORMATION SYSTEMS

Garland Publishing, Inc.
New York & London
1993

Library of Congress Cataloging-in-Publication Data

Stone, Jon R., 1959–
    A guide to the end of the world : popular eschatology in America /
by Jon R. Stone.
        p.   cm. — (Religious information systems ; vol. 12)
(Garland reference library of the humanities ; vol. 1713)
    ISBN 0-8153-1312-8 (alk. paper)
    1. Millennialism—United States—History. 2. Millennialism—United
States—Bibliography. 3. United States—Church history. 4. United
States—Church history—Bibliography.   I. Title. II. Series. III. Series:
Religious information systems series ; vol. 12.
BR517.S76   1993
236'.9—dc20   92-35100
                                                                      CIP

Printed on acid-free, 250-year-life paper
Manufactured in the United States of America

For my nieces and nephews:

Lauren, Shawna,
Christopher, Brenton, Zachary, and Bethany

CONTENTS

INTRODUCTION

Since the day Jesus Christ ascended into the heavens with the promise to reappear in the Last Days, Christians have expected his return and watched for signs of his second coming. Even before Jesus left, his disciples, eager for the restoration of Israel's kingdom and glory, asked him when all these things would come to pass. But Jesus waived their question, remarking instead: "It is not for you to know times or epochs which the Father has fixed by his own authority" (Acts 1:7). In other words, it is the work of the kingdom that should consume your interest, not its future consummation.

Jesus' stern admonition did not discourage his disciples, however, nor did it discourage many later followers from expecting his soon return or the arrival of his coming millennial kingdom of peace. Indeed, since Jesus' time, many Christians have tried to discern the exact date of his second coming (the parousia) and, with it, the end of all things (the eschaton).

But as time passed, and as the Christian church emerged from centuries of persecution to become one of the strongest organizations to survive the disintegrating Roman empire, the Christian religion slowly began to shed its apocalyptic excesses. By the time Christian bishops convened at the Council of Nicea in 325 C.E., the belief in Christ's second coming had become one of the cardinal doctrines of the Christian church, but eschatological concern was no longer of central interest to Christians, both Greek and Roman. Expectation of Christ's imminent return to this world had taken second place to the business of running the kingdom of God on earth. Still, from time to time there were periods of heightened millennial expectation. These periods of expectation were generally short lived, typically coming at times of social and political turmoil.

In modern times, the millennial hope has been a notable and an enduring strand in the fabric of American religion, especially Protestant. It is, as Catherine L. Albanese once remarked, the "red thread" in the grand tapestry of American religious history. Indeed, seemingly every popular religious movement in American history (e.g., Shakers, Mormons,

Adventists, Fundamentalists, and even the "New Age") has sprung from the soil of the New World with the expectation that a golden age -- a millennium of peace -- was on the horizon, ready to burst forth and usher in a new world order.

But while the millennialist impulse has been a strong force within American history, the direction that that impulse has taken has differed markedly among Protestants of varying shades. For some groups, the historical process has been speeding forward in an upward progression, moving naturally toward a "harmonic convergence" that would one day unite nature and humanity with supernature and the transcendent. For others, however, the road to the millennial kingdom of peace has been an increasingly downward spiral -- a free fall -- towards the complete destruction of the present evil age. The former vision of history and the social order tends to be optimistic, while the latter view tends to be pessimistic, bordering on nihilism. In the latter view, however, all is not doom and destruction. Individuals who do repent of evil deeds and embrace righteousness can still hope for salvation from the fiery pit of hell or annihilation. Society itself, however, is irretrievably lost; there is no saving the world from an inevitable, apocalyptic denouement.

The Nature and Organization of this Book

Since the turn of the century, popular eschatology (or millennialism) has developed into somewhat of a cottage industry, spinning out books and pamphlets at a dizzyingly rapid rate of speed. As a movement, American Millennialism has more or less been a loose collection of assorted conservative Protestants of varying stripes, clustered around a few key individuals, and held together by the belief that these were indeed the Last Days spoken about in the prophetic visions recorded in the Bible.

But one might well ask, How did these millennialists come by their conviction that their days were the Last Days?; and, How are their convictions reinforced and strengthened over time and not weakened through renewed disappointment? To put it more simply, How does the conviction that Christ may return *today* remain convincing from one generation to the next? One clue to the present tense "perhaps today!" conviction of American millennialists can be found in the common interpretive frame of reference from which both pre- and post-millennialists view the world. As one can detect from their writings, millennialists tend to share the belief that the Bible, though a collection of Hebrew and Greek texts, is essentially *one* book, written with *one* purpose in mind; it is to be read and interpreted, therefore, as though it were one book with one central message. What is more, millennialists believe that the whole text of the Christian Bible is the inspired word of God and, as such, is to be read and understood as literally, not figuratively, true.

What is more, for both pre- and post-millennialists, who look forward to a literal millennial kingdom on this earth, the Bible is not merely a sacred book that helps people live to the glory of God and for the betterment of humanity. It is much more. The Bible is a blueprint for history, a history predetermined by the will of God, a history revealed by holy prophets who have been to the mountain and seen what lies ahead of the journey. To millennialists, then, the Bible is not simply a blueprint that tells us how history should proceed; rather, it records the processes through which history will unfold -- however ambagious a path history may take and however ambiguous its meaning may appear.

As we will discover in the literature discussed in this book, millennialists often read the Bible as if it were the daily newspaper, comparing world events with sacred text. By matching prophetic signs with historical facts, millennialists attempt to divine the course of history and, ultimately, to predict the end of history. Indeed, as premillennialists have been wont to say, Bible prophecy is history written in advance.

To demonstrate this point and illustrate this prophetical reading of history by premillennialists, I have divided the literature of popular American eschatology into ten periods, each period influenced by several key historical events and shaped by a few leading figures. The first period of literature, roughly 1798-1848, witnessed the renewed interest in Bible prophecy, sparked by events during the reign of Napoleon Bonaparte and the consequent rise of nationalism in Europe. It was also during this period that the Jews were emancipated from the ghettoes of Europe, to begin their slow migration back to their ancient homeland in Palestine. These events prompted a flurry of British and, later, American millennialist speculation about the impending millennium of Christ. The literature of this period also reflects growing interest in adventism among American Protestants generally.

The second period (1849-1877) began roughly after the Great Disappointment, when William Miller's prediction of Christ's second coming in October 1844 did not take place. Plymouth Brethren John Nelson Darby's dispensational theology emerged during this period as well, gaining a number of devoted followers in the United States.

The third period (1878-1895) saw the organization of a series of Bible and Prophecy conferences, the most famous of those being the Niagara Conferences. The programs of most Bible and Prophecy conferences focused most eschatological discussion on current events in the light of Bible prophecy.

The emergence of World Zionism in the 1890s and the liberation of Palestine by the British during the First World War frame the fourth period of millenarian literary activity (1896-1918).

During the fifth period (1919-1939), world events took a sharp turn for the worst. Inflation, followed by worldwide depression, devastated the economies of a Europe whose population had been decimated by the deadly military machines of the First World War. The economic downturn and massive shortages in jobs and basic commodities directly contributed to both the rise of fascism in Italy in the 1920s and the advent of German national socialism (the Nazis), and, to a lesser extent, Russian Stalinism in the 1930s. These various forms of totalitarianism would once more hurl the world recklessly into the destructive path of another total war.

The sixth period of millenarian literary activity began during the second of this century's world wars and ended with the establishment of the Jewish state of Israel in 1948.

The seventh (1949-1957) and eighth (1958-1966) periods discussed in this book were marked by the global threat of nuclear holocaust brought about by the Cold War between the United States and the Soviet Union. The division between East and West, and their respective support of the Arabs and Israelis, set in motion a great flurry of speculation as to when the East/West tensions would give vent to nuclear Armageddon and, with it, the end of the world.

Limited war in the Middle East between Arabs and Israelis in 1967 and 1973 highlighted the ninth period of millennial activity (1967-1978). Peace initiatives, the recent war in the Persian Gulf region, and renewed Mideast peace talks mark the tenth and current period of popular eschatological literature that this volume highlights (1979-1992).

A separate section of selected journals and periodicals will follow section ten. For comparative purposes, I have also included a section listing works by amillennial, post-millennial, and anti-premillennialist authors.

In addition, a separate section of selected biographical sketches of the more influential millennialists in the evangelical tradition (*pre, post,* and *a*) will appear at the end of this volume as well.

To avoid the fatigue of repetition when referring to individuals within popular eschatological circles, I will use interchangeably the terms millennial, millennialist, millenarian, millenarianist, and premillennial, premillennialist. At times I will also use the terms dispensational and dispensationalist, but sparingly, as not all premillennialists hold a dispensational view of the Bible and history. When mentioning individuals who are not premillennial, I will use the specific terms amillennial and post-millennial.

A Note on the Sources

Although in compiling this *Guide to the End of the World* I have attempted to be as comprehensive as possible, many gaps still remain. I have tried to stay within the mainstream evangelical tradition, a tradition that since the turn of the century has almost wholly embraced some type of premillennial view of the endtimes. The multiplication of evangelical premillennial works after 1900 and the numerous reprintings of their works seem to bear this observation out.

In addition, it will be quite noticeable that in listing the bibliographic entries neither have I included the page sizes of the books nor have I distinguished between books and pamphlets. There are two reasons for this: first, almost all of the works listed in this volume are easily obtainable from the several libraries listed below through InterLibrary Loan services; second, in the case of pamphlets, I have included only those works which have been authored by the more prominent millennialist writers or those booklets that have influenced the development of American millennialism within their respective periods. Regarding pamphlets, I have listed only a score or two of them, all of which are bound and catalogued.

One problem I found was in separating out materials that do not properly "fit" into the dispensationalist-millenarian camp. Much to my fascination (and annoyance), I found that many works did not fall neatly into one category or another. For instance, some authors have changed their views over time, sometimes partially and sometimes even completely (e.g., Philip Mauro). Not uncommon, others have tended to fall in between conflicting millennialist positions. Curious as these inconsistencies may be, it is not the purpose of this work to unravel these intricate knots but simply to point them out wherever appropriate. Happily, I leave the kinks for others to work out and untangle.

Dividing the literature by periods, as I have, presents its own set of problems. For one thing, many of the books are not dated, while others have been reprinted numerous times, making exact placement a guessing game at best. In these instances, I have tried my best to place these works within their appropriate eras, basing my decision on internal evidence (e.g., the context) and external evidence (e.g., the inclusive dates of their authors). To be sure, this method is not fool-proof; I grant that in many cases I have undoubtedly made the wrong decision where to place these undated and reprinted books. However, I think it the better solution to either listing these works separately at the end of the text or leaving them out altogether.

One last comment about the bibliographic entries in this volume. I have intentionally excluded Adventist works and writings from groups not generally included within the mainstream evangelical tradition, groups such as British-Israelists, Jehovah's Witnesses, and the Latter-Day Saints (Mormons). I plan to examine this body of literature in a projected companion volume to this present work.

Several large holdings of Protestant dispensationalist and millennialist writings exist conveniently spread throughout the continental United States. The three major centers are: Biola University in La Mirada, California; Dallas Theological Seminary in Texas; and the Moody Bible Institute in downtown Chicago. There are also sizable holdings at Grace Theological Seminary in Winona Lake, Indiana, and at the Philadelphia College of the Bible. There are smaller collections at Westmont College in the hills above Santa Barbara and at Wheaton College in the Chicago suburbs, among many others.

In addition, many of the more important works listed in this book can be found as part of the collection at the Institute for the Study of American Religion. In preparing this work, I used the ISAR collection extensively. Access to this collection can be obtained through application to: Director, ISAR, Santa Barbara, CA 93190-0709.

Acknowledgments

This project began several years ago while I was still a doctoral student in Religious Studies at the University of California at Santa Barbara. If I had had any inkling then of the deeply cavernous and deceptive labyrinths that lay beneath the seemingly cohesive evangelical premillennial subculture, I probably would not have committed myself to such an insanely frustrating task as this one at times became. There is certainly much more there than meets the eye.

Dr. J. Gordon Melton, Director of the American Institute for the Study of American Religion, has been especially helpful to me and I wish here to express my appreciation to him for his time and for the unlimited use of his Institute's collection. He and his collection are an invaluable resource for the study of American religious traditions.

I would also like to acknowledge the reference librarians and staff at Biola University, the Billy Graham Center Archives, the Moody Bible Institute, Westmont College, and Wheaton College for their assistance. I would especially like to thank Faye Denny, Susan Johnson, Beth Patton, and Rodney Vliet (all reference librarians or associates of the Rose Library at Biola), Gerald E. Lincoln (associate director of the Morgan Library at Grace Theological Seminary), and Laurie Johnson (a reference librarian at Moody), for going out of their way to make my task easier.

I would also like to acknowledge receipt of a generous travel grant from the Institute for the Study of American Evangelicals to visit the Billy Graham Center Archives, with especial thanks to Larry Eskridge for his friendly assistance (D. G. Hart providing comic relief).

Last of all, I would like to thank my family and friends in Southern California who put up with me during my many visits to complete this project, especially after my sudden and reluctant move to the Iowa prairie in 1990. By name: Robert and Bobbie Stone, Richard and Dawn Stone, David and Mary Stone, R. Bruce Evans, Phillip E. Hammond, John and Carrie Birmingham, and Thomas and Karin Bryan. It is to my nieces and nephews, however, that I lovingly dedicate this book.

Jon R. Stone
University of Northern Iowa
Cedar Falls, Iowa
August 1992

A Guide to the End of the World

The created World is but a small Parenthesis in Eternity.

-- Sir Thomas Browne

PART ONE

BACKGROUND DISCUSSION ON POPULAR ESCHATOLOGY IN AMERICA

In its most basic sense, eschatology refers to the study of last things or of the endtimes. Just as time began with the creative act of God, Christians believe that time will end with a final recreative act of the Divine. Eschatology, then, deals with the conclusion of time and the processes through which that ending will take shape and effect. In Christian eschatology, Jesus plays a central role in the endtimes in that his return coincides the creation of a new world order.

Of the various types of Christian eschatologies that have existed throughout the centuries, the most persistent and currently the most pervasive is millennialism. In simplest terms, Christian millennialism is the belief that Christ will someday return, bringing with him peace to the earth for a thousand years (hence "millennial" or "one thousand years"). But even here there is disagreement among millennialists. The point Christian millennialists have typically quibbled over has not been *whether* Jesus would return but *when* and *how* his return would come about -- the timing and order of events.

Post-millennialists believe that Christ will return *after* the millennial age, the success of the Gospel of Peace having transformed the social order. Until the mid-nineteenth century, the post-millennial position held the greatest sway among most Protestants.

Premillennialists, on the other hand, believe that Christ will return *before* the millennial age to reign personally from the ancient city of Jerusalem, thus himself initiating the golden era of peace. Prior to Christ's return, however, the social and moral order will decline, making peace impossible apart from divine intervention. By the twentieth century, this premillennial view became the more popular position of the two among the mainstream evangelical churches, almost completely eclipsing post-millennialism.

A third position held among American Protestants is amillennialism or non-millennialism, the belief that there will be no millennium, no earthly reign of Christ. Individuals holding this view reject the idea of an actual thousand-year period of earthly peace. Indeed, amillennialists believe that the so-called millennium is not some future period in human history but is, in fact, the church age. The millennium, amillennialists argue, is not future; the millennium is now. When Christ does return, say the amillennialists, he will come not to establish peace on earth but to end human history altogether, to usher in Eternity.

Not surprisingly, amillennialism has been the least popular of the three positions, tending, as it does, to "spiritualize" Bible prophecy, thus rendering the dramatic doomsday prophecies of the Bible as merely symbolic. Although three opposing positions exist, there is at least one point on which premillennialists and post-millennialists will agree: that there will be a millennium, an actual 1,000-year period of peace. The differences, then, are essentially over chronology and logistics.

The Premillennial Vision of the Last Days

Because the most popular and prolific form of millennialism is premillennial (often mixed with a dispensational view of the Bible and history), this volume will focus almost exclusively on the writings of modern Protestant premillennialists. Central to the premillennialists' understanding of the end times is their belief that the Christian scriptures predict the events of the Last Days and the signs that herald the second coming of Christ. To apprehend these signs, say the millenarians, believers need only read their Bibles. But in truth, this is not as simple as it sounds. For one thing, millennialists come to the Bible with a set of interpretive assumptions or codes. One assumption they make about the Bible is that it must be read literally, not figuratively, and thus its symbols are not merely figures of speech but codes that help them unlock the mysteries of future world events.

Premillennialism is a religious subculture. For this reason its literature tends to be highly idiomatic and jargon-laden, written, as it were, by insiders for insiders. Millennialist authors make constant reference to biblical themes and often punctuate their writings with biblical imageries and symbols, making their works rather inaccessible to the uninitiated. What follows, then, is a brief look at some of the key Bible passages referenced by millennial writers from which they draw their premillennial endtimes views. I will outline the traditional premillennial reading of several passages from the Book of Daniel as well as a passage from the Prophet Ezekiel, both of which claim to record visions of the latter days. I will also give a summary of the premillennialist reading of the Book of Revelation, the central text millennialists look to for their elaborate chronology of the Last Days.

King Nebuchadnezzar's Dream

The first passage is from Daniel 2 in which Daniel offers an interpretation of a disturbing dream dreamed by the Babylonian king Nebuchadnezzar. In his dream, a great image appeared before the king. This great image had a head of gold, arms and a chest of silver, a belly and thighs of bronze, legs of iron, and feet of iron mixed with clay. Suddenly, a huge rock appeared in the sky, one not hewn by human hands. The rock struck the image at its base, destroying it utterly.

In his interpretation, Daniel told the king that the head represents the king himself and his own kingdom. After him, however, there would rise three successive kingdoms, all weaker than the one before. The last kingdom, the one of iron and iron and clay, would be destroyed by the huge stone.

Traditionally, this passage has been interpreted as referring to the four great empires of the ancient world: Babylon, Medea-Persia, Greece, and Rome, the last empire being overtaken by the spread of Christendom. While many scholars have held that the feet of iron and clay were merely an extension of the Roman empire in its long period of decline, contemporary millenarians have taught that the feet do not symbolize ancient Rome but represent a revived Roman empire in the Latter days, in the form of a ten-nation confederation. The ten toes, we are told, represent the ten nations of this confederation.

To the uninitiated, this interpretation of Nebuchadnezzar's dream is not obvious from a simple reading of the text. Fifteen hundred years have passed since the end of the old Roman Empire, making a "revival" difficult to imagine. In addition, the text speaks of these empires as following one after the other; in fact, each conquered its predecessor. Neither would hold true for this predicted revived Roman Empire. To avoid this inconsistency, millennialists often point to the Roman Catholic Church as the link between the old Roman Empire and its endtimes revival.

Daniel's Vision

In Daniel 7, Daniel himself has a vision in which he sees four creatures coming out of the sea: a winged lion; a bear chewing on three ribs; a winged four-headed leopard; and a dreadful creature unlike the previously three with ten horns and iron teeth. From the head of the fourth creature springs up a little horn that tears out three horns from the original ten. This little horn has "eyes like the eyes of a man, and a mouth speaking great things" (7:8). As it turns out, this little horn speaks blasphemy against God. From Daniel we also learn that this little horn is destined to rule for a short span of time, that is "for a time, two times, and half a time" (7:25). After the allotted period, the little horn is judged by Heaven and destroyed.

Traditionally, scholars have seen this vision as essentially parallel to Nebuchadnezzar's dream in chapter two of Daniel, with the identity of the fourth creature less than certain. However, the Premillennial gloss on this passage holds that the little horn in the vision is the Antichrist of the Last Days, a ruler springing up from the ruins of ancient Rome to rule a revived Roman Empire. According to the premillennialist view, in the Last Days this revived Roman Empire under the Antichrist will persecute believers and put them to death, as did the former Roman Empire.

This interpretation illustrates the premillennialist's unitive understanding of the Bible. "Antichrist" is a New Testament designation for the evil spiritual forces in the world (1John 2:18), with no apparent parallel in the Hebrew Bible (i.e., the Old Testament). But Millenarians, in their attempt to read history in and through the pages of the Bible, identify the "little horn" of Daniel with the "antichrist" of the Johannine epistle and with the "Beast" of the Revelation (13:1), as well as with St. Paul's "man of sin" (2 Thessalonians 2:3, KJV). This hermeneutic of linking Old and New Testament prophecies is repeated again and again by millennialists, often unscrupulously. To be sure, the writer of the Revelation drew many of his images from the Hebrew prophetic tradition, making the millennialist hermeneutic understandable. But this interpretive method, when applied indiscriminately to the rest of the Bible, is not particularly reliable or sound.

The Seventy Weeks of Daniel

The last text I will discuss from the Book of Daniel records another vision by the prophet Daniel. This text is perhaps the most crucial passage supporting the dispensational premillennial position. It is also fraught with the most interpretive problems of the three.

In this passage, Daniel 9:24-27, Daniel is told by an angel:

> Seventy weeks are determined upon thy people and upon thy holy city.... Know therefore and understand, that from the going forth of the commandment to restore and to build Jerusalem unto the Messiah the Prince shall be seven weeks, and threescore and two weeks.... And after threescore and two weeks shall Messiah be cut off, but not for himself: and the people of the prince that shall come shall destroy the city and the sanctuary.... And he shall confirm a covenant with many for one week: and in the midst of the week he shall cause the sacrifice and the oblation to cease, and for the overspreading of abominations he shall make it desolate... (KJV).

This text is known as Daniel's vision of the Seventy Weeks. The weeks are traditionally understood to represent weeks or sets of years, the calculation being 70 sets of seven years or a total of 490 years.

Christian scholars over the centuries have usually understood this prophecy as a prediction of the Messiah's coming and subsequent crucifixion (i.e., "cut off"), taking place some 483 years after Jerusalem and the temple were restored (or ca. 444 B.C.E.). Calculating from a lunar cycle, Christian scholars have dated the sixty-ninth week of Daniel as having occurred some time on or near 32 C.E.

But what of the final week of years? Traditionally, the final week was assumed to have elapsed during the first years of the early Church. But millenarians have not been satisfied with the traditional interpretation, regarding the last week of years as future, the church age being somewhat of a parentheses between the 69th and 70th weeks. For premillennialists, the final week of the seventy sevens corresponds to the seven-year period of tribulation spoken of in the Book of Revelation (see Revelation 12 and 13).

According to the premillennialist view, during this last week of years, a third temple in Jerusalem will be built on the site where the great Mosque of Omar presently sits. Animal sacrifices will be reinstituted and Jews from around the world will regather in Jerusalem to celebrate this momentous occasion. At the midpoint of this seven-year period, however, the rebuilt temple will be desecrated by the Antichrist, who will erect an image of himself in the temple and command the people to worship him in place of God. People loyal to this Antichrist will then be marked with the number 666. This action will bring about the wrath of Heaven and, ultimately, the destruction of the world.

Ezekiel's Vision of Gog and Magog

Ezekiel 38 and 39 are taken by the millennialists to refer to the future apocalyptic Battle of Armageddon and the countries that array themselves against Israel. In this section of Ezekiel, the prophet receives a vision by which he predicts that a great army from the north, led by Gog, from the land of Magog, prince of Rosh, Meshech, and Tubal, will invade Israel. Though a massive force of men and materiel, the armies of Gog will be repulsed and destroyed by the armies of Heaven.

Traditionally, biblical scholars have not been able to pinpoint with any certainty the identity of the northern kingdom to which Ezekiel refers. Many posit that because Ezekiel had been a prophet of Northern Israel (Samaria), his declamation might therefore be against the Assyrians, a vast and ruthless empire on Israel's northern border.

Millennialists assume, however, that Ezekiel is seeing a vision of the endtimes. Hence, the references he makes are not to nations and peoples in in his own time but to those in existence in the latter days. Working from this assumption, premillennialists try to match Ezekiel's geographical place names with modern countries and regions, looking for national and linguistic parallels to guide them. For example, a long line of noted premillennial writers, beginning with C. I. Scofield and including M. R. De Haan, Harry Rimmer, John Walvoord, Hal Lindsay, and Mike Evans, see striking parallels, among others, between the names *Rosh*, *Meshech*, and *Tubal* and the modern places *Russia*, *Moscow*, and *Tobolsk*. Arno Gaebelein saw a striking parallel between *Gomer* and *Germany*. Others have seen a linguistic connection between *Togarmah* and the *Turkoman* hordes (the Turks) or, with some strain, *Armenia* (Tog-armah = tribe of Armenia). To be sure, the average Christian probably could not pick up his or her Bible and connect these ancient place names with modern countries, at least not without the same a set of interpretive assumptions (or codes) that these students of prophecy bring with them to their reading the Bible.

The Revelation of St. John

The last text that one needs to understand in order to comprehend the literature of popular Protestant millennialism is the final book of the New Testament: the Apocalypse or Revelation of St. John (or simply, the Revelation).

As stated before, *premillennial* refers to the belief that human history is fast approaching an end point, an end that will be marked by increasing social and political turmoil. Only the physical return of Christ to this world and the establishment of an earthly kingdom will bring lasting peace to the world. Though premillennialists do not agree on all the details of how the endtimes will be played out, they are generally in agreement over the order events will take, as detailed in the highly symbolic Book of Revelation. A brief overview of this book and the vision it contains of the Last Days will shed some light on the premillennial view of the endtimes.

According to millennialists, the first event in the endtime scenario will be the rapture of true believers from the earth. The dead will be resurrected and, with the living, will be transported upwards to meet Jesus in the air. With the evacuation of the saints, the Holy Spirit will also depart from the earth. Whatever moral restraint existed prior to the rapture of the church and God's removal of the Holy Spirit from the earth will no longer exist, allowing men and women to pursue their evil human passions without restriction. Accordingly, a period of wickedness unparalleled in human history will begin. This period is generally referred to as the Tribulation.

The Tribulation will last seven years. During this period, a world ruler will emerge from one of the countries of the old Roman Empire. This world ruler (the Antichrist), assisted by a religious leader (the false prophet), will bring a semblance of peace to the earth. In effect, Antichrist will solve all the world's problems: social, political, economic, and religious.

Into this new united world order, two heaven-sent prophets will appear (perhaps Moses and Elijah), whose presence will bring about the conversion of 144,000 Jews to faith in Christ. These 144,000 converted Jews will, in turn, preach the Gospel to the nations. Enraged, the Antichrist will initiate a general persecution against Christians, ordering all citizens of the world to take an oath of loyalty and be branded with the mark 666. Those who refuse the mark will be hunted down as outlaws and executed.

At this point in the drama of the Last Days, events take a turn for the worse as God pours out his wrath on the earth. Wars, famine, pestilence, earthquakes, and other natural disasters will plague the earth for the remaining three and a half years of the Tribulation period. Frustrated over these great catastrophes and losing his grip on power, the Antichrist will order the invasion of Israel and the destruction of the Jewish nation. With a vast army, the world ruler will invade Palestine, where he and his allies will be met by the Jews at the valley of Megiddo. At the fateful moment, Christ and the armies of Heaven will appear and, with a single stroke, will completely annihilate the armies of the Antichrist. The massacre will be total, leaving only the birds to prey on the bodies of the slaughtered warriors, picking their mutilated carcasses clean to the bone.

After the Battle of Armageddon, both the Antichrist and his false prophet will be cast into the lake of fire. Jesus, now enthroned in Jerusalem, will judge the nations, separating out the righteous from the unrighteous. Sinners will be cast into the lake of fire. Satan, Christ's archenemy, will be chained and then cast into a pit for a thousand years, the duration of the millennium. It is at this point in the endtimes scenario that the millennium of peace will begin. Christ will rule the earth from the throne of King David in Jerusalem and the prophecy of Isaiah will be fulfilled: "the wolf will lay down with the lamb and a child shall lead them" (11:6).

After Jesus has reigned for 1,000 years, Satan will escape his bondage and gather an army to make one last attempt to defeat Christ and win the epic struggle between good and evil. But Satan and his followers will be defeated for the last time. They will then be cast forever into the lake of fire. After this, God will pass final judgment on the lost, who will be condemned to eternal hell. The last event in the apocalyptic drama will be the destruction of the old creation and the recreation of a new heaven and a new earth.

As before, the specific details of the premillennial chronology of the Last Days vary from author to author but the order of events is largely the same. Some millennialists, however, hold that the vision of St. John is a vision of the church age from the first century to the consummation of time. Amillennialists, for their part, believe that the Revelation of St. John is not a sketch of the Last Days but merely an exhortation to the Christian to keep the faith, no matter what the trial or tribulation.

Whatever the case may be, it is the premillennialist position, with its literalistic and futuristic interpretation of Bible prophecy, that has remained the most popular and the most pervasive eschatological view over the past century. While this highly literalistic reading of the Bible is at times difficult for those outside the system to follow, let alone comprehend, at the same time, in order for one to understand and appreciate the literature of American premillennialism, it becomes necessary for one to grasp the millennialist's attempt to make sense of highly symbolic and enigmatic language through a literal hermeneutic. If anything, their literalistic assumptions allow premillennialists to attach clear meaning to ambiguous predictions from unrelated passages, fitting them into their prophetic picture of the Last Days.

REFERENCES AND SOURCES

1. Alnor, William M. *Soothsayers of the Second Advent.* Old Tappan, NJ: Power Books, 1989.

2. Banki, Judith. *Christian Responses to the Yom Kippur War.* New York: The American Jewish Committee, 1974.

3. Bass, Clarence B. *Backgrounds to Dispensationalism: Its Historical Genesis & Ecclesiastical Implications.* Grand Rapids, MI: Baker Book House, 1978.

4. Barkun, Michael. *Crucible of the Millennium: The Burned-Over District of New York in the 1840s.* Syracuse, New York: Syracuse University Press, 1986.

5. _____. *Disaster and the Millennium.* Syracuse, NY: Syracuse University Press, 1986.

6. Beegle, Dewey M. *Prophecy and Prediction.* Ann Arbor: Pryor Pettengill, 1978.

7. Berry, George R. *Premillennialism and Old Testament Prediction: A Study in Interpretation.* Chicago: University of Chicago Press, 1929.

8. Bettis, Joseph and S. K. Johannesen (eds.). *The Return of the Millennium.* International Religious Foundation, 1984.

9. Bryant, M. Darrol and Donald W. Dayton (eds.). *The Coming Kingdom: Essays in American Millennialism and Eschatology.* Barryton, New York: International Religious Foundation; New York: Rose of Sharon Press, 1983.

10. Case, Shirley Jackson. *The Millennial Hope: A Phase of War-Time Thinking.* Chicago: University of Chicago Press, 1918.

11. _____. *The Revelation of John.* Chicago: University of Chicago Press, 1919.

12. Cherry, Conrad (ed.). *God's New Israel: Religious Interpretations of American Destiny.* Englewood Cliffs, NJ: Prentice-Hall, Inc., 1971.

13. Clabaugh, Gary K. *Thunder on the Right: The Protestant Fundamentalists.* Chicago: Nelson-Hall Co., 1974.

14. Clouse, Robert G. (ed.). *The Meaning of Millennium: Four Views.* Downers Grove, IL: InterVarsity Press, 1977.

15. Coad, F. Roy. *A History of the Brethren Movement* (2nd ed.). Exeter: The Paternoster Press, 1976.

16. _____. *Prophetic Developments: With Particular Reference to the Early Brethren Movement.* Middlesex: Christian Brethren Research Fellowship Publications, 1966.

17. Cohn, Norman. *The Pursuit of the Millennium* (rev. & enlarged ed.). New York: Oxford University Press, 1970.

18. Cross, Whitney R. *The Burned-Over District: The Social and Intellectual History of Enthusiastic Religion in Western New York, 1800-1850.* Ithaca: Cornell University Press, 1950.

19. Dollar, George W. *A History of Fundamentalism in America.* Greenville, SC: Bob Jones University Press, 1973.

20. Ehlert, Arnold D. *A Bibliographic History of Dispensationalism.* Grand Rapids, MI: Baker Book House, 1965.

21. Festinger, Leon, et al. *When Prophecy Fails.* Minneapolis, MN: University of Minnesota Press, 1956.

22. Fishman, Hertzel. *American Protestantism and a Jewish State.* Detroit: Wayne State University Press, 1973.

23. Gaebelein, Frank E. *The Story of the Scofield Reference Bible, 1909-1959.* New York: Oxford University Press, 1959.

24. Gaustad, Edwin Scott (ed.). *The Rise of Adventism: A Commentary on the Social and Religious Ferment of Mid-Nineteenth Century America.* New York: Harper & Row, 1974.

25. Glasson, T. Francis. *His Appearing and His Kingdom: The Christian Hope in the Light of Its History.* London: Epworth, 1953.

26. Glick, Edward B. *The Triangular Connection: America, Israel, and American Jews.* London: George Allen & Unwin, 1982.

27. Grier, W. J. *The Momentous Event: A Discussion of Scripture Teaching on the Second Advent and Questions Related Thereto.* Belfast: The Evangelical Book Shop, 1945; London: The Banner of Truth Trust, 1970.

28. Griffin, William (ed.). *Endtime: The Doomsday Catalog.* New York: Collier Books, 1979.

29. Gritsch, Eric W. *Born Againism: Perspectives on a Movement.* Philadelphia: Fortress Press, 1982.

30. Harrison, John F. C. *The Second Coming: Popular Millenarianism, 1750-1850.* New Brunswick, NJ: Rutgers University Press, 1979.

31. Hatch, Nathan O. *The Sacred Cause of Liberty: Republican Thought and the Millennium in Revolutionary New England.* New Haven: Yale University Press, 1977.

32. *Israel According to Holy Scriptures.* Cedar Rapids, IA: Ingram Press, n.d.

33. Johnson, Paul E. *A Shopkeeper's Millennium: Society and Revivals in Rochester, New York, 1815-1837.* New York: Hill & Wang, 1978.

34. Jorstad, Erling. *The Politics of Doomsday.* Nashville: Abingdon Press, 1970.

35. Kraus, C. Norman. *Dispensationalism in America: Its Rise and Development.* Richmond: John Knox Press, 1958.

36. Malachy, Yona. *American Fundamentalism & Israel: The Relation of Fundamentalist Churches to Zionism*. Jerusalem: The Institute of Contemporary Jewry, The Hebrew University of Jerusalem, 1978.

37. Marsden, George M. *Fundamentalism and American Culture*. New York: Oxford University Press, 1980.

38. Miller, Irving. *Israel, the Eternal Ideal*. New York: Farrar, Strauss, and Cudahy, 1955.

39. Minear, Paul S. *Christian Hope and the Second Coming*. Philadelphia: Westminster Press, 1954.

40. Moorhead, James H. *Protestants and the Civil War, 1860-1869*. New Haven: Yale University Press, 1975.

41. Nijim, Basheer K. (ed.). *American Church Politics and the Middle East*. Belmont, MA: Association of Arab-American University Graduates, 1982.

42. Oesterley, William Oscar Emil. *The Doctrine of the Last Things: Jewish and Christian*. London: John Murray, 1908.

43. Peters, Ted. *Fear, Faith, and the Future: Affirming Christian Hope in the Face of Doomsday Prophecies*. Minneapolis: Augsburg Publishing House, 1980.

44. _____. *Futures, Human and Divine*. Atlanta: John Knox Press, 1978.

45. Pragai, Michael J. *Faith & Fulfilment: Christians and the Return to the Promised Land*. London: Valentine, Mitchell & Co., 1985.

46. Pruter, Karl. *Jewish Christians in the United States, A Bibliography*. New York: Garland Publishing Inc., 1987.

47. Rausch, David A. *Arno C. Gaebelein, 1861-1945, Irenic Fundamentalist and Scholar*. New York: The Edwin Mellen Press, 1983.

48. _____. *Messianic Judaism: Its History, Theology & Polity*. New York: The Edwin Mellen Press, 1982.

49. _____. *Zionism Within Early American Fundamentalism, 1878-1918.* New York: The Edwin Mellen Press, 1979.

50. Richards, Jeffrey J. *The Promise of Dawn: The Eschatology of Lewis Sperry Chafer.* Lanham, MD: University Press of America, 1991.

51. Rist, Martin. *The Modern Reader's Guide to the Book of Revelation.* New York: Association Press, 1961.

52. Robinson, John Arthur Thomas. *In the End, God: A Study of the Christian Doctrine of the Last Things.* London: James Clarke, 1958.

53. _____. *Jesus and His Coming: The Emergence of a Doctrine.* London: SCM Press LTD, 1957.

54. Rubinsky, Yuri and Ian Wiseman. *A History of the End of the World.* New York: Quill, 1982.

55. Rutgers, William H. *Premillennialism in America.* Goes, Holland: Oosterbaan & Le Cointre, 1930.

56. St. Clair, Michael J. *Millenarian Movements in Historical Context.* New York: Garland Publishing, Inc., 1992.

57. Sandeen, Ernest R. *The Origins of Fundamentalism.* Philadelphia: Fortress Press, 1968.

58. _____. *The Roots of Fundamentalism: British and American Millenarianism, 1800-1930.* Chicago: University of Chicago Press, 1970.

59. Sheldon, Henry C. *Studies in Recent Adventism.* New York: The Abingdon Press, 1915.

60. Shelley, Bruce. *What the Bible Says about the End of the World: A Historical Look at How End-time Beliefs Developed.* Wheaton, IL: Victor Books, 1978.

61. Sobel, B. Z. *Hebrew Christianity: The Thirteenth Tribe.* New York: John Wiley & Son, 1974.

62. Thomas, N. Gordon. *Millennial Impulse in Michigan, 1830-1860: The Second Coming in the Third New England.* Lewiston, NY: The Edwin Mellen Press, 1989.

63. Travis, Stephen H. *I Believe in the Second Coming of Jesus.* Grand Rapids, MI: Wm B. Eerdmans, 1982.

64. _____. *The Jesus Hope.* Downers Grove, IL: InterVarsity Press, 1974.

65. Tuveson, Ernest L. *Millennium and Utopia: A Study in the Background of the Idea of Progress.* Berkeley: University of California Press, 1949.

66. _____. *Redeemer Nation: The Idea of America's Millennial Role.* Chicago: University of Chicago Press, 1968.

67. Vanderwaal, Cornelius. *Hal Lindsey and Biblical Prophecy* (Theodore Plantinga, trans.). St. Catherine's, ONT: Paideia Press, 1978.

68. Weber, Timothy P. *The Future Explored.* Wheaton, IL: Victor Books, 1978.

69. _____. *Living in the Shadow of the Second Coming: American Premillennialism, 1875-1982* (enlarged ed.). Chicago: University of Chicago Press, 1987.

70. Wilmore, Gayraud S. *Last Things First.* Philadelphia: Westerminster Press, 1982.

71. Wilson, Dwight J. *Armageddon Now!: The Premillenarian Response to Russia and Israel Since 1917.* Grand Rapids, MI: Baker Book House, 1977.

72. Zamora, Lois Parkinson (ed.). *The Apocalyptic Vision in America: Interdisciplinary Essays on Myth and Culture.* Bowling Green, OH: Bowling Green University Popular Press, 1982.

PART TWO

THE LITERATURE OF AMERICAN MILLENNIALISM

SECTION ONE

EARLY BRITISH AND AMERICAN MILLENNIALISM, 1798-1848

The revival of millennial interest, first in Britain and then in the United States, came as a result of two historic events: the American and French revolutions and, connected with the latter, the rise of Napoleon to power and dominance over Europe. With the republican revolution in America and democratic revolution in France came, respectively, the overthrow of a mighty imperial force by a rag-tag militia of colonists and the end of a monarchy that had ruled the French people for 1,000 years. These revolutions turned people's interests toward the possibility of a new world order, the hope of a new social order founded upon the virtues of "liberty, equality and universal brotherhood." Surely, many thought, a golden age of peace must be about to dawn upon humankind.

But the rise of Napoleon in the 1790s and his bold actions were events even more enthralling to those who read the Bible and anticipated the fulfillment of its prophetic passages. Two events commanded their interest. First of all, the French armies under Berthier and Napoleon dethroned Pope Pius VI in 1798, briefly ending papal control over the European continent. This event set the prophetic wheels into motion as many prophetically minded individuals read this bold and unprecedented move as a sign that the Church age was coming to a close and that the Last Days were upon them.

Ernest Sandeen observes that this first event was not unlike a prophetic Rosetta stone in that it provided those who had been puzzling over biblical prophecy with a key to its chronology. As Sandeen comments, "thus the French revolution accelerated millenarian interest in two ways. It upset notions of gradual progress and made apocalyptic expectations seem realistic. And it provided some scholars with confidence that they had found out where they were existentially located in the prophetic program and the historical present" (in Gaustad 1974: 108-109).

But the overthrow of the "antichrist" pope was not the only event of prophetic significance. In the wake of Napoleon's conquests, Jews all across Europe were being freed from their ghettoes, many migrating back to their promised homeland. For millenarians, this event fulfilled the predictions of the ancient Hebrew prophets who had foreseen the return of the Jews to Palestine in the latter days.

A flurry of literary activity followed these events, primarily among the British, who worked through the prophetic significance of these and other events of their time. In his summary of British millenarianism, Sandeen points to six major assumptions that underlie the thinking of these early millennialist works, which, to some extent, find later expression among millennialists in the United States (see Sandeen in Gaustad 1974: 109).

1. This dispensation or age will end cataclysmically in judgment and destruction of the church.

2. The Jews will be restored to Palestine during the time of judgment.

3. The judgment to come will fall principally upon the church.

4. When the judgment is past, the millennium will begin.

5. The Second Advent of Christ will occur before the millennium.

6. The 1260 years of Daniel 7 and Revelation 13 ought to be measured from the reign of Justinian to the French Revolution. The vials of wrath prophesied in Revelation 16 are now being poured out and the second advent is imminent.

As Sandeen points out, "This doctrinal summary makes plain that British millenarians believed that the course of history was inevitably downward trending, that the church as a public institution had been judged and found wanting, and that a cataclysm of judgment was imminent" (in Gaustad 1974: 109).

Not long after these events, dozens of books and pamphlets, relating these and other events to Bible prophecy, began to pour from presses all over the British Isles. A short while later, these same materials began to flood across the Atlantic, generating a revival of interest in prophecy and the endtimes among American Protestant clergy and laity as well. Though American millennialism would later become a fascinating blend of separatist Darbyite dispensationalism and popular Adventist (Millerite) speculation, many of the six points noted above did find their way into American millennial thought (e.g., points 2, 4, and 5), helping lay the foundation for the later work of Darby and others among the evangelical Protestant churches.

Below is a list of British and American millennialist writings from this early formative period.

73. Allwood, Philip. *A Key to the Revelation of St. John, the Divine: Being an Analysis of Those Parts of that Wonderful Book, Which Relate to the General State of the Christian Church, Through all the Times Since it was Written, and to the Peculiar Signs of Those Times.* London: C. J. G. & F. Rivington, 1829.

74. An American Layman. *The Second Advent; or Coming of the Messiah in Glory, Shown to be a Scripture Doctrine, and Taught by Divine Revelation, from the Beginning of the World.* Trenton, NJ: D. Fenton & Hutchinson, 1815.

75. Ash, Edward, M.D. *Four Lectures on the Apocalypse.* Fletcher J. Norwich; London: Hamilton, Adams & Co., 1848.

76. Bedell, Gregory Townsend. *Lectures on the Epistles to the Seven Churches of Asia.* Philadelphia: William Stavely, 1835.

77. Birks, Thomas Rawson. *First Elements of Sacred Prophecy* , 1844.

78. _____. *The Four Prophetic Empires and the Kingdom of Messiah.* London: Seeley, 1844.

79. _____. *The Two Later Visions of Daniel: Historically Explained.* London: Seeley, 1846.

80. _____. *The Mystery of Providence: or The Prophetic History of the Decline and Fall of the Roman Empire.* London: Nisbet, 1848.

81. Blunt, Henry. *A Practical Exposition of the Epistles to the Seven Churches of Asia* (2nd ed.). London: J. Hatchard and Sons, 1839.

82. Brooks, Joshua William (Abdiel, pseud.). *Essays on the Advent and Kingdom of Christ and the Events Connected Therewith* (4th ed., enlarged); London: Simpkin, Marshall & Co., 1843.

83. Brown, John (Minister at Haddington). *Harmony of Scripture Prophecies and History of Their Fulfilment.* Glasgow: John Bryce, 1784.

84. Burnet, William. *An Essay on Scripture-Prophecy, Wherein it is Endeavoured to Explain the Three Periods Contain'd in the XII Chapter of the Prophet Daniel: With Some Argument to Make it Probable that the First of the Periods Did Expire in the Year 1715, etc.* New York: William Bradford, 1724.

85. Bush, George. *A Treatise on the Millennium in Which the Prevailing Theories on that Subject are Carefully Examined, and the True Scriptural Doctrine Attempted to be Elicited and Established.* New York: J & J Harper, 1832.

86. Chamberlin, Richard. *New Discoveries, Concerning the Millennium Set Forth in an Original Treatise, etc.* Poughkeepsie, New York: Pub. by author, 1805.

87. *The Conversion of the Jews: A Series of Lectures Delivered in Edinburgh by Ministers of the Church of Scotland.* Edinburgh: J. Johnstone and London: R. Groombridge, 1842.

88. Crawford, Charles. *Observations Upon the Downfall of the Papal Power, and Consequent Events* (new ed.). Philadelphia: Printed and Sold by Zachariah Poulson, 1788.

89. Cunninghame, William. *A Dissertation on the Seals and Trumpets of the Apocalypse, and the Prophetical Period of Twelve Hundred and Sixty Years.* London: J. Hatchard, 1813.

90. _____. *Letters and Essays, Controversial and Critical on Subjects Connected with the Conversion and National Restoration of Israel.* London: J. Hatchard and Son, 1822.

91. _____. *The Scheme of Prophetic Arrangement of the Rev. Edward Irving and Mr. Frere Critically Examined, with Some Remarks on the Present Aspect of Affairs in Reference to the Fulfilment of Prophecy.* Glasgow: University Press, 1826.

92. Darby, J. N. *The Hopes of the Church of God, in Connection with the Destiny of the Jews and the Nations as Revealed in Prophecy: Eleven Lectures Delivered in Geneva, 1840* (new ed., rev.). London: Morrish, n.d.

93. Davis, Timothy. *Anti-Christian Religion Delineated, in a Treatise on the Millennium; or The Fulfillment of the Old Testament Prophecies Completed.* Leominster, MA: Published by author, 1807.

94. Davis, William. *The Millennium; or A Short Sketch on the Rise and Fall of Antichrist, etc.* Frankfort, KY: Berard & Berry, 1815.

95. *The Destiny of the Jews, and Their Connexion with the Gentile Nations; Viewed Practically in a Course of Lectures Delivered at St. Bride's Church, Liverpool.* London: John Hatchard & Sons, 1841.

96.   *Dialogues on the Bible, Relating to the Customs and Manners of the Israelites, and the Fulfilment of Prophecy* (2nd ed., enlarged). London: Harvey and Darton, 1830.

97.   Drummond, Henry. *A Defense of the Students of Prophecy.* London: James Nisbet, 1828.

98.   Drummond, Henry (ed.). *Dialogues on Prophecy* (3 vols). London: James Nisbet, 1827-1829.

99.   Duffield, George. *Dissertations on the Prophecies Relative to the Second Coming of Jesus Christ.* New York: Dayton & Newman, 1842.

100.   _____. *Millenarianism Defended: A Reply to Prof. Stuart's 'Strictures on the Rev. G. Duffield's Recent Work on the Second Coming of Christ,' in Which the Former's False Assumptions are Pointed Out, and the Fallacy of his Interpretation of Different Important Passages of Scripture are Both Philologically and Exegetically Exposed.* New York: Mark H. Newman, 1843.

101.   Eliot, Edward Bishop. *Horae Apocalypticae: Commentary on the Apocalypse, including also an Examination of the Chief Prophecies of Daniel.* London: Seeley, Burnside, & Seeley, 1846.

102.   Emerson, Joseph. *Lectures on the Millennium* (2nd ed.). n.p.: Philip Shaw, Pub., 1830.

103.   Faber, George Stanley. *A Dissertation on the Prophecies that have been Fulfilled, Are Now Fulfilling, or will Hereafter be Fulfilled, Relative to the Great Period of 1260 Years; the Papal and Mohammedan Apostacies; the Tyrannical Reign of Anti-Christ..; and the Restoration of the Jews* (2 vols.; 2nd American ed.). New York: Duckinck & Ward, 1811.

104.   _____. *Eight Dissertations on Certain Connected Prophetical Passages of Holy Scripture: Bearing, More or Less, Upon the Promise of a Mighty Deliverer.* London: Seeley, Burnside and Seeley, 1845.

105. _____. *A General and Connected View of Prophecies Relative to the Conversion, Restoration, Union and Future Glory, of the House of Judah and Israel: The Progress and Final Overthrow, or the Antichristian Confederacy in the Land of Palestine; and the Ultimate Diffusion of Christianity* (2nd ed., rev. and corrected). London: F. C. and J. Rivington, 1809.

106. _____. *Napoleon III, the Man of Prophecy; or The Revival of the French Emperorship Anticipated from the Necessity of Prophecy.* New York: D. Appleton, 1859.

107. _____. *The Sacred Calendar of Prophecy: or A Dissertation on the Prophecies which treat of the Grand Period of Seven Times, and especially of its Second Moiety, or the Latter Three Times and a Half.* London: C. & J. Rivington, 1828.

108. Fairbairn, Patrick. *The Interpretation of Prophecy* (2nd ed.). London: Banner of Truth Trust, 1865 (1st ed., 1856); (Reprinted ed.). T. & T. Clark, 1964.

109. _____. *Prophecy Viewed in Respect to its Distinctive Nature, its Special Function, and Proper Interpretation.* London: Banner of Truth Trust, 1865; New York: Carlton & Porter, 1866; (Reprinted ed.). T. & T. Clark, 1976.

110. _____. *The Prophetic Prospects of the Jews; or Fairbairn Vs. Fairbairn: Two Articles, the First One Originally Published in 1840 as the Author's Contribution to Lectures on the Jews, and a Second Published in 1864 as a Part of His 'Fairbairn on Prophecy'* (intro. by Albertus Pieters). Grand Rapids, MI: Wm. B. Eerdmans Publishing Co., 1930. [reprinted]

111. Folsom, Nathaniel Smith. *Critical and Historical Interpretation of the Prophecies of Daniel.* Boston: Crocker & Brewster, 1842.

112. Habershon, Matthew. *A Dissertation on the Prophetic Scriptures, Chiefly those of a Chronological Character; Showing their Aspect on the Present Times and on the Destinies of the Jewish Nation, etc.* London: James Nisbet, 1834.

113.   Hawley, Daniel. *Hawley's Millennium Declaring the Restoration of the Hebrews into the Holy Land, and Many Infallible Proofs of the Prophetical Doctrine, ...and Containing the Principles of a Perpetual Self-moving Engine.* New York: George Forman, 1818.

114.   Hershcell, Ridley Haim. *A Brief Sketch of the Present State and Future Expectations of the Jews* (5th ed.). London: J. Unwin, 1841.

115.   Hopkins, Samuel. *A Treatise on the Millennium: Shewing from Scripture Prophecy, that It is Yet to Come; When It will Come; in what It will Consist; and the Events which are First to Take Place, Introductory to It.* Edinburgh: Ogle & Aikman, 1806; (reprinted ed.). New York: Arno Press, 1972.

116.   Hunter, Henry. *The Rise, Fall, and Future Restoration of the Jews, to Which is Annexed Six Sermons Addressed to the Seed of Abraham by Several Evangelical Ministers, Concluding with an Elaborate Discourse by the Late Dr. Hunter entitled, 'The Fulness of the Gentiles Coeval with the Salvation of the Jews.'* London: W. Button, 1806.

117.   Hurd, Richard. *An Introduction to the Study of the Prophecies Concerning the Christian Church; and, in Particular, Concerning the Church of Papal Rome.* London: Bowyer and J. Nichols, 1772.

118.   Irving, Edward. *Babylon and Infidelity Foredoomed of God: A Discourse on the Prophecies of Daniel and the Apocalypse which Relate to These Latter Days and until the Second Advent.* Glasgow: Chalmers and Collins, 1826.

119.   Junkin, George. *The Little Stone and the Great Image: or Lectures on the Prophecies Symbolized in Nebuchadnezzar's Vision of the Golden Headed Monster.* Philadelphia: James M. Campbell & Co., 1844.

120.   Keith, Alexander. *The Signs of the Times: As Denoted by the Fulfilment of Historical Predictions Traced Down from the*

Babylonish Captivity to the Present. New York: Jonathan Leavitt, 1832.

121. Kett, Henry. *History, the Interpreter of Prophecy: or A View of Scriptural Prophecies and Their Accomplishment in the Past and Present Occurrences of the World with Conjectures Respecting Their Future Completion* (2nd ed.). Oxford: University Press, 1799.

122. King, John. *Observations on the Prophecies Which Relate to the Rise and Fall of Antichrist and Such as Appear to Point to the Events of Our Times: With Some Calculations on Prophetical Members to Show that His Fall May Not Now be Far off.* Chambersburg, PA: George Kenton Harper, 1809.

123. Lacunza, Manuel. *The Coming of Messiah in Glory and Majesty, by Juan Josafat Ben-Ezra, pseud.* (2 vols.; Rev. Edward Irving, trans). London: L.B. Seeley & Son, 1827.

124. Leach, W. B. *Lectures on Fulfilled Prophecy, as Verified in the Destruction of Ancient Nations, the Vicissitudes of the Jews, the Messiah and the Genius and Triumphs of Christianity.* London: Ward & Co., 1844.

125. Macleod, A. *Unfulfilled Prophecy , Respecting Eastern Nations, Especially the Turks, the Russians, and the Jews.* London: John Snow, 1841.

126. Maitland, Samuel Roffey. *A Second Enquiry into the Grounds on which the Prophetic Period of Daniel and St. John has been Supposed to Consist of 1260 years, etc.* London: C & J. Rivington, 1829.

127. Marshall, Benjamin. *A Chronological Treatise Upon the Seventy Weeks of Daniel, etc.* London: James Knapton, 1725.

128. McNeile, Hugh. *Popular Lectures on the Prophecies Relative to the Jewish Nation.* London: J. Hatchard and Son; 1830; London: The Christian Book Society, 1878.

129.   Morrison, Charles. *The Question, Will Christ's Reign During the Millennium be Personal?: Answered from Scripture*. Edinburgh: William Oliphant & Son, 1839.

130.   Myers, Thomas. *The Prophecies Delivered by Christ Himself, and the Miraculous Gifts exercised by His Apostles, applied to the Present State and Future Prospects of the Church of God (Two Dissertations)*. London: James Nisbet, 1836.

131.   Nares, Robert. *A Connected and Chronological View of the Prophecies Relating to the Christian Church, ...preached in Lincoln's Inn Chapel*. London: F. C. & J. Rivington, 1805.

132.   Newton, Sir Isaac. *Observations Upon the Prophecies of Daniel and the Apocalypse of St. John, in two parts*. London: J. Darby and T. Browne, 1733.

133.   Newton, Thomas (Bp.). *Dissertations on the Prophecies which have Remarkably been Fulfilled and at this Time are Fulfilling in the World* (13th ed.). London: W. Haynes & Son, 1823; London, J. F. Dove, 1838; (reprinted ed.) Crissy & Markley, 1850.

134.   _____. *The Pope, the Man of Sin, the Son of Perdition: A Dissertation on the Prophecy of the Apostle Paul Concerning the Man of Sin*. Fayetteville: Edwind C. Church, 1836.

135.   Priest, Josiah. *A View of the Expected Christian Millennium, Which is Promised in the Holy Scriptures, and is Believed to be Nigh its Commencement, and must Transpire before the Conflagration of the Heavens and the Earth, Embellished with a Chart, of the Dispensations from Abraham to the End of Time, etc.* Albany, New York: Loomis' Press, 1828.

136.   Scott, John. *The Conversion of the Jews and Their Restoration to Their Own Land*. Hull, England: J. Pulleyn, 1813.

137.   Shimeall, Richard C. *Age of the World; as Founded on the Sacred Records Historic and Prophetic, and the 'Signs of the Times', viewed in the Aspect of Premonition of the Speedy Establishment on the Earth of the Millennial State, by the Second, Personal Premillennial Advent of Christ, with an*

Introductory Essay, Vindicating the Claims of Sacred Chronology Against the Cavils of the Atheist, Antiquarian, and Infidel. n.p.: Swords, Stanford, 1842.

138.   Smith, Ethan. *A Dissertation on the Prophecies Relative to Antichrist and the Last Time, Exhibiting the Rise, Character, and Overthrow of the Terrible Power and a Treatise on Seven Apocalyptic Vials.* Boston: Samuel T. Armstrong, 1811; (2nd ed.). Boston: Samuel T. Armstrong, 1814.

139.   Towers, Joseph Lomas. *Illustrations of Prophecy....* Philadelphia: William Duane, 1808.

140.   Wallace, J. A. *The Seven Churches of Asia.* London: John Nisbet & Co., 1842.

141.   West, Augustus Willam. *The Spiritual Condition of the Seven Churches of Asia Minor, Made Applicable to Christians of the Present Day in Nineteen Discourses.* London: B. Fellowes, 1846.

142.   Whowell, T. *The First Epistle to the Christian Church, on the Eve of the Millennial Kingdom of Christ: or A Complete Key to the Old and New Testament with the Fulfilment, in Succession of the Prophecies of Our Blesses Saviour, With Past and Present State of the Jews and the Appearance of Their Restoration* (2 vols., bound together). Nottingham: Richard Sutton, 1830.

143.   Willson, James. *The Shaking of the Nations, Alias the Anti-Christian Nation.* Pittsburgh: E. Pentland, 1809.

144.   Witsius, Herman. *The Restitution of Israel not Incompatible with the Spirituality and Universality of the Kingdom of Christ, Demonstrated from the Prophecies of Ezekiel* (John Wing, trans). London: Nisbet and Co., 1840.

145.   Wylie, James Aitken. *The Seventh Vial: Being an Exposition of the Apocalypse and in Particular of the Pouring Out of the Seventh Vial, with Special Reference to the Present Revolutions in Europe, etc.* London: J. Johnstone, 1848.

SECTION TWO

POST-MILLERITE MILLENNIALISM AND THE SPREAD OF DISPENSATIONALISM, 1849-1877

American culture during the antebellum years of religious revivals and awakenings was fertile soil for millennial expectation and prophetic speculation. As one of the many fruits of American revivalism, millennialism tended to take one of two directions: the first, postmillennialism, was characteristically optimistic; and the second, premillennialism, was generally pessimistic. Postmillennialists could see evidence of peace and progress bursting forth all around them as flowers in the Spring and they concluded that the millennium would arrive as the culmination of their efforts to christianize human civilization. Those who saw the historical process through premillennial lenses tended to interpret the deterioration of morality and increase of sin and savagery around them as evidence that things were not getting better at all but were, in fact, getting worse. This corresponded to their belief that the Bible had predicted that in the Last Days, the spirit of antichrist would dominate the earth, a spirit antithetical to the Gospel of righteousness and love.

Millerite Millennial Expectation

The movement that would cause the greatest stir during this period began as a result of the prophetic prognostications of a New England farmer, William Miller (1782-1849). At first a Deist, Miller was converted by Baptists in 1816. For the next two years Miller studied the Bible intensely, especially its prophetic passages. By 1818, Miller had concluded that Christ would return in 1843. Confident in his calculations yet shy of the limelight, Miller did not publish his prediction until 1835. By 1839, however, Miller had been joined by Joshua V. Himes, a man with a knack for publicity, and Miller's message began to spread throughout the region. Soon, Miller and Himes drew together a considerable following, ranging from the curious to the convinced and the committed.

By early 1843, the expectations of several thousand believers, and perhaps as many as a hundred thousand other hopeful souls, began to run high. But after the original date passed, Miller had to refigure his calculations. He then set October 22, 1844 as the final date. When that day came and went in what became known as the "Great Disappointment," the movement collapsed. Adventism itself did not die, however. Though chastened, Miller recovered from the disappointment, returned to Vermont, and founded an Adventist church there.

Other followers, notably Hiram Edson and Ellen Harmon (later Ellen G. White), began to experience heavenly visions indicating to them that something of divine significance had indeed taken place on Miller's predicted day. Those events, however, had taken place in heaven, not on the earth as previously expected. Out of the seeds of the "Great Disappointment" sprang the Seventh-Day Adventist movement, whose leaders, though still expecting Christ's return, preached spiritual and physical preparedness over preoccupation with date-setting.

While later Protestants were also more careful about setting precise dates for Jesus' return, the notion that Christ's appearing was on the horizon encouraged others to take over where Miller and his followers had left off. The evangelical Protestant churches in America, for instance, became rich and fertile soil for the cultivation of millennial expectation, especially of the prophetic speculations and dispensational doctrines that followed soon after Miller's time.

Darbyite Dispensationalism

The revival of millennial expectation among British divines was expressed in varying ways. Among the most fascinating and persuasive speculative systems of prophetic interpretation was the dispensational teaching of the erstwhile Church of Ireland minister and leader of the non-conformist Separated Brethren of Plymouth, John Nelson Darby (1800-1882). In simplest terms, Darby's dispensationalism was a method of interpreting the Bible by marking human history into seven unequal periods, one for each of the days of creation in the Genesis account. As C. I. Scofield, Darby's most influential American disciple, explained in his book, *Rightly Dividing the Word of Truth* (1896), "these periods are marked off in Scripture by some change in God's method of dealing with mankind, or a portion of mankind, in respect to two questions: of sin, and of man's responsibility" (1896:8). In each of these periods, God gives a specific command, one intended to test humanity's obedience to God.

In every case, through their willful disobedience, men and women fail God. The result of their disobedience is judgment and calamity. This cycle of command, disobedience, and judgment is repeated from age to age, until the end of the sixth dispensation, when Christ returns. As Scofield reported, "five of these dispensations, or periods of time, have been fulfilled; we are now living in the sixth, probably toward its close, and have before us the seventh, and last -- the millennium" (1896:8). The seven dispensations, which follow the biblical history of the Hebrew people and their major covenantal agreements with God, are outlined as follows:

1. Innocence	=	Edenic Covenant
2. Conscience	=	Adamic Covenant
3. Human Government	=	Noahic Covenant
4. Promise	=	Abrahamic Covenant
5. Law$_1$	=	Mosaic Covenant
- Law$_2$	=	Palestinian Covenant
- Law$_3$	=	Davidic Covenant
6. Grace	=	New Covenant of Jesus
7. Fulness of Times	=	Millennial Kingdom of Christ

Nineteenth-century dispensational thought was not a new development within the history of Christian doctrine (or within Jewish thought, for that matter). For example, in the Books of Romans and Galatians, St. Paul distinguishes between the dispensation of Law and that of Grace. The Barnabas letter, written about 96 C.E., speaks of six thousand years of human history before the millennium, a thousand-year period of rest corresponding to the Sabbath day when God rested from his creative activity. Furthermore, St. Irenaeus was among the first of the Ante-Nicene fathers to write specifically of an *Old* and a *New* Testament, distinguishing these dispensations. It was the Venerable Bede (673-735 C.E.) who later divided historical time between B.C. and A.D., separating the Christian era from the pagan era at the nativity of Christ.

What Darby did, however, was to separate out two peoples -- the Israel of God and the Church of God -- each with its own divine program. Thus, in addition to his division of human history into periods of human failure and divine judgment, Darby also divided the people of God into primary and secondary groupings (with a third grouping being everyone else). Darby believed that God's primary concern was for Israel, the Jewish people. Jesus had come originally to save the Jews. Though thwarted, Christ would return in the latter days to complete his work among the Jews. Accordingly, when Christ returned, his reign would be an earthly reign from an earthly kingdom in Israel. The Church, however, was of secondary importance in the divine scheme of things, being largely an afterthought.

But Darby's signature doctrine was his belief that before the return of Christ and before the last judgment of the world, the Christian church (the "true" believers) would be whisked away toward heaven to meet Jesus in the air. This event was termed the secret "Rapture" of the saints. Because this event, this rapture, could happen at any moment, believers were strongly encouraged to be spiritually prepared at all times, lest they be left behind to suffer wrath during the coming tribulation period.

In large part, Darby's dispensationalism seems to stem more from his ecclesiology, his view of the Church, than from anything purely eschatological. Darby believed that the true church was spiritual, not institutional, and thus all institutional religions, even Christian denominations, were thoroughly corrupted. Wherever Darby went, he ardently entreated Christians to separate themselves from their churches so as to escape the apostate Church's damning corruption or be condemned to hell through association with apostate Christians. Not surprisingly, Darby's negative experiences in the state church in the English Church of Ireland had led to his own departure from it in 1827.

Between 1862 and 1877, Darby traveled extensively throughout the United States spending six years' time teaching his distinctive dispensationalist system and urging Christians to forsake their apostate churches. While many American Protestants openly embraced his dispensational system as well as his doctrine of the secret rapture of the saints, much to Darby's dismay, they did not adopt his strict separatist ecclesiology. Even so, Darby's ideas spread throughout the American churches, gaining a sizable following. A series of Bible and Prophetic conferences followed in the wake of the Darby's final visit to the United States, as well as a sizable outpouring of books and pamphlets on dispensational themes.

146. *Apocalyptic Sketches: Being a Condensed Exposition of the Views of the Most Eminent Writers Upon the Prophecies of Revelation, Daniel, Isaiah, etc., Respecting the Second Coming of Our Lord with all His Saints at the First Resurrection.* Canada: Galt, 1860.

147. Baker, William Adolfus. *The Day and the Hour, Notes on Prophecy: A Sketch of the Future, Extracted from the Bible.* London: William McIntosh, 1868.

148. Baxter, Michael Paget. *Coming Wonders: Expected between 1867 and 1875.* Philadelphia: J.B. Lippincott & Co., 1873.

149. _____. *Forty Coming Wonders, with Fifty Illustrations* (5th ed., enlarged). London: Christian Herald Office, n.d.; (14th ed.). London: Pub. by the author, 1880; (15th ed.). London: Christian Herald Co.; London: Thynne & Jarvis, 1923.

150. _____. *Forty Future Wonders of Scripture: Predicted in Daniel and Revelation* (15th ed.). London: The Christian Herald, n.d.

151. _____. *Louis Napoleon, the Destined Monarch of the World, and Personal Antichrist, Foreshown in Prophecy to Confirm a Seven Years' Covenant with the Jews about, or Soon after 1863, and Then, ...Subsequently to Become Completely Supreme Over England and most of America, and All of Christendom, ...Until He Finally Perishes at the Descent of Christ at the Battle of Armageddon, about or soon after 1870, etc* (3rd ed., enlarged). Philadelphia: J.B. Lippincott & Co.,1866.

152. Beale. *Armageddon; or A Warning Voice from the Last Battlefield of Nations, Proclaiming by the Mouths of Prophets and Apostles that the Close of the Times of the Gentiles, the Second Personal Advent, and Millennial Reign of our Lord and Saviour Jesus Christ are Nigh at Hand....* London: Wertheim, Macintosh, and Hunt, 1858.

153. Bickersteth, Edward. *On the Four Prophetic Empires and the Kingdom of Messiah.* n.p., n.d.

154.   _____. *The Restoration of the Jews to Their Own Land* (3rd ed.) London: n.p., 1852.

155.   Birks, Thomas Rawson. *Outlines of Unfulfilled Prophecy: Being an Inquiry into the Scripture Testimony Respecting the 'Good Things to Come.'* London: Seeley, 1854.

156.   Bonnar, James. *The Great Interregnum: An Exposition of Daniel and the Apocalypse.* Glasgow: Hugh Hopkins, 1871.

157.   Bonar, Horatio. *The Coming and Kingdom of the Lord Jesus Christ.* London: J. Nisbet and Co., 1849.

158.   Caldwell, John R. *Things to Come: Being a Short Outline of the Great Events of Prophecy.* Edinburgh: City Bible House, 1875; (10th ed.) Glasgow: Pickering & Inglis, 1900.

159.   Case, Ira. *Comments on the Revelation, and Other Prophecies.* Providence, RI: Providence Press Co., 1871.

160.   Chamberlain, Walter. *The National Resources and the Conversion of the Twelve Tribes of Israel: or Notes on Some Prophecies Believed to Relate to Those Two Great Events, and Intended to Show that the Conversion Will Take Place After the Restoration, and that the Occasion of it has been Uniformly Predicted, etc.* London: Wertheim and Macintosh,1854.

161.   Cheever, George Barrell. *The Powers of the World to Come.* New York: R. Carter, 1853.

162.   Cox, John. *The Future: An Outline of Events Predicted in the Holy Scriptures; Being a Revised Edition of 'Themes for Thought in the Prophetic Page.'* London: Nisbet & Co., 1862.

163.   Cumming, John. *Apocalyptic Sketches: or, Lectures on the Seven Churches of Asia Minor.* London: Arthur Hall, Virtue & Co., 1851.

164.   _____. *The Destiny of Nations as Indicated in Prophecy.* London: Hurst and Blackett, 1864.

165. _____. *The End: or The Proximate Signs of the Close of This Dispensation.* Boston: John P. Jewett, 1855.

166. _____. *God in History.* New York: Lane and Scott, 1852.

167. _____. *The Great Consummation: The Millennial Rest, or the World as it Will Be.* New York: Carleton, 1863.

168. _____. *The Great Preparation: or Redemption Draweth Nigh.* New York: Rudd & Carleton, 1861.

169. _____. *The Great Tribulation: or The Things Coming on the Earth.* New York: Rudd & Carleton, 1860.

170. _____. *The Last Warning Cry: With Reasons for the Hope that is in Me.* New York: G.W. Carleton, 1867.

171. _____. *Prophetic Studies: Lectures on the Book of Daniel.* Philadelphia: Lindsay and Blakiston, 1854.

172. _____. *Signs of the Times: or The Present, Past, and Future.* Philadelphia: Lindsay and Blakiston, 1855.

173. _____. *The Soundings of the Last Trumpet: or The Last Woe.* London: James Nisbet, 1867.

174. Cunninghame, William. *The Fulfilling of the Times of the Gentiles, A Conspicuous Sign of the End: Being an Analytical Survey of the Times of the Four Kingdoms of Daniel and of Jerusalem from the Year Before Christ, 606, to the Present Year, 1847; Which is Shown to be Their Common Point of Concentration and Fulness.* London: Seeley, Burnside, and Seeley, 1857.

175. Darby, J. N. *Collected Writings*, 34 vols and index. (William Kelly, ed.). London: G. Morrish, 1934.

176. _____. *Lectures on the Second Coming.* London: G. Morrish, 1909.

177. _____. *Notes on the Apocalypse.* London: G. Morrish, n.d.

178.   _____. *Notes on the Book of the Revelation.* London: W. H. Broom, 1876.

179.   _____. *The Restoration of the Jewish Nation (Matt. 24, 25).* London: Morrish, n.d.

180.   _____. *Will the Saints Be in the Tribulation?* New York: Loizeaux Brothers, n.d.

181.   Demarest, John T. and William D. Gordon. *Christocracy; or Essays on the Coming and Kingdom of Christ: With Answers to the Principal Objections of Postmillenarians.* Lloyd, 1867.

182.   Dods, Marcus. *The Epistles of our Lord to the Seven Churches of Asia.* Edinburgh: John Maclaren, 1867.

183.   Ewbank, William Withers. *The National Restoration of the Jews to Palestine, Repugnant to the Word of God.* Liverpool: Deighton and Laugthon, 1849.

184.   Goodwyn, Henry, Maj. General. *Antitypical Parallels: or The Kingdom of Israel and of Heaven, by Gershom* (pseud.). London: S. W. Partridge, 1866.

185.   _____. *The Substance of Things Hoped For: A Contrast to the Immaterial and Speculative System of Anti-millenarianism, etc.* London: Kellaway & Co., n.d.

186.   Govett, Robert. *The Saints' Rapture to the Presence of the Lord Jesus: Refutation of Dr. Cumming's Tract, Entitled 'The Pope, the Man of Sin.'* London: James Nisbet, 1864; (reprinted ed.). Miami Springs, FL: Conley & Schoettle, 1984.

187.   _____. *The Secret Presence and the Rapture Defended: A Letter to Pastor Frank White* [and] *Babylon Mystical.* Norwich: Fletcher, n.d.

188.   _____. *Seek the Sabbath Rest to Come* [and] *Christians! Seek the Rest of God in His Millennial Kingdom.* n.p.: n.p., n.d.

189. _____. *The Two Witnesses*. Norwich, UK: Fletcher & Sons, 1852. [reprinted as *The Locusts, The Euphratean Horsemen, and the Two Witnesses*. Miami Springs, FL: Conley & Schoettle, 1985].

190. Grant, James. *The End of All Things: or The Coming and Kingdom of Christ* (3 vols). London: Darton & Co., 1866.

191. Harris, Samuel. *The Kingdom of Christ on Earth: Twelve Lectures Delivered Before Students of the Theological Seminary, Andover*. Andover, MA: n.p., 1874.

192. *A Harmony of the Prophecies of Daniel and St. John, With Collateral Prophecies: Intended to Assist Students in the Comparison of the Different Predictions, and in Determining Their Order of Succession*. London: Seeley and Griffiths, 1861.

193. Hill, Henry F. *The Saints' Inheritance: or The World to Come* (6th ed.). Boston: Damrell & Moore, 1861.

194. _____. *The Prophetical Works of Edward Irving* (2 vols; Gavin Carlyle, ed.). London: Alexander Strahan, 1867-1870.

195. Keith, Alexander. *Evidence of the Truth of the Christian Religion Derived from the Literal Fulfilment of Prophecy, Particularly as Illustrated by the History of the Jews, and by the Discoveries of Recent Travelers*. Philadelphia: Presbyterian Board of Publication, 1835; (6th ed.). New York: Harper & Brothers, 1850; (6th Edinburgh ed.). New York: Harper & Brothers, 1871 and 1915.

196. _____. *The Harmony of Prophecy: or Scriptural Illustrations of the Apocalypse*. New York: Harper & Brothers, n.d.

197. _____. *The History and Destiny of the World and of the Church According to Scripture*. London: T. Nelson and Sons, 1861.

198. Kelly, William. *Elements of Prophecy*. London: Morrish, 1876.

199.   Ker, William. *A Series of Discourses on the Prophecies of 'the Last Days,' etc.* London: W. H. Laxton; Simpkin, Marshall, 1868.

200.   _____. *The Things Which Must Shortly Come to Pass: A Series of Discourses on the Prophecies of 'The Last Days.'* London: W. H. Laxton, 1868.

201.   *'The Kings of the East,' An Exposition of the Prophecies, Determining From Scripture and From History the Power for Whom the Mystical Euphrates is Being 'Dried Up;' With an Explanation of Certain Other Prophecies Concerning the Restoration of Israel* (2nd ed., enlarged). London: Seeleys, 1849.

202.   Knight, William. *Lectures on Some of the Prophecies Concerning the Rise and Character of the Power Commonly Called Antichrist; and their Reference to the Church of Papal Rome.* London: Seeley, Jackson, and Halliday; Bristol: Chilcott, 1855.

203.   Labagh, Isaac P. *Twelve Lectures on the Great Events of Unfulfilled Prophecy, which Still Await Their Accomplishment and are Approaching Their Fulfillment.* New York: n.p., 1859.

204.   Lee, Samuel. *Eschatology: or The Scripture Doctrine of the Coming of the Lord, the Judgment, and the Resurrection.* Boston: J. E. Tilton & Co., 1859.

205.   Neatby, Thomas. *Our Lord's Coming Again: His Appearing and Reign.* London: John F. Shaw & Co., 1877.

206.   Neil, James. *Palestine Re-Peopled: or Scattered Israel's Gathering, a Sign of the Times* (2nd ed., enlarged). London: James Nisbet & Co., 1877.

207.   Newton, Benjamin Wills. *Aids to Prophetic Enquiry* (3rd ed., considerably enlarged). London: The Sovereign Grace Advent Testimony, 1881 (1st ed., 1848; 2nd ed., considerably enlarged, 1850).

208. _____. *Elementary Studies on the Facts of Prophetic Scripture in the Book of Daniel and the Book of Revelation* [and] *Studies in 1 John.* Aylesbury: Hunt, Barnard & Co., n.d.

209. _____. *The First Resurrection and the Reign of Righteousness.* London: The Sovereign Grace Advent Testimony, n.d.

210. _____. *How B. W. Newton Learned Prophetic Truth: Reprinted From Watching and Waiting.* London: The Sovereign Grace Advent Testimony, n.d.

211. _____. *Israel and Jerusalem.* London: Houlston & Wright, 1867.

212. _____. *The Judgment of the Court of Arches and of the Judicial Committee of the Privy Council in the Case of Rowland Williams.* London: The Sovereign Grace Advent Testimony, 1866.

213. _____. *The New World Order, or The Pre-Millennial Truth Demonstrated: An Answer to the Post-Millennial, A-Millennial, and Anti-Millennial Theories.* London: The Sovereign Grace Advent Testimony, n.d.

214. _____. *The Prospects of the Ten Kingdoms of the Roman Empire.* London: Houlston & Wright, 1863; (2nd ed., rev.) London: Houlston and Sons, 1873.

215. Phillipps, Ambrose Lisle. *Mahometanism in its Relation to Prophecy: or An Inquiry into the Prophecies Concerning Antichrist with Some Reference to Their Bearing on the Events of the Present Day.* London: Charles Dolman, 1855.

216. Phillips, Joseph Scott. *Approximations of Prophecy: or Speculative Geography of the Holy Land.* London: James Nisbet, 1854.

217. Pitts, F. E. *A Defence of Armageddon; or Our Great Country Foretold in the Holy Scriptures: In Two Discourses Delivered in the Capitol of the United States, at the Request of Several Members of Congress, on the Anniversary of Washington's Birthday, 1857.* n.p.: J. W. Bull Publishers, 1859.

218.   Pond, Enoch. *The Seals Opened: or The Apocalypse Explained.* Portland, ME: Hoyt, Fogg, and Breed, 1871.

219.   *The Prophetic Chapters (VI to XX inclusive) of the Apocalypse Interpreted on the Infallible Basis, etc...., by A Student of Prophecy.* Bristol: W. Mack, 1873.

220.   Rabett, Reginald. *Lateinos (from Lateninus) is 'the Mark of the Beast,' ....the Solution of St. John's Enigma, also a Necessary Refutation.* London: William Edward Painter, 1849.

221.   Ralston, Samuel S. *The Revelation of John the Divine: or A New Theory of the Apocalypse, Corroborated by Daniel and Other Prophets.* Philadelphia: Smith, English & Co., 1858.

222.   Read, Hollis. *The Coming Crisis of the World; or The Great Battle and the Golden Age: The Signs of the Times Indicating the Approach of the Great Crisis and Duty of the Church.* Columbus: Follet, Foster & Co., 1861.

223.   Reid, William. *Things to Come, Practically Considered.* Edinburgh: Wm Oliphant & Co., 1871.

224.   Riley, Henry A. *The Restoration at the Second Coming of Christ: A Summary of Millenarian Doctrines.* Philadelphia: J. B. Lippincott & Co., 1868.

225.   Royse, Pleasant E. *The Predictions of the Prophets, Which Have Been Most Wonderfully Fulfilled Since the Commencement of the Christian Era, and Especially Those Predictions Concerning the United States.* Cincinnati: Pub. by Author, 1864.

226.   Ryle, J. C. *Coming Events and Present Duties: Being Miscellaneous Sermons on Prophetical Subjects.* London: Wm. Hunt & Co., 1867.

227.   Seiss, Joseph A. *The Apocalypse: A Series of Special Lectures on the Revelation of Jesus Christ with Revised Text.* New York: Charles C. Cook, 1900 (first published in 1865).

228.   _____. *The Last Times and the Great Consummation: An Earnest Discussion of Momentous Themes* (6th ed. rev. & enlarged). Philadelphia: Smith; London: Wertheim, Macintosh & Hunt, 1866; (7th ed.) Louisville, KY: Pickett Publishing Co., 1878 [retitled *The Last Times: or Thoughts on Momentous Themes*. Louisville, KY: Pentecostal Publishing Co., 1878; and Louisville, KY: Pickett Publishing Co., 1901.

229.   _____. *Millennialism and the Second Advent*. Louisville, KY: Pickett Publishing Co., n.d.; Louisville, KY: Pentecostal Publishing Co., n.d.

230.   Shepheard, H. *The Tree of Life: or Redemption, and its Fruits in Grace and Glory* (2nd ed.). London: James Nisbet, 1866.

231.   Shimeall, Richard C. *Christ's Second Coming; Is It Pre-millennial or Post-millennial?* n.p.: Trow, 1865.

232.   Simpson, David. *A Key to the Prophecies: or A Concise View of the Predictions Contained in the Old and New Testaments, Which Have Been Fulfilled, Which are Now Fulfilling, or Are Yet to be Fulfilled in the Latter Ages of the World*. London: Milner & Co., n.d.

233.   Slight, Benjamin. *The Apocalypse Explained, in Two Series of Discourses on the Entire Book of the Revelation of St. John*. Montreal: R. & A. Miller, 1855.

234.   Smith, George Vance. *The Prophecies Relating to Ninevah and the Assyrians* (trans. from Hebrew). London: Longman, Brown, Green, Longmans and Roberts, 1857.

235.   Smith, James. *Plain Thoughts on the Sealed Book*. London: Houlston & Sons, 1872.

236.   Snell, Hugh Henry. *Prophetical Outlines: Seven Lectures on the Second Coming and Kingdom of the Lord Jesus Christ, delivered in Leeds*. London: W.H. Broom, 1868.

237.   T. *Prophecy* (4th ed.). New York: John Polhemus, 1871.

238.   Thomas, John. *Eureka: an Exposition of the Apocalypse, in Harmony with 'the Things of the Kingdom of the Deity, and the Name of Jesus Anointed.'* West Hoboken, NJ: Pub. by the author, 1861-1869.

239.   Thompson, A. C. *Morning Hours in Patmos: The Opening Vision of the Apocalypse and Christ's Epistles to the Seven Churches of Asia.* Boston: Gould and Lincoln, 1860.

240.   Tregelles, Samuel P. *The Hope of Christ's Second Coming.* London: Samuel Bagster & Sons, 1864; (2nd ed.) Aylesbury: Hunt, Barnard & Co., n.d.; London: Samuel Bagster & Sons, 1886.

241.   _____. *The Man of Sin.* London: The Sovereign Grace Advent Testimony, 1850.

242.   _____. *Remarks on the Prophetic Visions in the Book of Daniel (A new edition revised and greatly enlarged): With Notes on Prophetic Interpretation in Connection with Popery, and a Defence of the Authenticity of the Book of Daniel.* London: Samuel Bagster & Sons, 1852 (5th ed., 1864).

243.   Trevilian, Maurice Cely. *A Dissertation on the History of the 'Beast' as Derived from the Prophets Daniel and John, and of the Head of the Beast Especially, etc.* London: Wertheim, Macintosh, & Hunt, 1858.

244.   Tristram, Henry Baker. *The Seven Golden Candlesticks.* London: The Religious Tract Society, 1871.

245.   Trotter, W. *Eight Lectures on Prophecy* (new ed.). New York: Loizeaux Brother, Bible Truth Depot, n.d.

246.   _____. *Plain Papers on Prophetic and Other Subjects* (new, rev. ed.). New York: Loizeaux Brother, Bible Truth Depot, n.d.; New York: Fleming H. Revell, 1863.

247.   Waldegrave, Samuel (Bp. of Carlisle). *New Testament Millenarianism: or The Kingdom and Coming of Christ as*

Taught by Himself and His Apostles (2nd ed.). London: Wm. Hunt & Co., 1866.

248.   Wepf, Lewis. *The Church of God and Her Adversaries: or The Revelation of John Explained by a Scriptural and Historical Representation of the Origin, Character, and Reciprocal Warfare of the Two Great Parties in the World, in the Past, Present, and Future* (2 vols). Chicago: Lakeside Publishing Co., 1871.

249.   Wickes, Thomas. *An Exposition of the Apocalypse.* New York: M. W. Dodd, 1851.

250.   Windle, Henry E. *Lectures on the Epistles to the Seven Churches of Asia.* London: James Nisbet, 1870.

SECTION THREE

THE EARLY BIBLE AND
PROPHECY CONFERENCES, 1878-1895

Dispensational premillennialism did not catch on in any big way among American evangelical Protestants until the decades just before and just after the turn of the century, when those views were popularized through a series of Bible and Prophecy conferences. The Prophecy conference movement began in 1868, when a small group of millenarians, influenced by Darby's teachings, gathered informally in New York City to share their views on the Second Coming of Christ. These annual prophecy meetings proved such a success that millennialists and other evangelicals met officially in Chicago in 1885 to organize what became known as the Believers' Meeting for Bible Study (later renamed the Niagara Conference).

Convening for two weeks every summer until 1900, the Niagara Conferences featured the "Bible Reading," a new style of expositional preaching in which the speaker would string together Bible verses -- or "proof texts" -- making as few personal comments as possible so as not to obscure the plain meaning of the texts through human interpretations. While participants in these meetings discussed a range of theological topics, their greatest concern was how to check the cancer of liberalism which was spreading into the churches, seminaries, and onto the mission fields. It was not long before the meetings became dominated by premillennialists, however, who used the Bible conference forum both to clarify and develop their endtime theology further as well as to publicize it.

In working out their views on the endtimes, the speakers at these conferences took their cues from both Miller and Darby, blending these two streams of thought into what soon became known as dispensational premillennialism: dispensational in that human history, now in its sixth dispensation since creation, was rapidly coming to a close; and premillennial in that the second coming of Christ would not occur *after* the millennium of peace, as post-millennialists held, but *before* the millennium. That is, Christ's second coming would signal the beginning of the seventh and final divine dispensation, the Kingdom of God.

In 1878, James H. Brookes, a longtime president of the Niagara Conferences, published a fourteen-point creed spelling out the fundamental beliefs of those attending that year's Believers' Meeting. While the so-called Niagara Creed re-emphasized conservative Protestant doctrine, then under fire by exponents of the New Theology, the creed also published for the first time the new dispensational premillennialist reading of the Bible in light of current events. The creed's fourteenth point outlines the eschatology of these new premillennialists. It reads: "We believe that the world will not be converted during the present dispensation, but is fast ripening for judgment, while there will be a fearful apostasy in the professing Christian body; and hence that the Lord Jesus will come in person to introduce the millennial age, when Israel shall be restored to their own land, and the earth shall be full of the knowledge of the Lord; and that this personal and premillennial advent is the blessed hope set before us in the Gospel for which we should be constantly looking" (Sandeen 1970: 276-277).

The Niagara Conferences met annually from 1875 until 1900, when differences over the chronology of the doctrine of the secret rapture effectively split the conference platform and divided premillennialists into two camps. Though disagreement forced a cancellation of the Niagara Conference in 1901, its earlier popularity and success gave rise to other spin-off conferences. The most famous of those were the Prophecy Conferences held in Chicago, 1886; Allegheny, Pennsylvania, 1895; Boston, 1901; Chicago, 1914; Philadelphia, March 1918; and New York City, November 1918. The proceedings of these conferences have recently been reprinted by Garland Publishing Inc. in a four-volume series edited by Donald W. Dayton (see below). Unlike the Niagara Conferences, speakers at the Prophecy Conferences focused their attention exclusively on Bible prophecy and the signs of the times. Such occurrences and events as the Zionist movement and the First World War provided ample grist for the premillennialist prophecy mill, as these proceedings attest.

Published Conference Proceedings

251. *Addresses of the International Prophetic Conference.* Boston: Watchword and Truth, 1901.

252. *Addresses on the Second Coming of the Lord: Delivered at the Prophetic Conference, 1895.* Pittsburgh: W. W. Waters, 1896.

253. Dayton, Donald W. (ed.) *The Prophecy Conference Movement* (4 vols.) New York: Garland Publishing, Inc, 1988.

254. Gabelein, Arno C. (ed.). *Christ and Glory: Addresses delivered at the New York Prophetic Conference, 1918.* New York: Our Hope Publishers, 1918.

255. Gray, James (ed.). *The Coming and Kingdom of Christ: The Prophetic Bible Conference in Chicago, 1914, ...Including a List of Some Exponents of Premillennialism.* Chicago: The Bible Institute Colportage, 1914.

256. *Light on Prophecy: Proceeding and Addresses at the Philadelphia Prophetic Conference, 1918.* New York: The Christian Herald, 1918.

257. Needham, George (ed.) *Prophetic Studies of the International Prophetic Conference, 1886.* Chicago: Fleming H. Revell, 1886.

258. West, Nathaniel. *Premillennial Essays of the Prophetic Conference, 1878.* Chicago: Fleming H. Revell, 1879.

The 'Rapture' Question

Although Darby's eccelesiastical separatism did not gain wide acceptance among evangelical Protestants, his dispensationalism and doctrine of the any-moment secret rapture of believers prior to the tribulation period did capture the attention of a sizable number of conservative clergy and laity. Among the major exponents of Darby's views were individuals such as James H. Brookes, a Presbyterian minister from St. Louis. Brookes hammered out the specifics of Darby's "any moment" rapture doctrine by insisting that there were in fact two second comings. First, Jesus would come *for* his saints at the rapture, which could happen at any moment. Second, after a seven-year period of judgment (the Tribulation), Jesus would return *with* his saints to rule and reign on the earth for a literal 1,000-year period.

As before, the first appearing of Christ and rapture of the church could come at any moment. The second and final appearing, however, would be preceded -- indeed, presaged -- by the fulfillment of specific prophesies, what millennialists often refer to as "prophetic signs" or "signs of the times." No one could ever know with certainty when the rapture would take place, but once it did, the rest of the eschatological timetable would proceed like clockwork.

At this point, a tension in millennialism becomes apparent: the yearning once again to calculate when Christ will return, while, at the same time, admitting that no one can know with any certainty when, in fact, the second coming will take place. Interestingly, many premillennialists reasoned that if one could estimate with some precision when the seven-year Tribulation period might begin or end, one could then calculate, with reasonable accuracy, when the rapture might occur. True, Christ did say that "of this day and hour no one knows, not even the angels of heaven, not the Son, but the Father alone" (Matthew 24:36). But, as many millennialists reason, Jesus did not say that one could not at least know the month or year of his coming, leaving the door wide open for an endless avalanche of speculation.

As mentioned above, one of the disagreements that surfaced during the Niagara Conferences -- one that continues to the present day -- was over the doctrine of the secret rapture of the church, specifically its chronology. During this early formative period in popular American millennialism, there emerged three main positions on *when* the any-moment rapture would take place in the endtime scenario: *before, during,* or *after* the Great Tribulation of the Last Days.

The *Pre-tribulation Rapture* view is the position made popular by Brookes. It basically argues that Christ's return for his saints will come *before* the beginning of the Tribulation, thus sparing believers' from the suffering non-believers and apostates will experience during this period of intense global destruction. Not surprisingly, this view has become the most popular of the three.

The second view holds that the rapture will take place in the *middle* of the seven-year Tribulation period, hence its name, *Mid-tribulation Rapture.* Mid-tribbers (as they are sometimes called) believe that Christians will live through the first half of the Tribulation and will be taken from the earth just before things start to heat up and all hell breaks loose. Those holding this view often speak of two tribulations: the Little Tribulation and the Great Tribulation. True believers will escape the latter.

A third view is the *Post-tribulation Rapture* position, a position first defended by Robert Cameron. Those who argue for this interpretation of the Book of Revelation place the rapture of the church *after* the Great Tribulation. The secret rapture and the second coming of Christ are thus virtually one and the same event. Post-tribbers maintain that the Great Tribulation is not simply a period of judgment but a period of cleansing. Only true believers will persevere through this fiery time of trial. All others will be burned up like dross, their souls consigned to eternal hell. While this view has been the least popular of the three, this position has recently gained a renewed following among some premillennialist writers.

In addition to the rapture rift, one last main distinction that evident during this period was the noticeable split between historicist and futurist millenarians -- a split that also continues to this day. Historicists hold that the so-called latter-day prophecies in the Bible have been and are still being fulfilled in history. One need only consider world events since Jesus' time in the light of Daniel and the Book of Revelation to see that many of their prophecies "fit" those events. For instance, a prophecy about "a great horde swooping down from the east," historicists posit, seems to parallel the Mongol invasions led by Genghis Khan in the twelfth and thirteenth centuries.

Futurists, on the other hand, differ with historicists in that they argue that most, if not all, of the endtimes prophecies have yet to be fulfilled. There is essentially no correlation between the history of western civilization and the prophecies in either the Hebrew Bible or the Christian New Testament.

Unfortunately, for our understanding of popular American eschatology, neither historicists nor futurists hold firmly to their own positions, creating no little confusion. For example, futurists might point to earlier fulfillments of prophecy in history to undergird their belief in future fulfillments of other prophecies, while historicists might accept "multiple" fulfillments of a single prophesied event, meaning that some prophecies can be future as well as historical.

Whatever the case may be, one can find among the entries gathered below, a fairly representative sampling of all these conflicting positions. Among the many possible combinations, however, the one most commonly held by premillennialists has been the pretribulation rapture futurist view.

---

259.   Adkins, E. *The Age to Come: or The Future States.* New York: The Authors' Publishing Co, 1880.

260.   Anderson, Robert. *The Coming Prince.* London: Pickering & Inglis, n.d.; (5th ed. with subtitle: *or, The Seventy Weeks of Daniel, with an Answer to the Higher Criticism*) London: Hodder & Stoughton, 1895; (18th ed. with subtitle: *The Marvelous Prophecy of Daniel's Seventy Weeks Concerning the Antichrist*) Grand Rapids, MI: Kregel Publications, 1972.

261.   *The Apocalypse, Looked at as the Final Crisis of the Age.* London: Paternoster, 1890.

262.   *The Apocalyptic Drama.* New York: Fleming H. Revell Co., 1891.

263.   Baines, T. B. *The Lord's Coming, Israel, and the Church* (3rd ed., rev. and enlarged) London: W. H. Broom, 1878; New York: Loizeaux Brothers, 1896; London: A. S. Rouse,1900.

264.   Baxter, Michael Paget. *Forty Coming Wonders, Between 1890 and 1901, as Foreshadowed in the Prophecies of Daniel and Revelation.* London: The Christian Herald, 1887.

265. _____. *Forty Future Wonders of Scripture Prophecy.* (15th ed.) London: The Christian Herald, 1923.

266. _____. *Future Wonders of Prophecy from 1896-1908* (8th ed.). London: Christian Herald, 1894.

267. Birks, Thomas Rawson. *Thoughts on the Times and Seasons of Sacred Prophecy.* London: Hodder & Stoughton, 1880.

268. Blackstone, W. E. *Jesus is Coming!* New York: Fleming H. Revell, 1886; (rev. ed.). New York: Fleming H. Revell, 1898 and 1908); (re-revised ed.). Christian and Missionary Alliance, 1908.

269. Bland, F. C. *Twenty-one Prophetic Papers: A Suggestive Outline of the Whole Range of God's Dealings with the Jews, Gentiles, and the Church of God.* London: Pickering & Inglis, 1890.

270. Brookes, James H. *Bible Reading on the Second Coming.* Springfield, IL: Edwin A. Wilson, 1877.

271. _____. *I Am Coming: A Setting Forth of the Second Coming of Our Lord Jesus Christ as Personal -- Private -- Premillennial* (7th ed., rev.). Glasgow: Pickering & Inglis, n.d.

272. _____. *Israel and the Church.* St. Louis: Gospel Book and Tract Depository, n.d.

273. _____. *Maranatha; or, The Lord Cometh.* St. Louis: Edward Brendell, 1878; (9th ed.). New York: Fleming H. Revell, 1889.

274. _____. *Till He Come* [sic]. New York: Fleming H. Revell, 1895.

275. Brown, David. *The Apocalypse: Its Structure and Primary Predictions.* New York: Christian Literature Co., 1891.

276. _____. *Christ's Second Coming: Will It be Premillennial?* New York: Carter, 1856; (5th ed.). London: Hamilton, Adams & Co., 1859; (6th ed.). New York: Carter, 1876; (7th ed.). Edinburgh: T

& T Clark, 1882; (reprinted ed.). Edmonton, AB: Still Waters Revival Books, 1990.

277. _____. *The Restoration of the Jews: The History, Principles, and Bearings of the Question.* n.p., n.d.

278. Brown, Fortune Charles. *Christ on the Throne of Power and Antichrist: A Treatise on the Book of Book of Revelation to St. John the Divine.* Rochester, New York: Union and Advertiser Co., 1885.

279. Brown, Robert. *Outlines of Prophetic Truth Viewed Practically and Experimentally in the Light of the Divine Word: From Redemption to Final State.* London: S. W. Partridge, 1890, (first published in 1883).

280. Browne, Charles O. *The Gentile Powers.* London: James E. Hawkins, 1882.

281. Brunson, Alfred. *A Key to the Apocalypse.* Cincinnati: Walden & Stowe; New York: Phillips & Hunt, 1881.

282. Bryant, Alfred. *The Attraction of the World to Come* (5th ed.). New York: Dodd, Mead & Co., 1889.

283. Bullinger, E. W. *The Apocalypse.* Fleming H. Revell, n.d.

284. _____. *Ten Sermons on the Second Advent.* n.p., 1887; London: Pub. by Author, 1892; (3rd ed., rev.). Eyre & Spottiswoode, 1895.

285. _____. *The Witness of the Stars.* Grand Rapids, MI: Kregel Publications, 1967. [reprint of 1893 edition]

286. Cachemaille, Ernest P. *Daniel's Prophecies Now Being Fulfilled.* London: Hodder & Stoughton, 1888.

287. Campbell, David. *The Judgment Period Preparatory to the Establishment of the Kingdom of Heaven: Comprising Twelve Chapters on the Apocalypse.* Bangor, ME: Z. B. Chase, 1886.

288. Chalklen, T. *Sermons on the Apocalypse* (2 vols). London: James Speirs, 1878.

289. Crosby, Howard. *The Seven Churches of Asia: or Worldliness in the Church.* New York: Funk & Wagnalls, 1890.

290. Dennett, Edward. *The Blessed Hope: Being Papers on the Lord's Coming and Connected Events* (new ed.). Denver, CO: Wilson Foundation, 1879.

291. _____. *The Seven Churches.* London: G. Morrish, n.d.

292. Dewart, Edward Hartley. *Jesus the Messiah in Prophecy and Fulfilment: A Review and Refutation of the Negative Theory of Messianic Prophecy* (American ed.). Cincinnati: Cranston & Stowe; New York: Hunt & Eaton, 1891.

293. Drummond, Henry. *The City Without a Church.* New York: James Pott, 1893.

294. Evans, Howard Heber. *St. John: The Author of the Fourth Gospel.* London: James Nisbet, 1888.

295. Fraser, Donald. *Seven Promises Expounded.* London: James Nisbet, 1889.

296. Gordon, Adoniram Judson. *Ecce Venit: Behold He Cometh.* New York: Fleming H. Revell, 1889.

297. Govett, Robert. *Christians! Seek the Rest of God in His Millennial Kingdom* [and] *Babylon Mystical* (2nd ed.). Norwich: Fletcher, n.d.

298. _____. *Christ's Judgment of His Saints at His Return and Solution of the Main Argument Against Secret Presence.* Norwich: Fletcher & Sons, 1895; (reprinted ed.). Miami Springs, FL: Conley & Schoettle Publishers, 1985.

299. _____. *Entrance into the Millennial Kingdom: Four Letters to J. T. Moleworth* [and] *Christians! Seek the Rest of God in His Millennial Kingdom.* Norwich: Fletcher & Sons, 1883.

300. _____. *The Millennial Kingdom One of Reward* [and] *Christians! Seek the Rest of God in His Millennial Kingdom* (3rd ed.). Norwich: Fletcher and Son, n.d.

301. _____. *The Millennium Cannot Come in Gospel Times.* London: James Nisbet, n.d.

302. _____. *Will All Believers Have Part in the Thousand Years?* [and] *Babylon Mystical.* Norwich: Fletcher, 1895.

303. _____. *Romanism and the Reformation from the Standpoint of Prophecy.* A. C. Armstrong, 1887; Arnold Publishing, 1890.

304. Grant, F. W. *The Hope of the Morning Star; with a Review of Objections to an Immediate Expectation of the Coming of the Lord and the Taking Away of the Saints to Meet Him Before the Closing Tribulation.* New York: Loizeaux Brothers, n.d.

305. _____. *Lessons of the Ages.* New York: Loizeaux Brothers, n.d.

306. _____. *The Numerical Bible.* New York: Loizeaux Brothers, n.d.

307. _____. *The Numerical Structure of Scripture.* New York: Loizeaux Brothers, n.d.; Swengel, PA: Bible Truth Depot, 1887.

308. _____. *The Revelation of Christ.* New York: Loizeaux Brothers, n.d.

309. Guinness, H. Grattan. *The Approaching End of the Age, Viewed in the Light of History, Prophecy, and Science.* 1878; New York: A. C. Armstrong, 1881; London: Hodder & Stoughton, 1884; (rev. ed. by E. H. Horne). London: Marshall, Morgan & Scott, 1918.

310. _____. *The Divine Programme for the World's History.* London: Harley House, 1892.

311. _____. *Light for the Last Days.* London: Hodder & Stoughton, 1893.

312.   _____. *Romanism and the Reformation from the Standpoint of Prophecy.* A. C. Armstrong, 1887; Arnold Publishing, 1890.

313.   Harper, Jesse. *The Millennium: The Restoration, the Race Restored, the Earth Restored, the Earth a Home (entos) for All.* Danville, IL: n.p.,1892.

314.   Huidekoper, Frederic. *Indirect Testimony of History to the Genuineness of the Gospels* (5th ed.). New York: David G. Francis, 1886.

315.   Hutchison, John. *Our Lord's Messages to the Seven Churches of Asia.* Edinburgh: Andrew Eliot, 1881.

316.   Jack, Thomas G. *The Casting Out of Satan into the Earth and the Gathering of Israel* (2nd ed.). Folkestone, n.d.; (1st ed., 1891).

317.   Keith, Alexander. *The Evidence of Prophecy: Historical Testimony to the Truth of the Bible.* New York: American Tract Society, n.d.; (new and rev. ed.). London: The Religious Tract Society, 1882.

318.   Kellogg, Samuel H. *The Jews: or, Prediction and Fulfillment, an Argument for the Times.* New York: Anson D. F. Randolph & Co., 1883.

319.   MacKintosh, C. H. *Papers on the Lord's Coming.* A. W. Otto, 1894; London, G. Morrish; Chicago: The Bible Institute Colportage Association., n.d.

320.   _____. *The Lord's Coming.* Chicago: Moody Press, n.d.

321.   Marsh, Frederick E. *The Second Coming of Our Lord Jesus Christ in Relation to 'the Millennium.'* London: Thynne and Jarvis, n.d.

322.   _____. *Will the Church, or Any Part of It, Go Through the Great Tribulation?* London: Pickering & Inglis, 1894.

323.   Mason, John. *Why We Expect Jesus Now.* New York: Fleming H. Revell, 1893.

324.   Matheson, Robert Edwin. *Things Which Must Shortly Come to Pass: or Outlines of the Books of Daniel and Revelation, with Explanitory Maps and Diagrams.* London: James Nisbet & Co., n.d.

325.   Moir, James of Maybole. *The Mystery of the Seven Churches, being the Exposition of the Symbolic and Prophetic Elements in the Epistles to the Seven Churches in Asia.* Edinburgh: Edinburgh Publishing Co., 1873.

326.   Moody, Dwight L. *Our Lord's Return: A Sermon, 2 Timothy 3:16.* Erie, PA: Free Tract League, n.d.

327.   _____. *The Second Coming of Christ.* London: R.W. Simpson & Co., n.d.; (rev. ed.). Chicago: Fleming H. Revell, 1877; Chicago: Bible Institute Colportage Association, 1896.

328.   Munhall, Leander. *The Lord's Return* (8th ed., reprinted). Grand Rapids, MI: Kregel Publications, 1962.

329.   _____. *The Lord's Return & Kindred Truth.* Chicago: Fleming H. Revell, 1885; (7th ed.). Philadelphia: E. & R. Munhall, 1895; New York: Eaton & Mains, 1898.

330.   Murphy, James Gracey. *The Book of Daniel: or The Second Volume of Prophecy, etc.* London: James Nisbet & Co., 1884.

331.   Needham, George C. (ed). *Primitive Paths to Prophecy: Prophetic Addresses Given at the Brooklyn Conference to the Baptist Society for Bible Study (Nov. 18-21, 1890).* Chicago: Gospel Publishing Co., 1891.

332.   Nevin, Robert. *Studies in Prophecy, in Two Parts.* Londonderry: James Montgomery, 1890.

333.   Newton, Benjamin Wills. *Babylon: Its Future History and Doom: With Remarks on the Future of Egypt and Other Eastern Countries* (3rd ed.). London: Houlston and Sons, 1890.

334.   _____. *Europe and the East: Final Predominance of Russia Inconsistent With the Declaration of Scripture* (2nd ed.). London: Houlston & Sons, 1878.

335.   _____. *Prophecies Respecting the Jews and Jerusalem Considered: In the Form of a Catechism* (4th ed.). London: C. M. Tucker, 1888.

336.   _____. *The Prophecy of the Lord Jesus as Contained in Matthew XXIV and XXV Considered.* London: Houlston and Sons, 1879; (5th ed.). n.p.: E. J. Burnett, 1930.

337.   _____. *The World to Come* [and] *Ancient Truths Respecting the Deity and True Humanity of the Lord Jesus* (6th ed.). London: Houlston and Sons, 1897.

338.   *Notes on Some Prophecies, Indicating the Probable Relation Between England and Egypt in the Last Days.* London: James Nisbet & Co., 1887.

339.   Pember, George H. *The Antichrist, Babylon, and the Coming of the Kingdom* (2nd ed.). London: Hodder & Stoughton, 1888.

340.   _____. *The Great Prophecies Concerning the Gentiles, the Jews and the Church of God* (2nd ed., rev. and enlarged). London: Holder and Stoughton, 1885; (3rd ed., rev. and enlarged). New York: Christian Herald, 1887.

341.   _____. *The Great Prophecies of the Centuries: Concerning Israel and the Gentiles* (3rd ed., rev. and enlarged). New York: Christian Herald Office, 1887; London: Hodder and Stoughton,1895; (4th ed.). London: Hodder and Stoughton, 1909; (5th ed.). London: Hodder 1902 and 1911.

342.   *The Personal and Pre-millennial Coming of Our Lord and Saviour Jesus Christ* (Conference Papers). Edinburgh: n.p., 1888.

343.   Peters, George N. H. *The Theocratic Kingdom of Our Lord Jesus Christ.* New York: Funk and Wagnalls, 1884.

344.   Potts, James Henry (ed.). *The Golden Dawn: or Light on the Great Future in this Life, Through the Dark Valley, and in the Life Eternal, as seen in the Best Thoughts of Over Three Hundred Leading Authors and Scholars.* Philadelphia and Chicago: P. W. Ziegler and Co., 1884.

345.   Redford, Robert A. *Prophecy: Its Nature and Evidence.* London: The Religious Tract Society, 1882.

346.   Rees, Luther. *Behold! He Cometh!: The Scripture Teaching as to the Pre-millennial Coming of the Lord Jesus Christ to Earth.* Chicago: Evangelical Publishing Co., 1882.

347.   Reimensnyder, Junius B. *Doom Eternal.* New York: Funk, 1887.

348.   Roberts, Robert. *England and Egypt: Prophecy Fulfilled And Fulfilling; or Signs of the Nearness of Christ in the Events of the Past Thirty Years, Which Have Realized, etc.* Birmingham: Pub. by author, 1882.

349.   Russell, J. Stuart. *The Parousia: A Critical Inquiry into the New Testament Doctrine of Our Lord's Second Coming.* London: T. Fisher Unwin, 1887; (new ed.). Grand Rapids, MI: Baker Book House, 1983.

350.   Scofield, Cyrus I. *Rightly Dividing the Word of Truth: Being Ten Outline Studies of the More Important Divisions of Scripture.* New York: Loizeaux Bros., 1896 [1888]; (3rd ed.). Philadelphia: Sunday School Times, n.d.

351.   Seiss, Joseph A. (ed.). *Our Blessed Hope; or Select Tracts on the Advent.* n.p.: H. B. Garner, 1884.

352.   Simpson, Albert Benjamin. *The Gospel of the Kingdom: A Series of Discourses on the Lord's Coming.* New York: Christian Alliance Publishing Co., 1890.

353.   Stockinger, William M. *Lectures on the Revelation Containing Forty Chapters and Embracing Three Lines of Prediction.* Indianapolis, IN: Morning Star Publishing Co., 1886.

354.   Storie, John. *The Future as Revealed in Divine Prediction.* James Gemmell, 1887; Edinburgh: R. W. Hunter, n.d.

355.   Stowe, Harriet Beecher. *The Second Coming of Christ.* Chicago: Bible Institute Colportage Association, 1896.

356.   Sturt, Henry. *Prophetic Notes: Being An Exposition of the Chief Parts of Sacred Prophecy.* London: Elliott Stock, 1889.

357.   Tait, Andrew. *The Messages to the Churches of Asia Minor: An Exposition of the First Three Chapters of the Book of Revelation.* London: Hodder & Stoughton, 1884.

358.   Taylor, Daniel T. *The Great Consummation and the Signs that Herald its Approach.* Boston: Advent Christian Publication Society, 1891.

359.   _____. *The Reign of Christ on the Earth: or The Voice of the Church in All Ages, Concerning the Coming and Kingdom of the Redeemer.* London: Samuel Bagster & Sons, 1882; (rev. and enlarged ed.). n.p.: H. L. Hastings,1895.

360.   Terry, Milton S. *The Prophecies of Daniel.* New York: Hunt & Eaton; Cincinnati: Cranston & Curts, 1893.

361.   Tophel, Gustave. *The Seven Churches of Asia: Seven Discourses* (George E. Shipman, trans.). Chicago: Chicago Foundlings Home, 1883.

362.   Tower, Frances Emory. *The Advancing Kingdom: or Wonders of Foretold History.* Hartford, CT: American Publishing Co., 1890.

363.   Tregelles, S. P. *Remarks on the Prophetic Visions of the Book of Daniel.* London: Samuel Bagster & Sons, 1883.

364.   Trench, George Frederic. *After the Thousand Years. The Glorious Reign of Christ as Son of Man in the Dispensation of the Fulness of Times.* London: Morgan and Scott, 1908; (first ed., 1894).

365.   *Twenty Reasons for Believing that the Second Coming of the Lord Is Near.* New York: Fleming H. Revell, 1878.

366.   Tyng, Stephen H., Jr. *He Will Come; or Meditations Upon the Return of the Lord Jesus Christ to Reign Over the Earth.* New York: Muchlow and Simon, 1877.

367.   Varley, Henry. *Christ's Coming Kingdom: or The Lord's Reign on Earth*. London: Whiting, 1886; (2nd ed.). London: Whiting, 1887.

368.   Wale, Burlington B. *The Closing Days of Christendom as Foreshadowed in Parable of Prophecy* (2nd ed., enlarged). London: S. W. Partridge & Co., 1883.

369.   _____. *The Day of Preparation: or, the Gathering of the Hosts to Armageddon*. London: Elliot Stock, 1893.

370.   West, Nathaniel. *The Apostle Paul and the Any-Moment Rapture Theory*. Philadelphia: J.H. Armstrong, 1893.

371.   _____. *The Coming of the Lord in the 'Teaching of the Twelve Apostles.'* Philadelphia: J.H. Armstrong, 1892.

372.   _____. *Daniel's Great Prophecy: Its Twelve Chapters Explained*. Salisbury Square, London: Prophetic News Office, n.d. [also pub. as *Daniel's Great Prophecy: The Eastern Question, the Kingdom*. New York: The Hope of Israel, 1898].

373.   _____. *John Wesley and Premillennialism*. Louisville: Pentecostal Publishing Co., 1894.

374.   _____. *The Present Condition and Future Glory of Believers and the Earth*. St. Louis: Gospel Book and Tract Depository, n.d.

375.   _____. *The Thousand Years in Both Testaments: Studies in Eschatology; With Supplementary discussions Upon Symbolical Numbers, the Development of Prophecy, and its Interpretation Concerning Israel, the Nations, the Church, and the Kingdom, as Seen in the Apocalypses of Isaiah, Ezekiel, Daniel, Christ, and John*. New York: Fleming H. Revell, 1880 and 1889. [reprinted as *The Thousand Years: Studies in Eschatology in Both Testaments*. Fincastle, VA: Scripture Truth Book Co., 1967.]

376.   *When and Ought I to Expect My Lord?* New York: Loizeaux Brothers, 1890.

377.   Wilkerson, John. *God's Plan of the Jews* (reprint of 1894 ed.). London: Messianic Testimony, 1978.

378. Wilkinson, Samuel Hinds. *'Israel My Glory.'* London: Mildmay Mission to the Jews Book Store, 1894 [tract].

379. Withers, James. *The Messiah King.* London: Partridge & Co., 1884.

380. Wolston, W. T. P. *Behold the Bridegroom: Ten Lectures on the Second Coming of the Lord Jesus* (2nd ed.). London: James Nisbet, 1892.

SECTION FOUR

FROM ZIONISM TO THE
FIRST WORLD WAR, 1896-1918

Though one cannot speak of American millennialists as constituting a definable movement, one can still identify certain individuals as leading exponents of premillennial doctrines and point to educational centers where dispensational premillennialism developed and where it is still honored and taught. These unifying influences bring a measure of cohesion to an otherwise diverse and diversifying congeries of Protestant evangelicals.

Among the leading exponents of millenarian thought at the turn of the century were C. I. Scofield, Arno Gaebelein, James M. Gray, and I. M. Haldeman. In addition to the assorted Bible and Prophecy conferences held throughout the United States, the major educational centers from which premillennialism emanated included: the Philadelphia School of the Bible, founded by Scofield in 1914; the Moody Bible Institute, headed by Gray from 1904 to 1934; and the Bible Institute of Los Angeles, founded in 1908 with Reuben A. Torrey as its first dean. Later centers included the Evangelical Theological College (later Dallas Theological Seminary) founded in 1924 by Lewis Sperry Chafer and headed by him until his death in 1952.

Many of these centers were the off-spring of some of the earlier Bible and Prophecy conferences. For example, Grace College and Seminary (founded in 1937) grew out of the Winona Lake conferences held in Indiana from the turn of the century to the late 1940s.

Early in the twentieth century, the millennialist movement gained an added boost when it was joined by a sizable contingent from pentecostal and holiness churches and associations, whose leaders became zealous devotees of dispensationalism. One such group was the International Church of the Foursquare Gospel, founded in 1923 by evangelist Aimee Semple McPherson. McPherson and other pentecostals believed that their charismatic experiences, such as tongue-speaking and healing, were supernatural signs of the Last Days.

Their beliefs are based on "Old" Testament prophecies such as the one in Joel chapter 2 which predicts that in the Last Days, the spirit of the Lord will descend, and "your sons and your daughters shall prophesy and your young men shall see visions and your old men shall dream dreams." To them, this "Latter Day Rain of the Spirit" was a clear sign from the Holy Spirit that the millennial kingdom of Christ was just over the horizon. Some of the more prominent figures in the pentecostal and holiness movement after McPherson's time would include such revivalists and faith healers as William Branham, Gordon Lindsay, Ernest Angley, Oral Roberts, and Jimmy Swaggart.

During this period, millenarians were also active in missionary work, especially among the Jews. Millennialists believed that the Jews, who would become the major players in the endtime drama, would be regathered in Palestine. One example of earlier mission work among the Jews was the Hope of Israel Mission, headed by Arno Gaebelein, who also edited its publication *Our Hope*. Gaebelein directed perhaps the most successful of these Jewish mission associations, a success that gave rise to a score of other competing organizations within the United States as well as abroad.

But not all mission work was advanced through specialized parachurch organizations. Interest in Jewish mission work also spilled over into the local pastorates of many millennialist leaders. Of the pulpit ministers connected with the millennialist movement, none was perhaps more influential than the ardent fundamentalist and zionist, I. M. Haldeman. Indeed, most of Haldeman's books are simply edited collections of premillennial sermons he preached while he was pastor of New York City's First Baptist Church, a pastorate spanning nearly 50 years.

A main focus of the literature of this period is on the emergence of Zionism throughout Western Europe and the United States and the push by Theodor Herzl (1860-1904) for a separate Jewish State. The First World War and the liberation of Palestine by the British spirited premillennial confidence in their interpretation of the Scriptures. They believed that the Bible predicted that in the Last Days the Jews would return to the Promised Land; the Zionist movement bore this assumption out. As Haldeman confidently wrote in 1910 in his work, *The Signs of the Times*, "Zion and Zionism are in the air.... But this Zionist Movement is a witness that the coming of the Lord to rule and reign as king is not far away" (1919:452). Additionally, the literature of this period also reflects concern on the part of millennialists over the expanding German empire as well as the threat of German theological liberalism's corrosive influence on fundamental Protestant doctrines.

But without a doubt, the most influential work of this period, and of subsequent decades, was the Scofield Reference Bible, published by Oxford University Press in 1909, and expanded in 1917. This Bible contained detailed reference notes by Scofield, notes that presented to the reader clear and authoritative interpretations to otherwise obscure passages. The Scofield Bible soon became the most popular reference work among American millenarians and fundamentalists and has remained popular to this day.

381. Anderson, Robert. *Forgotten Truths*. London: James Nisbet & Co., 1913; (2nd ed.). London: James Nisbet & Co., 1914; (reprinted ed.). Grand Rapids, MI: Kregel Publication, 1977.

382. _____. *Human Destiny* (6th ed.). New York: Gospel Publishing House, n.d.; (9th ed.). Glasgow: Pickering and Inglis, 1913.

383. _____. *Unfulfilled Prophecy and 'The Hope of the Church.'* London: James Nisbet & Co., 1917; (2nd ed.) Glasgow: Pickering and Inglis, n.d.

384. Andrews, Samuel J. *Christianity and Anti-Christianity in Their Final Conflict*. New York: George Putnam's Sons, 1898; (rev. ed.). Chicago: The Bible Institute Colportage Association, 1898; (rev. and popular ed.). Chicago: The Bible Institute Colportage Association, 1937.

385. Arnaud, R. K. *The New Prophecy*. London: Hodder & Stoughton, 1917.

386. Auchincloss, William Stuart. *The Book of Daniel Unlocked*. New York: D. Van Nostrand, 1905.

387. _____. *The Only Key to Daniel's Prophecies*. New York: D. Van Nostrand, 1902.

388.   Austin, John S. *The Golden Age of the World Under the Personal Reign of King Jesus, with Concomitant Events.* Robert Smith Printing Co., 1916.

389.   _____. *The Revelation of Jesus Christ* (5th ed.). London: G. Morrish, 1911.

390.   Baillie, William. *History in Prophecy: Studies for Pilgrims in the Present Crisis.* London: C.J. Thynne, 1915.

391.   Baker, Caleb Jason. *The Things Which Are: A Sketch of the History and Character of the Professing Church (Revelation 2-3).* Kilmarnock, Scotland: John Ritchie, n.d.

392.   Baring-Gold, Sabine. *The Restitution of all Things: or 'The Hope That Is Set Before Us.'* London: Skeffington & Sons, 1907.

393.   Baron, David. *The Ancient Scriptures and the Modern Jew.* 1900; (3rd ed.). London: Hodder & Stoughton, n.d.; (new ed.). Findlay, OH: Dunham Publishing Co., n.d.

394.   _____. *Israel's Inalienable Possession: The Gifts and the Calling of God Which are Without Repentance.* London: Morgan & Scott, n.d.

395.   _____. *The Visions and Prophecies of Zechariah.* London: Morgan & Scott, 1918, (3rd ed., 1919).

396.   Barton, G. A. *Does the Bible Predict the Present War?* Chicago: American Institute of Sacred Literature, 1918.

397.   Bartz, Ulysses S. *Studies in Eschatology: or Existence after Death.* New York: Abbey Press, 1900.

398.   Bates, William H. *The Kingdom of God, the Kingdom of Heaven, the Church: A Biblical Study Defining and Distinguishing Them.* New York: C. C. Cook, 1916.

399.   Beet, Joseph Agar. *The Last Things.* London: Hodder & Stoughton, 1897; (3rd ed.). New York: Eaton and Mains; Cincinnati: Curts and Jennings, 1898.

400. _____. *The Last Things in Few Words*. London: Hodder & Stoughton, 1913.

401. Blackstone, W. E. *The Heart of the Jewish Problem*. Chicago: Chicago Hebrew Mission, n.d.

402. _____. *The Millennium: A Discussion of the Question, 'Do the Scriptures Teach that There Is to Be a Millennium?'* New York: Fleming H. Revell Co., 1904.

403. _____. *Satan: His Kingdom and Its Overthrow*. New York: Fleming H. Revell, 1900.

404. _____. *The 'Times of the Gentiles' and 'The Time of the End.'* n.p., n.d.

405. Blanchard, Charles A. *Light on the Last Days*. Chicago: Bible Institute Colportage Association, 1913.

406. _____. *The World War and the Bible*. Chicago: Bible Institute Colportage Association, 1918.

407. Bland, E. A. *Babylon, Past and Present: Papers Read at the Women's Branch of the Prophecy Investigation Society*. n.p., 1914.

408. Bramley-Moore, William Joseph. *The Church's Forgotten Hope: or Scriptural Studies of the Translation of the Saints* (3rd ed.). Glasgow: Hobbs & Co., 1905.

409. Bridwell, Charles W. *The Second Coming of Christ: A Discussion of This Truth and Related Subjects Which Vitally Concern Our Time*. n.p., The Pentecostal Union, 1915.

410. Bronkhurst, Louis. *The Book with the Seven Seals*. London: Rider & Co., n.d.

411. Brooke, Hubert. *The Fact and Features of the Lord's Return*. London: Scott, 1911 and 1917.

412.   Broughton, Len G. *The Second Coming of Christ.* Philadelphia:
       Pepper Publishing Co., 1902; (2nd ed.). New York: Fleming H.
       Revell, Co., 1907.

413.   Brown, William Bryant. *The Problem of Final Destiny: Studied in
       the Light of Revised Theological Statement.* New York: Thomas
       Whittaker, 1900.

414.   Bultema, Harry. *Maranatha!: A Study on Unfulfilled Prophecy.*
       (1917 edition). Grand Rapids, MI: Kregel Publications, 1985.

415.   Burridge, James H. *The Church, the Coming of Christ and the
       Great Tribulation.* Glasgow: Hulbert Publishing Co., n.d.

416.   _____. *God's Prophetic Plan: A Comprehensive View of God's
       Dealings with Man from the Creation to the New Heavens and
       New Earth.* St. Louis: Hammond Publishing Co., 1909.

417.   Burroughs, Joseph Birkbeck. *Titan, Son of Saturn: The Coming
       World Emperor, a Story of the Other Christ.* Cincinnati: The
       Forum Printing Concern, 1921 [1914].

418.   Burton, Alfred Henry. *The Future of Europe, Politically and
       Religiously, in the Light of Holy Scripture.* London: Alfred
       Holness, 1896; New York: C. C. Cook, 1915; New York: Bible
       Truth Press, 1915.

419.   _____. *Prophetic Outlines.* London: S. W. Partridge & Co., n.d.

420.   _____. *Russia's Destiny in the Light of Prophecy.* New York:
       C. C. Cook, 1915; New York: Gospel Publishing House, 1917.

421.   Cachemaille, Ernest P. *The First Two Visions of Daniel, With
       Continuous-historic Explanation and a Harmony of the Two
       Visions.* London: Charles J. Thynne, n.d.

422.   _____. *The Prophetic Outlook To-day: Where are We Now in
       Prophecy?* London: Morgan & Scott, 1918.

423.   _____. *XXVI Present Day Papers on Prophecy: An Explanation
       of the Visions of Daniel and of the Revelation.* London: Seeley,

1911; (reprinted in a new edition under the title, *The Visions of Daniel and of Revelation Explained*. London: Seeley, n.d.)

424.   Cameron, Robert. *The Doctrine of the Ages*. New York: Fleming H. Revell, 1896.

425.   Campbell, J. L. *The Patmos Letters: Applied to Modern Christianity*. London: Morgan & Scott, 1908.

426.   Campbell, William M. *Christ's Message to the Churches*. New York: Abbey, 1900.

427.   Chapman, J. Wilbur. *A Reason for My Hope*. New York: Our Hope, 1916.

428.   Charles, Benjamin H. *Lectures on Prophecy: An Exposition of Certain Scriptures with Reference to the History and the end of the Papacy; the Restoration of the Jews to Palestine, Their Repentance and Enlargement under the Reign of the Son of David; and the new State in the Millennium*. New York: Fleming H. Revell, 1897.

429.   Charles, R.H. A. *Critical History of the Doctrine of a Future Life: In Israel, In Judaism, In Christianity*. London: Adam and Charles Black 1913 [1899].

430.   Clarke, J. E. *The Coming of the King: A Study of the Teaching of Scriptures Concerning the Second Advent of Christ*. The Advance Publishing Co., n.d.

431.   St. Clement. *Christ's Return* (A.B. Simpson, ed.). New York: Christian and Missionary Alliance, 1906.

432.   Close, Albert. *Antichrist and His Ten Kingdoms*. London: Protestant Truth Society, 1917.

433.   Clouser, George B. M. *Coming Events: A Study of the Eschatology of Jesus*. Harrisburg: United Evangelical Publishing House, 1918.

434.   _____. *Dispensations and Ages of Scripture: A Study of the Divine Plan for the 'Ages [and] Times.'* n.p., 1903.

435.   Cook, Charles C. *End of the Age Themes.* New York: C. C. Cook, 1917.

436.   Cossum, William Henry. *Mountain Peaks of Prophecy and Sacred History.* Chicago: The Evangel Publishing House, 1911.

437.   Craig, Stephen Speers. *The Dualism of Eternal Life: A Revolution in Eschatology.* Rochester, New York: Pub. by author, 1916.

438.   Culross, James. *Thy First Love: Christ's Message to Ephesus.* London: Morgan & Scott, n.d.

439.   Davidson, A. B. *The Book of Ezekiel.* Cambridge, 1896.

440.   Dixon, A. C., et al. *Advent Testimony Addresses.* London: C. J. Thynne, 1918.

441.   Dodd, M. E. *Jesus is Coming to Earth Again; or The Signs of the Times: The Second Coming of Christ and the End of the World.* Chicago: Bible Institute Colportage Association, 1917.

442.   Duncklee, J. F. *The Development and Fulfillment of Prophecy; Being an Exposition of the Book of Daniel and of the Book of Revelation, Giving the Consecutive History of the Rise and Development of the Seven Heads and Ten Horns of the Great Prophetic Beast of These Prophecies, and Also the Application of 'the Man of Sin, the Son of Perdition,' as the Papal Power in its Dominion Over the Saints for 1260 Years.* Cranston & Curts, 1896.

443.   Eckman, George P. *When Christ Comes Again.* New York: Abingdon Press, 1917.

444.   Erdman, Fred. *What is the Lord's Coming?* New York: Charles C. Cook, 1903.

445.   Erdman, William J. *The Parousia of Christ, a Period of Time: or When Will the Church be Translated?* Chicago: Gospel Publishing Co., n.d.

446.   _____. *The Return of Christ*. Germantown, PA: Pub. by author, 1913.

447.   Fair, Francis. *Momentous Events: The Solemn Realization of Scripture Prophecy -- All Inter-related and Converging on the Coming Time*. London: Samuel E. Roberts, n.d.

448.   Fox, Rachel J. *Revelation on Revelation and the Latter Days*. London: Kegan Paul, Trench, Trubner & Co.; New York: E. P. Dutton & Co., 1916.

449.   Frith, William. *The Age to Come: or The Millennium*. London: S. W. Partridge & Co., n.d.

450.   Frost, A. J. *The Early Church was Premillennial*. Toronto: A. Sims, n.d.

451.   Gaebelein, Arno C. *Fulfilled Prophecy: A Potent Argument for the Inspiration of the Bible*. New York: Our Hope Publication Office, n.d.

452.   _____. *The Harmony of the Prophetic Word: A Key to Old Testament Prophecy Concerning Things to Come*. New York: Fleming H. Revell, 1907.

453.   _____. *Hath God Cast Away His People?* New York: Gospel Publishing House, 1905.

454.   _____. *The Prophet Daniel: A Key to the Visions and Prophecies of the Book of Daniel*. Los Angeles: Bible House of Los Angeles, 1911.

455.   _____. *The Prophet Ezekiel*. New York: Our Hope Publication Office, 1918.

456.   _____. *Studies in Prophecy*. New York: Our Hope Publication Office, 1918.

457.   _____. *The Work of Christ: Past, Present and Future*. New York: Our Hope Publication Office, 1913.

458.   Gardiner, F. P. M. *Can Ye Not Discern the Signs of the Times?: A Short Review of Certain Recent Political Events, and Current Social and Religious Affairs and of Their Significance in the Light of the Holy Scriptures* (rev. ed.). Kingston-on-Thames: Stow Hill Bible & Tract Depot, n.d.

459.   Girdlestone, Robert Baker. *The Grammar of Prophecy: A Systematic Guide to Biblical Prophecy.* 1901; (reprinted ed.). Grand Rapids, MI: Kregel Publications, 1955.

460.   Gordon, Samuel Dickey. *Quiet Talks About Our Lord's Return.* New York: Fleming H. Revell, 1912.

461.   Grant, F. W. *The Prophetic History of the Church.* New York: Loizeaux Brothers, 1902.

462.   Gray, James M. *The Audacity of Unbelief, and Other Papers.* Chicago: The Bible Institute Colportage Association, n.d.

463.   _____. *Great Epochs of Sacred History, and The Shadows They Cast.* Chicago: The Bible Institute Colportage Association, 1910.

464.   _____. *The Present Darkness and the Coming Light.* Chicago: The Bible Institute Colportage Association, n.d.

465.   _____. *Prophecy and the Lord's Return: A Collection of Popular Articles and Addresses.* New York: Fleming H. Revell, 1917.

466.   _____. *Satan and the Saints; or The Present Darkness and the Coming Light.* New York: Fleming H. Revell Co., 1909; Edinburgh: Oliphant, Anderson and Ferrier, n.d.

467.   _____. *The Second Coming of Christ; The Meaning, Period, and Order of Events [and] How I Came to Believe in the Lord's Return.* Chicago: The Bible Institute Colportage Association, n.d.

468.   _____. *Studying the Second Coming for Yourself* (Christian Faith Series # 6). Chicago: The Bible Institute Colportage Association, n.d.

469. _____. *A Text-Book on Prophecy*. New York: Fleming H. Revell Co., 1918.

470. Greet, William. *The Approaching 'Great Day': or The World's New Birth, etc.* London: Morgan & Scott LTD, n.d.

471. Guinness, H. Grattan. *History Unveiling Prophecy; or Time as an Interpreter*. New York: Fleming H. Revell, 1905.

472. _____. *Key to the Apocalypse: or The Seven Interpretations of Symbolic Prophecy*. London: Hodder & Stoughton, 1899.

473. _____. *The Last Hour of Gentile World Rule; Showing From the Word of God that the Sands Have Nearly All Run Out of the Hour-Glass of Gentile World Rule, etc.* Toronto: A. Sims, n.d.

474. Guinness, H. Grattan and Mrs. Guinness. *Light for the Last Days: A Study in Chronological Prophecy*. 1886. London: Marshall, Morgan & Scott, LTD, 1917; (new ed., rev. and ed. by E.P. Cachemaille, 1918).

475. Habershon, Ada R. *Babylon, the Metropolis of Satan*. n.p., n.d.

476. Haldeman, I. M. *The Coming of Christ, Both Pre-Millennial and Imminent*. New York: C. C. Cook, 1906.

477. _____. *The Coming of Christ: Is the Millennium to Come Before Christ?* New York: Pub. by author, n.d.

478. _____. *The Coming of Christ: The Two-fold Coming and the Immediacy*. New York: Pub. by author, n.d.

479. _____. *A Dispensational Key to the Holy Scriptures*. Philadelphia: Philadelphia School of the Bible, 1915.

480. _____. *The History of the Doctrine of Our Lord's Return*. New York: First Baptist Church, n.d.

481. _____. *How to Study the Bible: The Second Coming and Other Expositions*. New York: C. C. Cook, 1904.

482.   _____. *Is the Coming of Christ Before or After the Millennium?*
           New York: C. C. Cook, 1917.

483.   _____. *The Judgment Seat of Christ.* New York: C. C. Cook,
           1917.

484.   _____. *Professor Shailer Mathews's Burlesque on the Second
           Coming.* New York: Pub. by author, 1918.

485.   _____. *The Second Coming of Christ: In Relation to Doctrine,
           to Promise, and to Exhortation.* New York: Charles C. Cook,
           1917.

486.   _____. *The Signs of the Times.* (1910). Philadelphia:
           Philadelphia School of the Bible, 1919; (4th ed.). New York:
           Charles C. Cook, 1913; (5th ed.). New York: Charles C. Cook,
           1914; (8th ed.). New York: F. E. Fitch, 1929.

487.   _____. *Ten Sermons on the Second Coming.* New York:
           Fleming H. Revell, Co., 1916; (2nd ed.). Philadelphia:
           Philadelphia School of the Bible, 1917.

488.   _____. *This Hour Not the Hour of Peace.* New York: Charles
           C. Cook, 1915.

489.   _____. *The Thousand Years and After.* New York: Charles C.
           Cook, 1917.

490.   Hawkins, Robert M. *Outlines of Divine Purposes: A Dispensation
           of the Fulness of the Times, Israel's National Life, The Mosaic
           Economy.* London: Operative Converts' Institution, 1901.

491.   Heath, Alban. *The Prophecies of Daniel in the Light of History.*
           London: Covenant Publishing Co., n.d.

492.   Hill, Henry Erskine. *Apocalyptic Problems.* New York: Hodder &
           Stoughton, 1916.

493.   Hislop, Alexander. *The Two Babylons; or The Papal Worship
           Proved to Be the Worship of Nimrod and His Wife.* London: A.
           & C. Black, 1916; (2nd ed.). Neptune, NJ: Loizeaux Brothers,
           1959.

494.   Holden, John Stuart. *Behold, He Cometh.* London: Scott, 1918.

495.   _____. *Will the Christ Return? Addresses on the Second Coming of Our Lord.* New York: Fleming H. Revell, 1918.

496.   Holiday, Alfred J. *The Character of the Last Days: Six Lectures on Spiritualism, Lawlessness, Formalism, Rationalism, Imitations, Antichrists.* Kilmarnock, Scotland: John Ritchie, n.d.

497.   _____. *Maranatha ('The Lord Will Come'): The Second Advent of the Lord Jesus, With Answers to Common Objections to His Personal Coming FOR and WITH His Saints.* Kilmarnock, Scotland: John Ritchie, n.d.

498.   Houliston, William. *The Coming of the Great King: or An Examination and Discussion of the Subject of the Second Coming of Christ, and of Questions Thereto Related, with a concluding chapter on the Millennium and the Future Life.* Minneapolis: Great Western, 1897.

499.   Ironside, H. A. *Lectures on Daniel the Prophet.* New York: Loizeaux Brothers, 1911; (2nd ed., 1920).

500.   _____. *Lectures on the Revelation.* New York: Loizeaux Brothers, n.d.

501.   *Israel -- Past, Present and Future: Addresses Delivered at a Conference on Behalf of Israel Held...in Chicago.* Chicago: Chicago Hebrew Mission, 1915.

502.   Jannaway, Frank G. *Palestine and the Jews: or The Zionist Movement and Evidence that the Messiah Will Soon Appear in Jerusalem to Rule the Whole World Therefrom.* Birmingham: C. C. Walker, 1914.

503.   Jennings, Frederick Charles. *The End of the European War in the Light of Scripture.* New York: Charles C. Cook, 1915.

504.   _____. *The Seven Letters: or A Divine Church History.* New York: Our Hope, 1909.

505.   _____.   *The World Conflict in the Light of the Prophetic Word.*
        New York: Our Hope, 1917.

506.   *The Jew in History and Prophecy.* Chicago: Chicago Hebrew
        Mission, 1918.

507.   J. J.   *Clay and Stone: or Babylon the Great and the New Jerusalem.*
        London: S. W. Partridge & Co., n.d.

508.   Jordon, Willis F.   *The European War from a Bible Standpoint.* New
        York: Charles C. Cook, 1915.

509.   Kelly, William. *Babylon and the Beast.* London: W. H. Broom, n.d.

510.   _____.   *Christ's Coming Again, Chiefly on the Heavenly Side.*
        London: T. Weston, 1904.

511.   _____.   *Lectures on the Second Coming and Kingdom of the
        Lord and Savior Jesus Christ.* London: W. H. Broom, n.d.

512.   _____.   *Lectures on the Second Coming of the Lord Jesus Christ.*
        London: G. Morrish, n.d.; London: W. H. Broom, n.d.

513.   _____.   *The Lord's Prophecy on Olivet in Matthew 24 and 25.*
        London: T. Weston, 1903.

514.   _____.   *Notes on Daniel.* New York: Loizeaux Brothers, n.d.

515.   _____.   *Notes on Ezekiel.* London: G. Morrish, n.d.

516.   _____.   *The Revelation Expounded.* London: F. E. Race, n.d.

517.   _____.   *The So-Called Apostolic Fathers on the Lord's Second
        Coming.* London: T. Weston, 1904.

518.   _____.   *Three Prophetic Gems.* Charlotte, NC: Books for
        Christians, 1970 [combines in one volume: *The Lord's Prophecy
        on Olivet* ; *The Coming and the Day of the Lord* ; and *The
        Heavenly Hope*].

519.   King, H. P. *The Imperial Hope: A Restatement of the Doctrine of the Return of Jesus Christ.* New York: Fleming H. Revell, 1918.

520.   Lancaster, G. Harold. *Prophecy, the War, and the Near East* (5th impr., popular ed.). London & New York: Marshall Brothers, 1918.

521.   Langston, Earle L. *How God is Working to a Plan.* London: Thynne & Co., n.d.; Chicago: Westminster Press, n.d.; (4th ed., rev.). London: Marshall, Morgan & Scott, n.d.

522.   _____. *Ominous Days!; or The Signs of the Times.* London: Thynne, 1914; (5th ed). London: Thynne, 1918; (6th ed.). London: Chas. J. Thynne & Jarvis, 1925.

523.   MacDonald, Thomas A. *The Mighty Conflict of the Ages: Minted From Bible Prophecy and Profane History.* Paterson, NJ: Pub. by author, 1898.

524.   MacNeil, John. *Even So, Come.* New York: Fleming H. Revell, 1897.

525.   _____. *Some One is Coming.* London: Marshall Brothers, 1896.

526.   Marvin, E. P. *Maranatha.* Louisville: Pickett Publishing Co., 1902.

527.   McCartney, Richard H. *The Anti-Christ* (a poem). New York: C. C. Cook, 1914.

528.   _____. *The Coming of the King.* New York: Fleming H. Revell, 1897.

529.   McClure, W. J. *The Seven Churches of Asia.* Kilmarnock, Scotland: John Ritchie, n.d.

530.   McHardie, Mrs. E. *The Midnight Cry, 'Behold the Bridegroom Cometh,' etc.* London: John Kensit, 1898.

531.   Moggridge, E. H. *The Antichrist: Personal and Future.* London: Seeley, 1914.

532.   Moore, E. C. S. *'History in Advance,' or 'Things That Must Shortly Come to Pass.'* Aylesbury: Hunt, Barnard & Co., n.d.

533.   Moorhead, William G. *Studies in the Book of Revelation.* Pittsburgh: United Presbyterian Board of Publishers, 1908.

534.   Morgan, G. Campbell. *'Behold, He Cometh!': An Introduction to a Study of the Second Advent.* New York: Fleming H. Revell, 1912. (reprinted ed.). Grand Rapids, MI: Baker Book House, 1976.

535.   _____. *A First Century Message to Twentieth Century Christians: Addresses Based Upon the Letters to the Seven Churches of Asia.* New York: Fleming H. Revell, 1902.

536.   _____. *God's Methods with Man, In Time: Past, Present & Future.* New York: Fleming H. Revell, 1898.

537.   _____. *The Letters of Our Lord: A First Century Message to Twentieth Century Christians.* London: Pickering & Inglis, n.d.

538.   _____. *Sunrise; 'Behold, He Cometh!': An Introduction to a Study of the Second Advent.* London: Hodder and Stoughton, 1912.

539.   Morris, Alvin Marion. *The Prophecies Unveiled: or Prophecy a Divine System.* Winfield, KS: The Courier Press, 1914.

540.   Morrison, Henry Clay. *Lectures on Prophecy.* Louisville: Pentecostal Publishing Co., 1915.

541.   _____. *The Second Coming of Christ.* Louisville: Pentecostal Publishing Co., 1914.

542.   _____. *The World War in Prophecy.* Louisville: Pentecostal Publishing Co., 1917.

543.   Murray, Marr. *Bible Prophecies and the Plain Man, With Special Reference to the Present War.* London and New York: Hodder & Stoughton, 1915.

544.   _____. *Bible Prophecies and the Present War*. London: Hodder and Stoughton, 1915.

545.   Myland, D. Wesley. *The Latter Rain Covenant and Pentecostal Power*. Chicago: Evangel Publishing House, 1910.

546.   Needham, Mrs. Elizabeth Annabel (Mrs. George Needham). *The Antichrist*. St. Louis: C. B. Cox, 1881; New York: Charles C. Cook, 1901.

547.   Neighbour, Robert E. *Pre and Post Millennialism: Vital Issues at Stake*. Swengel, PA: Bible Truth Depot, n.d.

548.   Nelson, Thomas Hiram. *The Doom of Modern Civilization: or The Great Tribulation and the Millennial Kingdom that Follow*. n.p., n.d.

549.   Newton, Benjamin Wills. *The Antichrist Future* [and] *The 1260 Days of Antichrist's Reign Future* (2nd ed.). London: Houlston and Sons, 1900; London: The Sovereign Grace Advent Testimony, 1900.

550.   _____. *Expository Teaching on the Millennium and Israel's Future*. London: The Sovereign Grace Advent Testimony, 1913.

551.   _____. *Jerusalem: Its Future History*. London: L. Collins, 1908.

552.   Norris, Harold. *When Will Our Lord Return?: Prophetic Times and Warning Events* (3rd ed.). London: Chas J. Thynne, 1916.

553.   Oliphant, Mrs. John Stewart. *The End of the Bible: A Book of Prophecy for Young Christians*. London: Marshall Brothers, 1902.

554.   Ottman, Ford C. *God's Oath: A Study of an Unfulfilled Promise of God*. New York: G. H. Doran, 1911; New York: Our Hope, 1911.

555.   _____. *Imperialism and Christ*. New York: Our Hope; New York: C. C. Cook, 1912.

556.   _____. *The Unfolding of the Ages.* New York: Baker and Taylor,
         1915.

557.   Overton, John. *'Shall So Come': A Plea for Faith in the
         Premillennial Advent of the Lord Jesus Christ* (rev. ed.).
         Chicago: Bible Institute Colportage Association, 1916.

558.   Page, Alfred. *Rejoicing and Glory: Present-day Words for Believers.*
         London: Samuel E. Parks, n.d.

559.   *Papers on the Lord's Coming, by C. H. M.* Chicago: The Moody
         Press, n.d.

560.   Parlane, W. A. *Elements of Dispensational Truth.* New York:
         Charles C. Cook, 1905.

561.   Paterson-Smyth, John. *The Gospel of the Hereafter.* New York:
         Fleming H. Revell, 1910. [also listed under Smyth, John
         Paterson]

562.   Peck, A. C. *Christ's Return: The Key to Prophecy and Providence.*
         New York: Alliance Press Co., 1906.

563.   Pettingill, William L. *Brief Prophetic Messages.* Waterloo, IA: The
         Cedar Book Store, n.d.

564.   _____. *The Coming One According to Scripture.* New York:
         Charles C. Cook, 1916.

565.   _____. *God's Prophecies for Plain People.* Philadelphia: The
         Philadelphia School of the Bible, 1905, (reprinted, 1923).

566.   _____. *Israel: Jehovah's Covenant People.* Harrisburg, PA: F.
         Kelker, 1905.

567.   _____. *Simple Studies in Daniel.* Philadelphia: The Philadelphia
         School of the Bible, 1909, (reprinted, 1920).

568.   _____. *Simple Studies in Matthew* (6th ed.). Philadelphia: The
         Philadelphia School of the Bible, 1910.

569.   _____. *Simple Studies in Revelation.* Philadelphia: The
        Philadelphia School of the Bible, 1916, (7th ed., 1933).

570.   Pickering, Hy (ed.). *100 World-known Witnesses to the Second
        Coming of the Lord: Personal, Premillennial.* London: Pickering
        & Inglis, n.d.

571.   Pickett, Leander L. *The Blessed Hope of His Glorious Appearing.*
        Louisville: Pentecostal Publishing Co., 1901.

572.   _____. *The Renewed Earth: or The Coming and Reign of Jesus
        Christ.* Louisville: Pentecostal Publishing Co., 1903.

573.   Pierson, Arthur T. *The Coming of the Lord.* London: Passmore &
        Alabaster, 1896; Chicago: Fleming H. Revell, 1896.

574.   _____. *The Second Coming of Our Lord.* Altemus, 1896.

575.   Pollock, Algernon J. *The Amazing Jew* (5th ed.). London: The
        Central Bible Truth Depot, n.d.

576.   _____. *The Apostasy of Christendom.* The Central Bible Truth
        Depot, n.d.

577.   _____. *May Christ Come at Any Moment? or Will the Church
        of God Go Through the Great Tribulation.* The Central Bible
        Truth Depot, n.d.

578.   _____. *'Things Which Must Shortly Come to Pass'* (2nd ed.).
        London: The Central Bible Truth Depot, 1936.

579.   _____. *Why Does God Allow This War?* New York: Loizeaux
        Brothers, n.d.

580.   Ramsay, William Mitchell. *The Letters to the Seven Churches of
        Asia and their Place in the Plan of the Apocalypse.* London:
        Hodder and Stoughton, 1904.

581.   Reed, John K. *That Blessed Hope.* New York: Charles C. Cook,
        1914.

582.   Reitzel, Charles Francis. *The Identity of the Antichrist.* Altoona, PA: Pub. by author, n.d.

583.   Riggle, Herbert M. *The Kingdom of God and the One Thousand Year's Reign.* Moundville, WV: Gospel Trumpet Publishing Co., 1899.

584.   Riley, William B. *The Coming and the Kingdom.* Kansas City, MO: The Western Baptist Publishing Co., n.d.

585.   _____. *The Evolution of the Kingdom.* Chicago: Charles C. Cook, 1913 [enlarged version of *The Coming and the Kingdom*].

586.   _____. *The Seven Churches of Asia.* New York: Christian Alliance Publishing Co., 1900.

587.   Rodd, John E. *The Last Days: Text Book on the Second Coming of Christ, and Events Which Shall be Hereafter.* Chicago: The Evangelical Publishing Co., n.d.

588.   _____. *Our Lord's Second Coming: A Comprehensive, Consecutive and Emphasized New Testament Reading on this Momentous Subject.* New York: Charles C. Cook, n.d.

589.   Rohold, S. B. *The War and the Jew.* Toronto: The Macmillan Co. of Canada, 1915.

590.   Ross, Alexander. *A Protest Against a Change of Creed, Denying Our Lord's Coming to Establish His Kingdom, Teaching a Merely Spiritual Millennium Contrary to All the Historical Creeds of Christendom.* n.p., n.d.

591.   Rowland, Edward G. *After Civilization -- What?* (rev. ed.). Williamsport, PA: Bible Truth Depot, 1911.

592.   Rutledge, David D. *Christ, Anti-Christ and Millennium.* London: Marshall Brothers, 1903.

593.   St. Dalmas, H. G. Emeric de. *The Time of the End and the 'Weeks' of Daniel: A Discovery and Restatement.* London: Thynne, 1917.

594.   Salmon, T. H. *Christ is Coming: How? and When?* London: Samuel E. Roberts, n.d.

595.   _____. *Waiting the Coming One: Listening for the Shout (1 Thess. IV.16).* London: Samuel E. Roberts, 1915.

596.   Saphir, Adolph. *Christ and Israel.* London: Morgan, 1911.

597.   Savage, John A. *The Scroll of Time; or Epochs and Dispensations of Scripture, A Key to the Chart, with Special References to the Book of Revelation and Other Prophecies.* London: A. S. Rouse, 1893; London: G. Morrish, 1918.

598.   _____. *The Voice of the Watchman.* London: G. Morrish, n.d.

599.   Scofield, Cyrus I. *Addresses on Prophecy.* Los Angeles: Bible House of Los Angeles, n.d.; Swengel, PA: Bible Truth Depot, 1910; New York: Charles C. Cook, 1914.

600.   _____. *Dr. C. I. Scofield's Question Box* (compiled by Ella E. Pohe). Chicago: Bible Institute Colportage Association, 1917.

601.   _____. *Prophecy Made Plain: Addresses on Prophecy.* Glasgow: Pickering & Inglis; London: Alfred Holness, n.d. [British edition of *Addresses on Prophecy*].

602.   _____. *Things New and Old* (compiled and edited by Arno Gaebelein). New York: Publication Office of Our Hope, 1920.

603.   _____. *What Do the Prophets Say?* Philadelphia: The Sunday School Times Co., 1916.

604.   _____. *Will the Church Pass Through the Great Tribulation?: Eighteen Reasons Which Prove that It Will Not.* Philadelphia: Philadelphia School of the Bible, 1917.

605.   _____. *The World's Approaching Crisis.* New York: Our Hope, n.d.; Philadelphia: Philadelphia School of the Bible, 1913.

606.   Scofield, Cyrus I. (ed.). *The Scofield Reference Bible.* New York: Oxford University Press, 1909, (expanded ed., 1917).

607.   Scofield, Cyrus I., and Arno Gaebelein. *The Jewish Question.* New York: Our Hope, 1912.

608.   Scott, James. *After These Things -- What?* Glasgow: Pickering & Inglis, n.d.

609.   Scott, Walter. *'At Hand'; or Things Which Must Shortly Come to Pass: The Prophetic Future Comprehensively Set Forth, with Concise Details of Coming Events.* London: Pickering & Inglis, n.d.; London: A. Holness, 1908; (2nd ed., carefully revised). London: A. Holness, 1909.

610.   _____. *Coming Glories: or Plain Answers to Seventy-Six Prophetic and Other Questions* (2nd ed., rev.). Glasgow: Allan, n.d.; (3rd ed.). Glasgow: Allan; London: Holness, n.d.; (new ed.). Glasgow: Allan, n.d.

611.   _____. *Exposition of the Revelation of Jesus Christ.* London: Pickering & Inglis, n.d.

612.   _____. *Future Events with Numerous Prophetic Details.* London: Alfred Holness, n.d.; (new ed.). R. L. Allan & Son, n.d.

613.   _____. *Palestine Restored; or The Near Restoration of the Jewish Commonwealth in Palestine: The Question of the Twentieth Century.* London: Pickering & Inglis, n.d.

614.   Scroggie, W. Graham. *The Great Unveiling.* London: Marshall, Morgan & Scott, n.d.

615.   _____. *Prophecy and History with Reference to the Jews, the Gentiles, and the Church of God.* London: Marshall, Morgan & Scott, 1915.

616.   Seiss, Joseph A. *The Letters of Jesus* (Lenten Lectures). New York: Charles C. Cook, 1903.

617.   Shackleton, Edmund. *Will the Church Escape the Great Tribulation?* [and] *Sound an Alarm!* (3rd ed.). London: John F. Shaw, n.d.

618. Shipman, C. A. *Unfulfilled Prophecy.* London: Samuel E. Roberts, 1908; (rev. and enlarged ed.). London: Samuel E. Roberts, 1915.

619. Silver, Jesse F. *The Lord's Return, Seen in History and in Scripture as Pre-millennial and Imminent.* New York: Fleming H. Revell, 1914.

620. Simpson, Albert Benjamin. *Back to Patmos: Prophetic Outlooks on Present Conditions.* New York: Christian Alliance Publishing Co., 1914.

621. _____. *The Coming One.* New York: Christian Alliance Publishing Co., 1912.

622. _____. *The Midnight Cry.* Pub. by author, 1914.

623. Sims, Albert. *Beacon Lights of Prophecy; For Heaven-bound Travellers Amid the Deepening Shadows.* Toronto: A. Sims, n.d.

624. _____. *The Coming Golden Age: When Lost Eden Will Have Been Restored, and God's Redeemed Family Shall Reign on the Earth* (3rd ed.). Toronto: A. Sims, n.d.

625. _____. *Deepening Shadows and Coming Glories.* Toronto: A. Sims, 1905.

626. _____. *The Great Tribulation: What Does it Mean? When Will it Commence? How Long Will it Last?* (2nd ed.). Toronto: A. Sims, n.d.

627. _____. *The Near Approach to Antichrist.* Toronto: A. Sims, n.d.

628. _____. *The World's Desperate Cry for a Super Man: An Unveiling of the Satanic Forces Behind the Screen, The Universal Commotion Explained.* Toronto: A. Sims, n.d.

629. Smyth, John Paterson. *The Gospel of the Hereafter.* New York: Fleming H. Revell, 1910 and 1930. [also listed under Paterson-Smyth, John]

630. Soltau, George. *Past -- Present -- Future; or Scripture Fulfilled,
      Fulfilling, Unfulfilled: A Series of Lectures on the 'Plan of the
      Ages.'* London: Christian Herald, 1912.

631. Speer, Robert E. *The Second Coming of Christ.* New York: Gospel
      Publishing Co., 1903.

632. Stevens, William Coit. *The Book of Daniel: A Composite
      Revelation of the Last Days of Israel's Subjugation to Gentile
      Powers* (rev. ed.). New York: Fleming H. Revell Co., 1918.

633. _____. *Mysteries of the Kingdom.* Nyack, NY: Missionary
      Institute, 1904; San Francisco: M. G. McClinton & Co., 1915.

634. Stine, Milton H. *The Devil's Bride: A Present Day Arraignment of
      Formalism and Doubt in the Church and in Society, in the Light
      of the Holy Scriptures, Given in the Form of a Pleasing Story.*
      Harrisburg, PA: Minter, 1910.

635. Stowe, Harriet Beecher, et al. *He's Coming To-morrow, and Other
      Papers.* New York: Fleming H. Revell, 1901.

636. Stroh, Grant. *The Next World Crisis, in the Light of the Former
      World Crises.* Chicago: Bible Institute Colportage Association,
      n.d. [Formerly *When God Comes Down to Earth*]

637. _____. *When God Comes Down to Earth: or Epochal Crises,
      Past and Future.* Chicago: Bible Institute Colportage
      Association, 1914.

638. Sunday, William Ashley. *The Second Coming.* Fort Wayne, IN:
      E.A.K. Hackett, 1913.

639. Sutcliffe, B. B. *The Responsibility of the Church in Relation to
      Israel.* Chicago; Chicago Hebrew Mission, n.d.

640. Tanner, Joseph. *Daniel and the Revelation: the Chart of Prophecy
      and Our Place in it; A Study of the Historical and Futurist
      Interpretation.* London: Hodder & Stoughton, 1898.

641. Taylor, J. M. *The Second Coming of Christ and Some Reasons
      Why I Think It Is Near.* Bismarck, ND: Pub. by author, 1917.

642. Thomas, E. H. *The Remnant of Israel, the Church, and the Coming of Christ.* London: James Nisbet, 1903.

643. Tinling, James Forbes Bisset. *The Great Prophecy -- in Fulfilment: A Sketch of the Parallel Lines of Prophecy and History.* London: Marshall Brothers, LTD, n.d.

644. Torrey, R. A. *The Personal Return of Christ.* London: James E. Hawkins, n.d.

645. _____. *The Return of the Lord Jesus: The Key to the Scripture and Solution of All Our Political and Social Problems; or The Golden Age That is Soon Coming to the Earth.* Los Angeles: The Bible Institute of Los Angeles, 1913.

646. _____. *What War Teaches: The Greatest Lesson of the Year 1917.* Los Angeles: The Bible Institute of Los Angeles, 1918.

647. Townsend, J. H. *'After this I will Return': or The Threefold Outlook.* London: Marshall Brothers, LTD, 1907.

648. Trench, Richard C. *Commentary on the Epistles to the Seven Churches in Asia: Revelation II and III* (6th ed., revised & improved). Kegan Paul, Trench, Truber & Co., LTD, 1897; (reprinted ed.). Minneapolis: Klock & Klock Christian Publishers, 1978.

649. Turner, Charles W. *Outline Studies in the Book of Revelation and Key to the Chart of the Age.* Plain City, OH: Pub. by author, 1916.

650. Urquhart, John. *What are We to Believe?: The Testimony of Fulfilled Prophecy.* London: Marshall Brothers, n.d.

651. _____. *The Wonders of Prophecy: or What are We to Believe?* (3rd ed., revision of *What Are We to Believe?*). New York: Gospel Publishing House, 1906; (9th ed.). Harrisburg, PA: Christian Publishers, n.d. (new rev. ed.). New York: Christian Alliance Publishing Co., 1948.

652.   Vine, W. E. *The Roman Empire in the Light of Prophecy; or The Rise, Progress, and End of the Fourth World Empire*. London: Pickering & Inglis, 1916.

653.   Waggoner, E. J. *Prophetic Lights: Some of the Prominent Prophecies of the Old and New Testaments Interpreted by the Bible and History* (4th ed.). London: International Tract Society LTD, 1899.

654.   Watson, George Douglas. *The Age to Come and Signs of its Approach*. Columbia, SC: Pike, n.d.

655.   Watson, Sydney. *In the Twinkling of an Eye.* Los Angeles: Bible Institute of Los Angeles, 1918; New York: Fleming H. Revell, 1933. [fiction]

656.   _____. *The Mark of the Beast*. London: Nicholson & Sons, 1911; Los Angeles: BIOLA, 1918; New York: Fleming H. Revell Co, n.d. [fiction]

657.   Waugh, Thomas. *When Jesus Comes*. London: Charles H. Kelly, 1901.

658.   Westerdale, T. L. Barlow. *The Coming Miracle, God and the Jews: A Little Book Dealing with the Great Prophecy of Isaiah and Jesus Concerning the Jewish Race and its Dramatic Fulfillment in History* (3rd ed.). New York: Marshall Brothers, n.d.

659.   Whalley, William H. *Light on the Judgment: Past, Present, and Future*. Glouster: Jennings, 1918.

660.   Wheeler, R. L. *The Age to Come*. Taunton: E. Goodman & Son, LTD, n.d.

661.   White, Frank H. *The Saints' Rest and Rapture: When and For Whom?* (5th ed.). Aylesbury: Hunt, Barnard & Co., n.d.

662.   Wilson, M. W. *Prophetical Suggestions, Being Expository of the Books of Revelation and Daniel*. London: Digby, Long & Co., 1906.

663.   Wilson, Robert Dick. *Studies in the Book of Daniel: A Discussion
        of the Historical Questions.* New York: G Putnam's Sons,
        1917; New York: Fleming H. Revell Co., n.d.; (reprinted ed.).
        Grand Rapids, MI: Eerdmans, 1972 .

664.   Wilson, W. H. *The Destiny of Russia and the Signs of the Times.*
        Chicago: Pub. by author, 1914.

665.   Wimberley, Charles F. *Behold the Morning!: The Imminent and
        Premillennial Coming of Jesus Christ.* New York: Fleming H.
        Revell, 1916.

666.   Wingate, Sir Andrew. *Palestine, Mesopotamia, and the Jews; the
        Spiritual Side of History with a Synopsis of the War.* Glasgow:
        Alfred Holness; London: Pickering and Inglis, n.d.

667.   Woods, F. H. *The Hope of Israel: A Review of the Argument from
        Prophecy.* T. & T. Clark, 1896.

668.   Woodward, E. P. *The Threefold Witness (Daniel, Christ, John):
        Concerning the Final Consummation.* Westbrook, ME: Pub. by
        author, 1912.

669.   Wright, Charles H. H. *Daniel and His Prophecies.* London:
        Williams and Norgate, 1906; (reprinted as *Studies in Daniel's
        Prophecies.* Minneapolis: Klock & Klock, 1983).

SECTION FIVE

INFLATION, DEPRESSSION, AND THE RISE OF TOTALITARIANISM, 1919-1939

The return of the Jews to the Holy Land gave dispensational millenarians a measure of credibility and a modicum of respect among many conservative Protestant churches. The World War had confirmed the premillennialist view that things were not getting better but were, indeed, getting much worse. What is more, the war had also dealt a body blow to post-millennialist optimism. Contrary to the post-millennialist anticipation of a better tomorrow, the war had made it clear that the sun was setting precipitously on Western civilization.

From 1919 to 1939, the world spun through two decades of dramatic changes which saw an era of tremedous social and economic turmoil. During the 1920s, Mussolini and his fascists party gained control of Italy. Then, in the 1930s, National Socialism took firm root, first in Germany, and, soon after, in Spain, as totalitarians such as Adolf Hitler and Francisco Franco came to power. In the new Soviet Union, Stalin ruthlessly dragged feudal Russian society into the modern industrial world. Before industrialization was achieved later in the 1940s, Stalin and his agents would send upwards to 12 million people to their graves.

Premillennialist literature of this period reflects the uneasiness many evangelical Protestants felt in the face of such political and economic uncertainty. For instance, several works focus on the rise of the Antichrist of the Last Days and his rule as world dictator. Many authors of this period wondered aloud if perchance Mussolini would become the leader of a revived Roman Empire -- "Il Duce Antichrist." Others nominated Hitler and Stalin as candidates for the Antichrist's mantle. Some authors pondered the significance of the newly formed League of Nations and its place in the endtimes. Still others speculated on the prophetic significance of the various pacts and treaties signed by Germany, Italy, the USSR, and the Vatican.

Though their individual concerns varied, their attempt to decipher the Divine timetable through their dispensational premillennial reading of history and prophecy remained the common link among them.

---

670. Adams, John Quincy. *Babylon: Just What Is It?: 'Reprinted from Mr. Adams' Larger Work, a Copyrighted Book.'* n.p., n.d.

671. _____. *The Time of the End.* Dallas: The Prophetical Society of Dallas, 1924.

672. Anderson, John A. *The Church, the Chart, and the Coming.* London: Morgan & Scott, n.d.

673. Baker, Ernest. *The Prophetic Lamp.* London: Pickering & Inglis, 1932.

674. _____. *The Return of the Lord* (2nd ed.). London: Seeley, 1916.

675. Ball, C. T. *Eschatology.* Forth Worth, TX: American Publishing Co., n.d.

676. _____. *The Victorious Christ.* Forth Worth, TX: American Publishing Co., n.d.

677. Baron, David. *The Jewish Problem: Its Solution; or Israel's Present and Future* (6th ed., carefully rev.). London: Morgan and Scott, n.d.

678.   Barton, Harold E. *It's Here: The Time of the End: A Comprehensive Study of Bible Prophecy Fulfilled and Unfulfilled.* New York: Exposition Press, 1963. [reprinted from an earlier edition]

679.   _____. *Why Time? God's Plan and Purpose.* San Jose, CA: Burbank Press, 1927; (reprinted ed.). San Jose, CA: Burbank Press, 1967.

680.   Bauman, Louis S. *God and Gog: or The Coming Meet Between Judah's Lion and Russia's Bear.* Long Beach, CA: Pub. by author, 1934.

681.   _____. *Shirts and Sheets: or Anti-Semitism, A Present-day Sign of the First Magnitude.* Long Beach, CA: Pub. by author, 1934.

682.   _____. *The Time of Jacob's Trouble.* Long Beach, CA: Pub. by author, 1938.

683.   Benham, Charles O. *101 Signs of Christ's Coming: X-Raying Today's Crisis* (3rd ed.). Joliet, IL: Pub. by author, 1937.

684.   Beskin, Nathan Cohen. *Return of the Jews and the End of the World: 'Consummation of Time.'* Chicago: The Peacock Press, 1931.

685.   Biederwolf, William Edward. *The Millennium Bible: Being a Help to the Study of the Holy Scriptures in Their Testimony to the Second Coming of Our Lord and Saviour Jesus Christ.* Chicago: Glad Tidings Publishing Co., 1924.

686.   _____. *The Millennium Bible (American Standard Bible).* Nashville: Thomas Nelson Co., 1924.

687.   _____. *The Second Coming of Christ.* Chicago: Glad Tidings Publishing Co., n.d.

688.   Bingham, David. *The Number of the Beast.* n.p., 1921.

689.   Bougher, J. T. *'In the Twinkling of an Eye,' Being the Word of God Concerning 'The Things Which Are and the Things Which*

Shall Be' (7th ed.). Findlay, OH: Fundamental Truth Publishers, n.d.

690.   Boyd, Frank M. *Ages and Dispensations*. Springfield, MO: Gospel Publishing House, 1935.

691.   _____. *The Budding Fig Tree*. Springfield, MO: Gospel Publishing House, n.d.

692.   Brandt, Johanna. *The Millennium: A Prophetic Forecast*. n.p., n.d.

693.   Brooks, Frederick L. *Prophetic Glimpses* (2nd ed.). Findlay, OH: Fundamental Truth Publishers, 1939.

694.   Brooks, Keith L. *The Age-end Prophecy of Our Lord: A Verse by Verse Comment on Matthew 24-25*. Los Angeles: American Prophetic League, n.d.

695.   _____. *The Consummation: Vital Prophetic Truth*. Los Angeles: Brooks Publishers, n.d.

696.   _____. *Harvest of Iniquity: Impending World Events as Revealed in the Book of Revelation*. Los Angeles: Brooks Publications, 1933.

697.   _____. *The Jews and the Passion for Palestine in the Light of Prophecy*. Grand Rapids, MI: Zondervan Publishing House, 1937.

698.   _____. *Prophecies of Daniel and Revelation*. Los Angeles: BIOLA, 1925.

699.   _____. *Prophecy and the Tottering Nations*. Los Angeles: BIOLA, 1935.

700.   _____. *Prophetic Text Book*. Los Angeles: BIOLA, 1933.

701.   Broomall, Wick. *The Antichrist: A Brief Scriptural Study of the Coming Satan-Inspired World Dictator*. Pub. by author, n.d.

702. Brown, Arthur I. *Into the Clouds*. Hoytville, OH: Fundamental Truth Publishers, 1938.

703. _____. *Light on the Hills*. Hoytville, OH: Fundamental Truth Publishers, 1934.

704. _____. *What of the Night?* Hoytville, OH: Fundamental Truth Publishers, 1933.

705. Brown, Harry M. *'The Morning Cometh.'* Brooklyn: William Haedrich & Sons, 1939.

706. Brownville, C. Gordon. *The Romance of the Future*. New York: Fleming H. Revell, 1938.

707. Burr, Willard Vail. *Bible Prophecy Made Easy to Understand: A Most Comprehensive Outline of Prophecy*. Los Angeles: Pub. by author, n.d.

708. Buroker, L. Peres. *Today in Bible Prophecy*. Laper, MI: W. E. Cole, 1937.

709. _____. *Yesterday in Bible Prophecy*. Laper, MI: W. E. Cole, 1938.

710. Buswell, J. Oliver Jr. *Unfulfilled Prophecies*. Grand Rapids, MI: Zondervan Publishing House, 1937.

711. Cameron, Robert. *Scriptural Truth About the Lord's Return*. New York: Fleming H. Revell, 1922.

712. Chafer, Lewis Sperry. *Dispensations*. Dallas, TX: Dallas Theological Seminary Press, 1936.

713. _____. *He That is Spiritual*. New York: Our Hope Publishing Co., 1918.

714. _____. *The Kingdom in History and Prophecy*. New York: Fleming H. Revell, 1915; Philadelphia: The Sunday School Times, 1922; Chicago: Moody Press, 1936.

715.   _____. *Must We Dismiss the Millennium?* Crescent City, FL: Biblical Testimony League, 1922.

716.   _____. *Seven Major Biblical Signs of the Times.* Philadelphia: The Sunday School Times, 1919.

717.   _____. *Signs of the Times.* Chicago: Bible Institute Colportage Association, 1919.

718.   Chalmers, Thomas M. *Israel in Covenant and History.* New York: Pub. by Author, 1916 and 1926.

719.   _____. *The Present Condition of Israel in the Light of Prophecy.* Philadelphia: American Society for Prophetic Studies, 1923.

720.   Chamberlain, M. H. *Comments on Daniel: A Revision of the Interpretations of the Prophecies of Daniel and Other Prophecies* (2nd ed., rev.). Los Angeles: Paul C. Brown, 1932.

721.   Childe, Frederick W. *Prophecies of Daniel and Revelation Compared: Being an Outline of Chart Lectures Given by the Author, including his Famous lecture 'Fifteen Reasons Why I Believe the Second Coming is Near.'* Los Angeles: Pub. by the author, n.d.; Glendale, CA: Glendale News Commercial Printing Co., 1927.

722.   Close, Albert. *The Hand of God and Satan in Modern History* (3rd ed.). London: Thynne & Co., 1938.

723.   Conradi, Ludwig R. *The Impelling Force of Prophetic Truth.* London: Thynne & Co. and the Daily Prayer Union, 1935.

724.   Cook, Charles C. *World Peace: Is It a Reasonable Hope or a Delusion?* Chicago: Bible Institute Colportage Association, 1924.

725.   Cooper, David L. *Future Events Revealed: An Exposition of the Olivet Discourse.* Los Angeles: Biblical Research Society, 1935, (reprinted, 1983).

726.   _____. *Is the Jew Still First on God's Prophetic Program?: Vital Questions Answered.* Los Angeles: Biblical Research Society, 1935.

727.   _____. *May Christ Delay His Return 1000 Years?* Los Angeles: Biblical Research Society, n.d.

728.   _____. *Preparing for the World-wide Revival.* Los Angeles: Biblical Research Society, 1938.

729.   Corey, William A. *Tomorrow: A Preview of the Millennial Kingdom.* Premillennial Prophetic Association, n.d.

730.   Cox, Herbert W. *Epochs Connected with the Second Coming of Christ.* London: Marshall, Morgan & Scott, 1928.

731.   Crowell, Henry E. *The Structure of the Bible: A Study of the Ages Followed by a Quest for Jesus Christ as Prophet, Priest and King* (Mary A. Scotten and Madeleine Eldred, eds.). New York: The Echoes Publishing Co., 1921.

732.   Davis, George T. B. *Fulfilled Prophecies That Prove the Bible.* Philadelphia: The Million Testaments Campaign, 1931.

733.   _____. *Rebuilding Palestine According to Prophecy.* Philadelphia: The Million Testaments Campaign, 1935.

734.   _____. *Seeing Prophecy Fulfilled in Palestine.* Philadelphia: The Million Testaments Campaign, 1937.

735.   Dawson, W. Bell. *The Hope of the Future.* London: Marshall, Morgan & Scott, n.d.

736.   _____. *The Time is at Hand, as Indicated by the Periods in Prophecy Already Fulfilled.* London: Thynne, 1926.

737.   Dean, Ibzan Rice. *The Coming Kingdom, the Goal of Prophecy.* Philadelphia: Philadelphia School of the Bible, 1928; Philadelphia: Approved Book Store, 1928.

738.   _____. *The Gospel of Matthew and the Seventy Weeks of Daniel.* New York: Our Hope, n.d.

739.   Dobyns, William R. *Pre-millennial -- Why?* Chicago: The Bible Institute Colportage Association, n.d.

740.   Dorman, Lucy Mary. *The Unveiled Future: An Interpretation of the Revelation Given to St. John.* London: Marshall, Morgan & Scott, LTD, 1936.

741.   Duffield, John T. *In Defence of Pre-millenarianism.* New York: Arno C. Gaebelein, n.d.

742.   Dunbar, James. *The Coming Glories of the Jewish Nation: Israel Restored to Palestine, and Made Head of the Nations. Their Marvellous City and the Temple of Gems and Gold.* London: Pickering & Inglis, n.d.

743.   _____. *Mesopotamia and Babylon: the Rebuilt City the Wonder of the Century.* New York: The Book Stall, 1919.

744.   _____. *The Two Witnesses: Who are They? Who do They Witness? When and Where?* New York: The Book Stall, n.d.

745.   Dunham, T. Richard. *The Great Tribulation.* Hoytville, OH: Fundamental Truth Publishers, 1933.

746.   _____(ed.).   *Unveiling the Future: Twelve Prophetic Messages.* Findlay, OH: Fundamental Truth Publishers, 1934.

747.   Ely, James E. *Glimpses of Bible Climaxes.* Garden City, KS: Businessman Gospel Association, 1927.

748.   Erdman, Charles R. *The Return of Christ.* New York: George H. Doran Co., 1922.

749.   Emmerson, George J. *The End in View.* London: Marshall Brothers, 1920.

750.   Evans, William. *Christ's Last Message to His Church: An Exposition of the Seven Letters of Revelation I-III.* New York: Fleming H. Revell, 1926.

751.   _____. *The Coming King: The World's Next Great Crisis.* New York: Fleming H. Revell Co., 1923.

752.   Feinberg, Charles L. *Premillennialism or Amillennialism?: The Premillennial and Amillennial Systems of Interpretation Analyzed and Compared.* Grand Rapids, MI: Zondervan Publishing House, 1936; (2nd ed., enlarged). Wheaton, IL: Van Kampen Press, 1954; (3rd ed., enlarged). Chicago: Moody Press, 1980.

753.   Frodsham, Stanley H. *The Coming Crises and the Coming Christ.* Springfield, MO: Gospel Publishing House, n.d.

754.   _____. *'Things Which Must Shortly Come to Pass.'* Springfield, MO: Gospel Publishing House, 1928.

755.   Frost, Frank Dutton. *The Appointed Time: or The Present World Crisis, the Disease and the Cure* (4th ed.). London: Pickering & Inglis, 1933.

756.   Frost, Henry W. *Matthew Twenty-Four and the Revelation.* New York: Oxford University Press, 1924.

757.   _____. *The Second Coming of Christ.* Grand Rapids, MI: Wm B. Eerdmans Publishing Co., 1934.

758.   Gaebelein, Arno C. *As it Was -- So Shall it Be.* New York: Our Hope Publication Office, 1937.

759.   _____. *The Conflict of the Ages: The Mystery of Lawlessness, Its Origin, Historic Development and Coming Defeat.* New York: Our Hope; London: Pickering & Inglis, 1933.

760.   _____. *The Hope of the Ages: The Messianic Hope in Revelation, in History, and in Realization.* New York: Our Hope Publication Office, 1938.

761.   _____. *Hopeless -- Yet There is Hope: A Study in World Conditions and Their Solution*. New York: Our Hope Publication Office; London: Pickering & Inglis, 1935.

762.   _____. *If Christ Should Return -- What?* New York: Our Hope, n.d.

763.   _____. *The League of Nations in the Light of Prophecy*. New York: Our Hope Publication Office, 1920.

764.   _____. *Maranatha Bells: The Blessed Hope in Prose and Poetry*. New York: Arno Gaebelein, Inc., 1935.

765.   _____. *Meat in Due Season: Sermons, Discourses and Expositions of the Word of Prophecy*. New York: A. C. Gaebelein, Inc., n.d.; New York: Our Hope Publication Office, 1933.

766.   _____. *Our Age and Its End* [bound with C. I. Scofield's *Lectures on Prophecy*]. New York: Our Hope, n.d.

767.   _____. *The Return of the Lord: What the New Testament Teaches About the Second Coming of Christ*. New York: Our Hope Publication Office 1925.

768.   _____. *The Revelation*. New York: Loizeaux Bros., n.d.

769.   _____. *'Things to Come.'* New York: Our Hope Publication Office, n.d.

770.   _____. *The Unfinished Symphony*. New York: Our Hope, n.d.

771.   _____. *World Prospects; How Is It All Going to End? A Study in Sacred Prophecy and Present Day World Conditions*. New York: Our Hope; London: Pickering & Inglis, 1934.

772.   Gardner, Preston Edwin. *Our Lord's Coming and His Kingdom*. Los Angeles: n.p., 1935.

773.   Gartenhaus, Jacob. *The Jew and Jesus Christ*. Nashville: Southern Baptist Convention, 1934.

774. _____. *The Rebirth of a Nation: Zionism in History and Prophecy.* Nashville: Broadman Press, 1936.

775. Gordon, Samuel Dickey. *Quiet Talks on the Deeper Meaning of the War and Its Relation to Our Lord's Return.* New York: Fleming H. Revell, 1919.

776. Grautoff, B. M. W. *They That are Left!* London: Thynne & Co., n.d. [fiction]

777. Gray, J. M., et al. *How I Came to Believe in Our Lord's Return and Why I Believe the Lord's Return is Near.* Chicago: Bible Institute Colportage Association, 1935.

778. Gray, James M. *My Faith in Jesus Christ.* Chicago: Bible Institute Colportage Association, 1927.

779. Gray, Mrs. Carl R. *The Lord's Return According to the Scriptures.* Pub. by author, 1925.

780. Gudebrod, George H. *Bible Problems Solved: A Logical Interpretation.* New York: G. P. Putnam's Sons, 1937.

781. Guille, G. E. *That Blessed Hope.* Chicago: Bible Institute Colportage Association, 1920.

782. Haldeman, I. M. *The Kingdom of God: What Is It? --When Is It? --Where Is It?* NY: C. C. Cook, 1931.

783. _____. *A Review of Mr. Philip Mauro's Book 'The Gospel of the Kingdom': A Defence of Dispensational Truth and the Scofield Bible.* New York: F. E. Fitch, 1931.

784. _____. *Why I Preach the Second Coming.* New York: Fleming H. Revell, Co., 1919.

785. Ham, Mordecai Fowler. *The Jews.* n.p., n.d.

786. _____. *The Second Coming of Christ.* n.p., n.d.

787.   Hardie, Alexander. *The World Program According to the Holy Scriptures, etc.* Los Angeles: The Times-Mirror Press, 1923.

788.   Harrison, Norman B. *His Right to Rule.* Chicago: The Bible Institute Colportage Association, 1933.

789.   Haslam, William. *The Lord is Coming: A Plain Narrative of Prophetic Events in their Order.* London: Morgan & Scott, n.d.

790.   Heffren, H. C. *The Sign of His Coming.* Canada: Pub. by author, n.d.

791.   Herrstrom, William Dewey. *War Preparations and International Suicide.* Findlay, OH: Fundamental Truth Publishers, 1937.

792.   *He Shall Come Again, by an Unknown Christian.* London: Marshall, 1922.

793.   Hicks, W. P. *The Anti-Christ To-day.* New York: The Christian Herald Office, n.d.

794.   Hogg, Charles Frederick. *The Mystery of Iniquity: Suggestions Towards the Interpretation of Revelation 13.* London: Pickering & Inglis, n.d.

795.   _____. *The Promise of His Coming: Chapters on the Second Advent.* London: Pickering & Inglis, n.d.

796.   Hogg, C. F. and W. E. Vine. *The Church and the Tribulation: A Review of the Book Entitled, 'The Approaching Advent of Christ.'* London: Pickering & Inglis, 1938.

797.   _____. *Touching the Coming of the Lord.* Edinburgh: Oliphants, 1919.

798.   Hole, Frank Binford. *Will All the Saints be Caught Up When the Lord Comes?* London: The Central Bible Truth Depot, n.d.

799.   Holt, Basil F. *What Time Is It?: The Second Coming of Christ and the Signs of the Times* (Introduction by William Biederwolf). Cincinnati: Standard Publishing Co., 1936.

800. Horsefield, Frederick J. *The Church and the Coming King*. London: Marshall Brothers, 1926.

801. _____. *Parables of the Second Coming.* n.p., n.d.

802. _____. *The Return of the King.* n.p., n.d.

803. _____. *The Voice of Prophecy.* London: Marshall Brothers, n.d.

804. Hottel, W. S. *The Lord Coming for and With His Saints.* Grand Rapids, MI: Zondervan Publishing House, 1937.

805. Houghton, Thomas. *The Faith and the Hope of the Future.* London: The Sovereign Grace Advent Testimony; Scottdale, PA: Evangelist Fellowship, n.d.

806. *How Can We Haste His Coming?* New York: Christian Alliance Publishing Co., n.d.

807. Hudgings, Franklyn. *Zionism in Prophecy: The Return of Israel to Palestine a Fulfilment of Biblical Prophecy.* New York: Pro-Palestine Federation of America, 1936.

808. Huffman, Jaspar A. *The Progressive Unfolding of the Messianic Hope.* New York: George H. Doran Co., 1924.

809. Hughes, Albert. *Is There Anything in It?* Toronto: Evangelical Publishers, 1934.

810. Ironside, H. A. *Four Golden Hours at Kingsway Hall, London.* London: Marshall, Morgan & Scott, LTD, 1939.

811. _____. *Looking Backward Over a Third of a Century of Prophetic Fulfilment.* New York: Loizeaux Brothers, 1930.

812. _____. *The Midnight Cry!* Western Book and Tract Co., [1914]; New York: Loizeaux Brothers, 1928.

813. _____. *The Mysteries of God.* New York: Loizeaux Brothers, n.d.

814.   _____. *Not Wrath, But Rapture: or Will the Church Participate in the Great Tribulation?* New York: Loizeaux Brothers, n.d.

815.   _____. *Setting the Stage for the Last Act of the Great World Drama.* New York: Loizeaux Brothers, n.d.

816.   _____. *Wrongly Dividing the Word of Truth: Ultra-dispensationalism Examined in the Light of Holy Scripture* (3rd ed.). Oakland, CA: Western Book & Tract, 1938.

817.   Johnson, Andrew, and L. L. Pickett. *Postmillennialism and the Higher Critics.* Chicago: Glad Tidings Publishing Co., 1923.

818.   Kaye, James Ross. *The Coming Crisis: Are We Approaching the End of the Age?* Chicago: Buxton-Westerman Co., 1927.

819.   Keefer, Glen Elgin. *Definite Signs of This Age Closing, by 'A Business Man.'* Westport, CT and Antwerp, OH: G. E. Keefer, 1925.

820.   Kellogg, Howard W. *A-Millennialism. How Does it Differ From Pre-Millennial Views?: A Fresh Examination of Prophecy as it Bears Upon the A-Millennial Position.* Los Angeles: American Prophetic League, 1939.

821.   _____. *The Coming Kingdom and the Re-Canopied Earth.* Los Angeles: American Prophetic League, 1936.

822.   Kellogg, Jay C. *The Midnight Cry: Do We Face the Golden Age or the World's Darkest Midnight?* (2nd ed.). Tacoma: The Whole Gospel Crusaders of America, 1932.

823.   _____. *This Tech-noc-crazy Old World in the Light of Prophecy; Where are We Headed? Do We Face the Dawn of a New Age?* Tacoma: The Whole Gospel Crusaders of America, 1933.

824.   Kellogg, Samuel H. *An Abridgement of The Jews; or Prediction and Fulfillment, an Argument for the Times. With a Supplementary Chapter by Henry S. Nesbitt.* Madras: Milton

Stewart Evangelistic Funds, 1927; Scottdale, PA: Evangelical Fellowship, 1954.

825. _____. *A-millennialism; How Does It Differ from Premillennial Views?: A Fresh Examination of Prophecy as it Bears Upon the A-millennial Position.* Los Angeles: American Prophetic League, 1939.

826. _____. *Are Premillennialists Right?* (new ed.). New York: Fleming H. Revell Co., 1923.

827. Kelly, William. *The Coming of the Lord* (new ed.). London: F. E. Race, 1919.

828. _____. *The Day of the Lord: 2 Thess. ii. 1, 2* (new ed.). London: F. E. Race, 1919.

829. Keyes, Henry S. *World Peace Through Satan: This is not a Complete Treatise but an Exposition of Certain Scripture Relating to the 'Times of the End,' ...* (3rd ed., rev.). Los Angeles: Pub. by author, 1937.

830. Kingston, Charles J. E. *The Coming of Christ -- and After* (rev. & enlarged). London: Victory Press, 1929.

831. Kirk, E. (ed.) *The Millennium Manifested* (a collection of pamphlets). London: The Sovereign Grace Advent Testimony, n.d.

832. Klerekoper, Moses. *An Answer to Philip Mauro's Book 'The Hope of Israel -- What is it?'* n.p., n.d.

833. Kressly, Paul E. *The Destiny of Man.* San Marino, CA: Pub. by author, 1935.

834. Kuldell, Alexander R. *The Difficulties of a Post-millennialist on His Way to Pre-millennialism.* Washington, D.C.: Pub. by author, n.d.

835. Lamb, William. *Great Future Events Which Must Shortly Come to Pass.* Sydney, AUS: Winn & Co. Printers of Sydney, n.d.

836.   _____. *The Great Tribulation; Has the Church to Go Through It?* Sydney, AUS: The Worker Trustees, n.d.

837.   _____. *Signs Showing the Return of the Lord to be at Hand.* Sydney, AUS: The Worker Trustees, 1929.

838.   _____. *Studies in the Book of Revelation.* Sydney, AUS: The Worker Trustees, 1928; Chicago: The Bible Institute Colportage Association, n.d.

839.   _____. *The Times of the Nations.* Chicago: The Bible Institute Colportage Association, n.d.

840.   _____. *The Wise Shall Understand.* Sydney, AUS: The Worker Trustees, 1932.

841.   Larkin, Clarence. *The Book of Daniel.* Philadelphia: Pub. by author, 1929.

842.   _____. *The Book of Revelation.* Philadelphia: Pub. by author, 1919.

843.   _____. *Dispensational Truth: or God's Plan and Purpose in the Ages* (rev. and enlarged ed.). Philadelphia: Pub. by author, 1920.

844.   _____. *The Second Coming of Christ* (3rd ed.). Philadelphia: Pub. by author, 1918; Philadelphia: Pub. by author, 1922.

845.   Leckie, Joseph H. *The World to Come and Final Destiny* (2nd ed.). Edinburgh: T & T Clark, 1922.

846.   Lindberg, Conrad Emil. *Beacon Lights of Prophecy in the Latter Days.* Rock Island, IL: Augustana Book Concern, 1930.

847.   Lindberg, Milton B. *Gog all Agog 'in the Latter Days': News From Russia and Palestine in the Light of Ezekiel 38 & 39.* Chicago: Hebrew Mission, 1938; Findlay, OH: Fundamental Truth Publishers, 1939.

848.   _____. *Is Ours the Closing Generation of the Age?* Chicago:
           Chicago Hebrew Mission, 1938; Findlay, OH: Fundamental
           Truth Publishers, n.d.

849.   _____. *Palestine and the Jew Today in the Light of Prophecy.*
           Los Angeles, CA: A. J. Johnson, 1935; (8th ed., rev.). Findlay,
           OH: Fundamental Truth Publishers; Chicago: Moody Press,
           1973.

850.   Lowry, Oscar. *The Second Coming of Christ: Signs of the
           Approaching End of the Age.* Chicago: Bible Institute Colpor-
           tage Association, 1936.

851.   MacKenzie, Herbert. *Jerusalem and the Jews, What Next?*
           Cleveland. Erieside Publishing Co., 1918.

852.   MacKintosh, H. R. *Immortality and the Future.* New York: Doran,
           n.d.

853.   Marsh, F. E. *What Will Take Place When Christ Returns?* (2nd ed.).
           London: C. J. Thynne; Brooklyn: Christian Alliance Publishing
           Co., 1919.

854.   _____. *Why Will Christ Come Back?* Los Angeles: BIOLA, n.d.

855.   Massee, J. C. *The Second Coming.* Philadelphia: Philadelphia
           School of the Bible, 1919.

856.   Masselink, William. *Why Thousand Years?* Grand Rapids, MI:
           Eerdmans Publishing Co., 1930; (4th ed., includes subtitle: *or
           will the Second Coming be Premillennial?*). Grand Rapids, MI:
           Eerdmans Publishing Co., 1953.

857.   Matthews, John. *Will the 'Times of the Gentiles' End in 1934-35?*
           Hollywood, CA: KNX, n.d.

858.   Matthews, Mark. *The Second Coming of Christ.* New York: The
           Book Stall, n.d.

859.   Mauro, Philip. *'After This' or the Church, the Kingdom, and the
           Glory.* New York: Fleming H. Revell, 1918.

860. _____. *Bringing Back the King*. New York: Fleming H. Revell, 1920.

861. _____. *Dispensationalism Justifies the Crucifixion*. Swengel, PA: Reiner Publications, n.d.

862. _____. *Dr. Shailer Mathews on the Christ's Return*. Swengel, PA: Bible Truth Depot, 1918.

863. _____. *The Gospel of the Kingdom* [or *God's Present Kingdom*]: *With an Examination of Modern Dispensationalism*. Boston: Hamilton Bros., 1928.

864. _____. *The Hope of Israel -- What is It?* Boston: Hamilton Brothers, 1929.

865. _____. *How Long to the End?* Boston: Hamilton Brothers, 1927.

866. _____. *The Last Call to the Godly Remnant*. Swengel, PA: Reiner Publications, n.d.

867. _____. *More Than a Prophet*. Swengel, PA: Reiner Publications, n.d.

868. _____. *The Number of Man -- The Climax of Civilization*. New York: Fleming H. Revell, 1909.

869. _____. *Of The Things Which Soon Must Come to Pass*. Swengel, PA: Reiner Publications, 1933.

870. _____. *The Seventy Weeks and the Great Tribulation: A Study of the Last Two Visions of Daniel, and of the Olivet Discourse of the Lord Jesus Christ*. Boston: Hamilton Brothers, Scripture Truth Depot, 1923.

871. _____. *Watch. Be Ready: The Parable of the Ten Virgins* (new and rev. ed.). New York: Christian Alliance Publishing Co., 1919.

872. _____. *The Wonders of Bible Chronology.* Swengel, PA: Reiner Publications, n.d.

873. _____. *The World War: How it is Fulfilling Prophecy.* Boston: Hamilton Brothers, 1918.

874. McBride, Joseph B. *In the Citadel -- On the Throne.* Louisville, KY: Pentecostal Publishing Co., 1920.

875. McCarrell, William. *Christ's Seven Letters to His Church.* Grand Rapids, MI: Zondervan, 1936.

876. McCartney, Richard H. *The Secret Rapture Delusion and Snare.* Chicago: James Watson & Co., 1926.

877. _____. *The Four Great Powers of the End Time and Their Final Conflict.* Los Angeles: American Prophetic League, 1938.

878. McConkey, James H. *The Book of Revelation.* Pittsburgh: Silver Publishing Co., 1921.

879. _____. *The End of the Age: A Series of Prophetic Bible Studies Upon the End of This Present Age.* Pittsburgh: Silver Publishing Co., 1918, (15th ed., 1925).

880. McCown, C. C. *The Promise of His Coming.* New York: The Macmillan Co., 1921.

881. McCrossan, Thomas J. *The World's Crisis and the Coming Christ.* Seattle, WA: Pub. by Author, 1934.

882. McDonald, M. B. *The Coming Christ and Signs of His Coming.* Findlay, OH: Fundamental Truth Publishers, 1935.

883. McGinlay, James. *Why Ours May be the Last Generation Before Christ's Return.* London, n.p., n.d.

884. McKey, Gus. *The End of Time.* Whittier, CA: Pub. by author, 1928.

885.   McLaren, Charles. *The Seed of the Serpent.* Forth Worth, TX: American Publishing Co., n.d.

886.   McManus, Karl C. *The Arc of Civilization.* New York: House of Field-Doubleday, 1947.

887.   McPherson, Aimee Semple. *The Second Coming of Christ.* Los Angeles: Pub. by Author, 1921.

888.   Messenger, Frank M. *The Coming Superman.* Kansas City, MO: Nazarene Publishing House, 1928.

889.   Michelson, Arthur U. *The Jews and Palestine in the Light of Prophecy.* Los Angeles: The Jewish Hope Publishing House, 1934, (rev. ed., 1939).

890.   Miles, Frederic J. *'Even at the Doors': The Coming King and the Coming Kingdom.* London: Marshall, Morgan & Scott, 1936 and 1937.

891.   Milligan, Ezra McLeod. *Is the Kingdom Age at Hand?: An Interpretation of Portions of Daniel's Prophecy and the Book of the Revelation of Jesus Christ.* New York: George H. Doran, 1924.

892.   Moseley, E. H. *The Jew and His Destiny.* Edinburgh: J. K. Souter & Co., 1930; Cleveland: U. G. Press, 1931.

893.   Moule, H. C. G. *The Hope of the Near Approach of the Lord's Return and Its Influence Upon Life: An Address Under the Auspices of the Advent Preparation Movement.* London: Charles J. Thynne, 1919.

894.   Naish, Reginald T. *The Last Call!: or 'The Trumpet Shall Sound'* (5th ed.). London: Thynne, 1935.

895.   _____. *The Midnight Hour and After!* (5th ed.). London: Chas J. Thynne and Jarvis, 1925.

896.   Neighbor, Robert Edward. *The Lamp, the Darkness and the New Day.* Cleveland: Union Gospel Press, 1927.

897. _____. *The Rider on the White Horse and Other Prophecy Sermons.* Cleveland: Union Gospel Printing Co., n.d.

898. Newell, William R. *The Book of Revelation.* Chicago: Moody Press, 1935; Chicago: Grace Publications, 1935.

899. _____. *The Church and the Great Tribulation* [and] *Will the Church Pass Through the Great Tribulation?* Chicago: The Scripture Press, Inc., 1933.

900. Newman, Elias. *The Jewish Peril and the Hidden Hand.* Minneapolis, MN: Pub. by author, 1934.

901. O'Hair, J. *At His Coming: Premillennialism.* Oak Park, IL: Pub. by author, n.d.

902. Oliphant, William Landon. *The Oliphant-Rice Debate.* Austin, TX: Firm Foundation Publishing House, 1935.

903. Olsen, Erling C. *Modern Complexes in the Light of Biblical Prophecy: Three Radio Addresses.* New York: National Radio and Missionary Fellowship Inc., 1938.

904. Orr, William W. *Jesus is Coming...This Year?* Findlay, OH: Dunham Publishing Co., n.d.

905. _____. *A Simple Picture of the Future.* Los Angeles: BIOLA, n.d.

906. Ostrom, Henry. *My Personal Experience with the Doctrine of Our Lord's Second Coming.* Chicago: The Moody Bible Institute, n.d.

907. Ottman, F. C. *The Coming Day.* Philadelphia: Sunday School Times, 1921.

908. Overley, E. R. *The Second Coming of the Lord.* Louisville, KY: Herald Press, n.d.

909. Overton, John. *'I Come Again.'* Chicago: The Bible Institute Colportage Association., n.d.

910. Owen, Frederick. *Abraham to Allenby.* Grand Rapids, MI: Eerdmans Publishing Co., 1939.

911. Palmer, Orson R. *'The Coming of the Lord Draweth Nigh.': A Message for Today.* Chicago: The Bible Institute Colportage Association., n.d.

912. _____. *What Next?* Press of Harris & Partridge, n.d.

913. Pankhurst, Christabel (Dame). *The Lord Cometh! The World Crisis Explained.* New York: The Book Stall, 1923.

914. _____. *Pressing Problems of the Closing Age.* London: Morgan & Scott, 1924.

915. _____. *Seeing the Future.* New York: Harper & Brothers, 1929.

916. _____. *Some Modern Problems in the Light of Bible Prophecy.* New York: Fleming H. Revell Co., 1924.

917. _____. *The Uncurtained Future.* London: Hodder & Stoughton, 1926.

918. _____. *The World's Unrest: Visions of the Dawn.* London: Morgan & Scott, 1926; Philadelphia: Sunday School Times, 1929.

919. Panton, David M. *The Judgment Seat of Christ* (2nd ed.). London: Chas. J. Thynne, 1921.

920. _____. *The Panton Papers: Current Events and Prophecy* (A Selection of Editorial Articles by D. M. Panton from his Magazine *The Dawn,* 2nd ed.). New York: T. M. Chalmers, 1928.

921. _____. *Rapture.* London: Alfred Holness, 1916; (2nd ed.) London: Charles J. Thynne, 1922.

922.   _____. *Satanic Counterfeits of the Second Advent* (2nd ed., rev. and enlarged). London: Charles J. Thynne and Jarvis, 1925.

923.   Panton, D. M., James McAlister, and A. Sims. *Startling Signs of Great World Changes Soon to Take Place.* Toronto: A. Sims, n.d.; (2nd ed.) Toronto: A. Sims, 1927.

924.   *Papers Read Before the American Society for Prophetic Study.* n.p., 1926.

925.   Patmont, Louis R. *Perils of the Latter Days: A Survey of Apocalyptic Events.* Findlay, OH: Fundamental Truth Publishers, 1936.

926.   Perret, Paul. *Prophecies I Have Seen Fulfilled* (J. D. Townsend, trans.). London: Marshall, Morgan & Scott, 1939.

927.   Pickett, L. L. *Armageddon; or The Next Great War.* Louisville: Pentacostal Publishing Co., 1924.

928.   Pink, Arthur W. *The Antichrist.* Swengel, PA: Bible Truth Depot, 1923; (reprinted ed.). Minneapolis, MN: Klock & Klock Publishers,1979.

929.   _____. *The Millennium.* Swengel, PA: Bible Truth Depot, n.d.

930.   _____. *The Redeemer's Return.* Swengel, PA: Bible Truth Depot, 1918.

931.   Piper, Fred L. *The Return of Christ: The Bible Basis of the Doctrine.* New York: Fleming H. Revell, 1922.

932.   Pitt, F. W. *Coming Events Cast Their Shadows in the Air.* London: Marshall, Morgan & Scott LTD, 1937.

933.   Price, Charles S. *The Battle of Armageddon.* Pasadena, CA: C. S. Price Publishing Co., 1938.

934.   _____. *The Next War.* Pasadena, CA: C. S. Price Publishing Co., 1936.

935.   *Prophecy Fulfilled; by a Student of Prophecy* (rev. & enlarged).
       London: H. B. Skinner, 1939.

936.   Putnam, C. E. *Jesus' Coming and the Kingdom.* Chicago: Bible
       Institute Colportage Association, 1920.

937.   _____. *Non-Millennialism vs. Premillennialism, Which Harmo-
       nizes the Word?* Chicago: Bible Institute Colportage
       Association, 1921.

938.   _____. *Where Now is Jesus?: And Nine Kindred Questions with
       the Word's Clear Answer.* Chicago: Bible Institute Colportage
       Association, 1924.

939.   Rader, Paul. *The Coming World Dictator.* Chicago: World Wide
       Gospel Couriers, 1934, (reprinted, 1943).

940.   _____. *The Midnight Cry.* Chicago: Chicago Gospel Taber-
       nacles, 1938.

941.   Reese, Alexander. *The Approaching Advent of Christ.* London:
       Marshall, Morgan & Scott, 1937.

942.   Reid, John G. *The Conversion of a 'Post': or How I Came to be a
       Premillennarian* [sic]. Chicago: The Bible Institute Colportage
       Association, n.d.

943.   Riggs, Ralph M. *The Path of Prophecy.* Springfield, MO: Gospel
       Publishing House, 1937.

944.   Riley, William Bell. *Daniel and the Doom of World Governments:
       Is there any Redemption?* Minneapolis: L.W. Camp, 1935.

945.   _____. *Is Christ Coming Again?* (4th ed.). Grand Rapids, MI:
       Zondervan, n.d.

946.   _____. *The Only Hope of Church and World: What is It?*
       London: Pickering & Inglis, n.d.

947.   _____. *Wanted -- A World Leader!* Pub. by author, 1939.

948.   Ritchie, John. *Impending Great Events: Addresses on the Second Coming of Christ and Subsequent Events* (2nd ed.). London: Pickering & Inglis, 1939.

949.   Robison, G. A. *God's Purpose in the War and After: What the Bible Says*. London: Marshall Brothers, 1920.

950.   Rogers, William Robert. *'The End from the Beginning': A Panorama of Prophecy or History, the Mold of Prediction*. New York: Arno C. Gaebelein Inc., 1938.

951.   Rollings, Elmer J. *The World Today in the Light of Bible Prophecy*. Findlay, OH: Fundamental Truth Publishers, 1935.

952.   Ross, John Jacob. *Daniel's Half-week Now Closing: A Study of Daniel's Prophecy of the Seventy Weeks, With Particular Attention Given to the Closing Three-and-a-half Days of the Seventieth Week*. New York: Fleming H. Revell, 1922.

953.   _____. *The Kingdom in Mystery: A Study of the Parables of Our Lord Concerning the Kingdom of Heaven*. New York: Fleming H. Revell, 1920.

954.   _____. *Our Glorious Hope: A Study of the Nature, Ground, Content, and Influence of the Glorious Hope of Our Lord's Second Coming*. New York: Fleming H. Revell, 1922.

955.   _____. *Pearls from Patmos (Revelation 2-3)*. New York: Fleming H. Revell, 1923.

956.   _____. *The Sign of His Coming: or The Near Approach of the End*. New York: Charles C. Cook, 1918.

957.   Rowlands, William J. *Our Lord Cometh* (2nd ed., enlarged). London: Pub. by author, 1939.

958.   Ruth, Thomas Elias. *The Advent Heresy and the Real Coming of Christ*. Melbourne: Hutchinson Printing, n.d.

959.   Sale-Harrison, L. *The Coming Great Northern Confederacy or the Future of Russia and Germany* (15th ed., rev.). New York: Sale-

Harrison Publications, 1928; (16th ed., rev., 1933); Wheaton, IL: Van Kampen, 1948 .

960.   _____. *Ethiopia in the Light of Prophecy.* London: Pickering & Inglis, 1935.

961.   _____. *Israel's Regathering: The Return of the Jew.* Chicago: Van Kampen Press, 1934 and 1948.

962.   _____. *The League of Nations.* Harrisburg, PA: Evangelical Press, 1930.

963.   _____. *The League of Nations and the Future of Europe.* London: Pickering & Inglis, n.d.

964.   _____. *Palestine: God's Monument of Prophecy; The Wonders of a Remarkable Book in a Remarkable Land.* Chicago: Bible Institute Colportage Association, n.d.; London: Pickering & Inglis, 1933; Harrisburg, PA: Evangelical Press, 1933.

965.   _____. *The Remarkable Jew: His Wonderful Future, God's Great Timepiece* (7th ed., rev.). Philadelphia: Sale-Harrison Publications, 1928; (10th ed., rev. and enlarged). Harrisburg, PA: Sale-Harrison, 1934.

966.   _____. *The Resurrection of the Old Roman Empire: The Future Confederation of the Ten Nation Empire.* New York: Sale-Harrison Publications, 1934; (12th ed., rev. & enlarged, with subtitle: *The League of Nations and the Future of Europe*). London: Pickering & Inglis, n.d.

967.   _____. *The Wonders of the Great Unveiling.* Philadelphia: Evangelical Press, 1930.

968.   Sampson, Holden Edward. *The Rise and Consummation of the Aeon: A Book of Interpretation and Prophecy Relating to the Present 'Last Times' of Antichrist.* London: Ek-Klesia Press, 1920; William Rider & Son, 1920.

969.   Sargent, Harry Neptune. *The Marvels of Prophecy.* London: The Covenant Publishing Co., 1938.

970. Schoeler, William. *Prophecy and Fulfillment: or The Word Proved True* (2nd ed., rev.). Columbus: The Book Concern, n.d.

971. Schor, Samuel. *The Everlasting Nation and Their Coming King.* London: Marshall, Morgan & Scott, 1935.

972. Scott, Walter. *Prophetic Scenes and Coming Glories: Answers to Numerous Prophetic Questions.* London: Pickering & Inglis, 1919; London: Morgan and Scott, 1919.

973. Scroggie, William G. *The Lord's Return.* London: Pickering & Inglis, 1939.

974. Sidersky, Philip. *Hitler, the Jews, and Palestine in Relation to the Second Coming of Our Lord* (2nd ed.). Grand Rapids, MI: Zondervan Publishing House, n.d.

975. Sims, Albert. (ed.). *The Coming Great War, the Greatest Ever Known in Human History.* Toronto: A. Sims, 1932.

976. Smith, A. J. *The Divine Program; or A Treatise of God's Plan for the Ages as Revealed in the Scriptures.* C. Hauser, Publishers, 1919.

977. Smith, J. Denham. *The Brides of Scriptures; or Foreshadows of Coming Glory* (2nd ed., rev. and enlarged). Walter G. Wheeler & Co., n.d.

978. _____. *The Prophet of Glory: or Zechariah's Visions of the Coming and the Kingdom of Christ.* London: Hawkins, n.d.

979. Smith, Oswald J. *Antichrist and the Future* (2nd ed.). Toronto: The People's Church, 1932.

980. _____. *The Clouds are Lifting* (pt 1: Studies in Prophecy; pt 2: The Visions of Daniel). London: Marshall, Morgan & Scott, 1937 .

981.   _____. *The Dawn is Breaking.* London: Marshall, Morgan & Scott, n.d.; Grand Rapids, MI: Zondervan Publishing House, 1937.

982.   _____. *Is the Antichrist at Hand?* (5th ed.). n.p.: The Tabernacle Publishing Co., 1926; (7th ed. adds subtitle: *What of Mussolini?*). New York: The Christian Alliance Publishing Co., 1927.

983.   _____. *Prophecies of the End Times.* Toronto: Toronto Tabernacle Publishers, 1932.

984.   _____. *The Rider on the Red Horse.* Toronto: The People's Church, 1934.

985.   _____. *Signs of His Coming* [and] *What Will Happen Next?* Toronto: The People's Church, 1933.

986.   _____. *The Visions of Daniel* (3rd ed.). Canada: The People's Church, 1932.

987.   _____. *When Antichrist Reigns.* New York: The Christian Alliance Publishing Co., 1927.

988.   _____. *When He is Come.* Chicago: World-wide Christian Couriers, 1929.

989.   _____. *When the King Comes Back.* Wheaton, IL: Sword of the Lord Publishers, n.d.

990.   _____. *World Problems in the Light of Prophecy.* London: Marshall, Morgan & Scott, n.d.

991.   Smock, C. M. *God's Dispensations Compared and Contrasted.* Chicago: Bible Institute Colportage Association, 1918.

992.   Snowden, James H. *The Coming of the Lord: Will it Be Premillennial?* New York: Macmillan, 1922.

993.   _____. *Is the World Growing Better?* New York: Macmillan, 1919.

994. _____. *Revelation, the Crown-Jewel of Prophecy.* New York: Christian Alliance Publishing Co., 1928.

995. Stamps, Drure Fletcher. *The Mystery of God's Wrath.* Grand Rapids, MI: Zondervan Publishing House, 1936.

996. Stanley, Charles. *The Millennial Reign of Christ* (a sequel to the tract, *What God Hath Said on the Second Coming of Christ and the End of the Present Age*). New York: Loizeaux Brothers, n.d.

997. Steen, J. Carleton. *God's Prophetic Programme, As Revealed in the Book of Daniel* (2nd ed.). Kilmarnock, Scotland: Ritchie, n.d.

998. Steven, F. A. *The Second Coming of Christ in Relation to Church Problems of Today.* Chicago: The Bible Institute Colportage Association, n.d.

999. Stevens, William Coit. *Revelation, the Crown-Jewel of Biblical Prophecy.* Harrisburg, PA: The Christian Alliance Publishing Co., 1928.

1000. Stewart, Alexander H. *Maranatha!: The Coming of Christ and Signs of the Times.* New York: Loizeaux Brothers, n.d.

1001. Stewart, Herbert. *The Stronghold of Prophecy: Irrefutable Evidence from Fulfilled Prophecy that the Scriptures are the Infallible Word of God.* London: Marshall, Morgan & Scott, 1935.

1002. Stover, Gerald L. (ed.). *The Plight of the Jews: A Compilation of Messages on Prophecy and the Jews, etc.* New York: Loizeaux Brothers, n.d.

1003. Talbot, Louis T. *The Army of the Two Hundred Million and the Lord's Return.* Los Angeles: Livingstone Press, 1931.

1004. _____. *The Book of Revelation.* Grand Rapids, MI: Eerdmans Publishing Co., n.d.

1005.   _____. *The Coming World Dictator: the Second in a Series of Addresses on Bible Prophecy.* Los Angeles: The Church of the Open Door, n.d.

1006.   _____. *The Feasts of Jehovah: Foreshadowing God's Plan of the Ages from the Past Eternity to the Future Eternity.* Los Angeles: The Church of the Open Door, n.d.

1007.   _____. *God's Plan of the Ages: A Comprehensive View of God's Great Plan from Eternity to Eternity illustrated with Chart.* Los Angeles: Pub. by author, 1936; Grand Rapids, MI: Eerdmans 1936, (reprinted 1974).

1008.   _____. *The Great Prophecies of Daniel.* Los Angeles: Pub. by author, 1934.

1009.   _____. *The Revelation of Jesus Christ: An Exposition on the Book of Revelation.* Los Angeles: The Church of the Open Door, 1937.

1010.   _____. *The Thousand Years' Reign of Christ on the Earth: The Characteristics of that Reign.* n.p.: The Livingstone Press, 1931.

1011.   Thomas, John, M.D. *A Brief Exposition of the Prophecy of Daniel.* Birmingham: C. C. Walker, 1921.

1012.   Thompson, Erik. *The Key to Revelation; or Jesus' Olivet Discourse: Jesus' Own Prophecy of His Second Coming and Final Judgment* (Jersing Thompson, ed.). Grand Rapids, MI: Zondervan Publishing House, 1935.

1013.   _____. *The Key to the Book of Revelation.* Grand Rapids, MI: Zondervan Publishing House, 1935.

1014.   Thurston, E. Temple. *Millennium.* Garden City, New York: Doubleday, Doran & Co., 1930.

1015.   Titterton, Charles H. *Armageddon: or The Last War* (2nd ed.). London: Chas. J. Thynne & Jarvis, 1923.

1016. Trumball, W. M. *The Shadow on the Sun-dial.* New York: Christian Alliance Publishing Co., n.d.

1017. Trumbull, Charles G. (ed.). *How I Came to Believe in Our Lord's Return and Why I Believe the Lord's Return is Near.* Chicago: Bible Institute Colportage Association, 1934.

1018. _____. *Prophecy's Light on Today.* New York: Fleming H. Revell, 1937.

1019. Tuggy, H. *He Cometh With Clouds: or Every Eye Shall See Him [and] Things Which are Coming: or The Bright and Morning Star* [and] *Changed in a Moment.* London: n.p., n.d.

1020. *Unfulfilled Prophecies.* Grand Rapids, MI: Zondervan Publishing House, 1937.

1021. Van Burkalow, J. T. *The Lost Prophecy.* New York: Fleming H. Revell, 1924.

1022. Van Ryn, August. *The Tribulation in Relation to the Church.* Fort Dodge, IA: Walterick, n.d.

1023. Vogt, Frederick. *The Divine Clock; With Visions of the Future.* London: Marshall, Morgan & Scott, 1929.

1024. Ware, Arthur E. *The Immediate Prospects of Mankind.* London: Pub. by author, 1933.

1025. _____. *The Hour of Translation: A Declaration from the Word of God.* London: Marshall, Morgan & Scott, n.d.

1026. Washington, Canon M. *The Period of Judgment and the Saved Remnant.* London: Thynne, 1919.

1027. Webber, E. F. *Signs of His Coming.* Wichita, KS: Defender Publishers, n.d.

1028. Welch, Charles H. *The Apostle of Reconciliation: or The Dispensational Position of the Acts and the Ministry and Epistles of Paul.* London: F. P. Brininger, 1923.

1029.   _____. *Dispensational Truth: or The Place of Israel and the
         Church in the Purpose of the Ages.* London: L. A. Canning,
         1927; London: Berean Publishing Trust, 1959.

1030.   Whitla, Sir William (ed.). *Sir Isaac Newton's Daniel and the
         Apocalypse: With an Introductory Study of the Nature and
         Cause of Unbelief, of Miracles and Prophecy.* London: J.
         Murray, 1922.

1031.   Whyte, H. A. *Where is the Antichrist?* Scarborough, Ont.: Pub.
         by author, n.d.

1032.   Wight, Francis Asa. *Babylon the Harlot.* Scottdale, PA: YMCA,
         1925.

1033.   _____. *The Beast, Modernism, and the Evangelical Faith.*
         Boston: The Stratford Co., 1926.

1034.   _____. *The Kingdom of God: or The Reign of Heaven Among
         Men.* New York: Fleming H. Revell Co., 1923.

1035.   Wight, Fred Hartley. *Israel -- Key to World Blessing: Israel's
         Miraculous Preservation, Present Plight, Future Trials,
         National Redemption.* Los Angeles: American Prophetic
         League, Inc, n.d.

1036.   Wilkinson, John. *God's Plan for the Jew* (rev. and ed. by H. L.
         Ellison). London: The Paternoster Press, 1946 (reprinted,
         1978).

1037.   Wilkinson, Samuel Hinds. *The Israel Promises and Their
         Fulfilment: An Examination of the Pronouncements Found in
         the Book Entitled, 'The Hope of Israel: What is It?' by Philip
         Mauro.* London: J. Bale, Sons & Danielsson LTD, 1936.

1038.   Williams, Samuel J. *The Jew, God's Timepiece.* Cincinnati:
         God's Bible School, 1935.

1039.   Wilson, James. *The Hour of His Judgment.* Belfast: Pub. by
         author, 1929.

1040.   Wilson, Philip Whitwell. *The Vision We Forget: A Layman's Reading of the Book of the Revelation of St. John the Divine.* New York: Fleming H. Revell Co., 1921.

1041.   Winrod, Gerald Burton. *The Hidden Hand: The Protocols and the Coming Superman.* Wichita, KS: Defender Publishers, 1933.

1042.   _____. *Hitler in Prophecy.* Wichita, KS: Defender Publishers, 1933.

1043.   _____. *Mussolini and the Second Coming of Christ* (9th ed.). Wichita, KS: Defender Publishers, n.d.

1044.   Wood, Ross. *The Present in the Light of Prophecy.* Cincinnati: Pub. by author, 1933.

1045.   Wyngarden, Martin J. *The Future of the Kingdom in Prophecy and Fulfillment: A Study of the Scope of 'Spiritualization' in Scripture.* Grand Rapids, MI: Zondervan Publishing House, 1934.

SECTION SIX

THE SECOND WORLD WAR
AND THE NEW JEWISH STATE, 1940-1948

The war years and their aftermath proved to be a prophetic windfall for millennialists, who watched with keen interest the rise and fall of the axis powers, the holocaust against European Jewry, and the unleashing of nuclear fire and brimstone upon the Japanese mainland. All of these events were interpreted, in one way or another, as prophetic signs pointing to the imminent return of Christ. But far and away, the one event of greatest prophetic significance to the continuing vitality of popular eschatology in America was the establishment of an independent Jewish nation on May 14, 1948. For, above all other events, the existence of a Jewish state became, for millennialists, the watershed dividing normative history from eschatological history. With this event, the "Time of the Gentiles" had come to an end; Israel would now take center stage in the apocalyptic drama of the Last Days.

In 1920, the British government had won the Mandate from the League of Nations, giving Britain control over Palestine and other regions of the old Ottoman Empire. The Mandate bound Britain to work diligently and effectively toward the independence of Palestine. The British had a rough go of it, however, as they attempted the impossible: to secure the peaceful coexistence of Palestinians and Jews. Exhausted by six years of world war and exasperated over renewed snipings by Arabs and Israelis after that war, the British government announced in January 1948 that the Mandate would end by May of that year. In accordance with the 1947 United Nations proposals for the Partition of Palestine, Britain would then transfer sovereignty of Palestine over to Israel.

To premillennialists, nothing else on the Bible's prophetic timeline could compare in importance with this event. It became the prophetic Rosetta stone for twentieth-century millenarians in that it marked with some precision where the world was in relation to Armageddon and the Second Coming. That is, the establishment of Israel was also the prophetic sign *par excellence* in that, for millennialists, it gave currency to Jesus' prophecy in the Olivet discourse. "Now learn the parable from the fig tree," Jesus told his disciples. "When its branch has already become tender, and puts forth its leaves, you know that summer is near; even so you too, when you see these things, recognize that He is near, right at the door." Jesus then predicted, in what has given rise to a plethora of speculation and date-setting: "Truly I say to you, this generation will not pass away until all these things take place" (Matthew 24:32-34).

Premillennialists then and now argue that the fig tree symbolizes Israel and that the budding leaves refer to its rebirth as a modern nation. Thus, they argue, within a generation of Israel's rebirth as a nation, Christ will assuredly return. As to the length of "this generation," they are less certain. Most premillennialists hold (or had held) that a biblical generation is forty years -- the length of time the Hebrews wandered in the wilderness until the first generation of Hebrews since their Exodus out of Egypt had died off. The implication for the millennialist is clear: the Tribulation period would take place sometime before 1988. The literature from this period to the present reflects this interpretation of Jesus' fig tree parable in the Olivet Discourse as well as the added conviction that the rapture would be the next event on God's prophetic calendar.

Another point of interest in this tour of popular eschatology in America is the support premillennialists voiced for Israel. To be sure, Jewish missions in both Britain and the United States had been in existence since the revival of millennial interest a century and a half before the Second World War. And, as noted above, many millennialists had been early exponents of Zionism in America. But in the 1940s, millenarian interest in Jewish missions was heightened.

In addition to Arno Gaebelein's organization, Our Hope of Israel, mentioned in an earlier section, several other major Jewish missions that incorporated dispensational premillennial beliefs in an attempt to angle for Jewish converts included: The Chicago Hebrew Mission, founded in 1889 (later the American Messianic Fellowship); the American Board of Missions to the Jews (1894); David Cooper's Biblical Research Society (1930); Hyman Appelman's American Association for Jewish Evangelism (1945);

and the International Board of Jewish Missions, founded and directed by Jacob and Lillian Gartenhaus in 1951.

1046.   Appelman, Hyman J. *The Battle of Armageddon*. Grand Rapids, MI: Zondervan Publishing House, 1942; Faith of Our Fathers Broadcast, 1944.

1047.   _____. *The Jew in History and Destiny*. Grand Rapids, MI: Zondervan Publishing House, 1947.

1048.   Atkinson, B.F. *The Millennium, A Necessity*. Louisville: The Herald Press, 1942.

1049.   Bauman, Louis S. *Light from Bible Prophecy: as Related to the Present Crisis*. New York: Fleming H. Revell Co., 1940.

1050.   _____. *Russian Events in the Light of Biblical Prophecy*. New York: Fleming H. Revell Co., 1942; Philadelphia: The Balkiston Co., 1952.

1051.   Beckwith, George D. *God's Prophetic Plan Through the Ages: An Explanation of the Beckwith Art Chart of Bible History and Prophecy* (2nd ed.). Grand Rapids, MI: Zondervan Publishing, 1942.

1052.   Bloomfield, Arthur E. *Bloomfield's Prophetic Atlas*. Angola, IN: Traveling Bible Institute, 1946.

1053.   Borden, Eli M. *The Millennium: or The Plan of the Ages*. Austin, TX: Firm Foundation Pub. House, 1941.

1054.   Bradbury, John W. (ed.). *Israel's Restoration: A Series of Lectures by Bible Expositors Interested in the Evangelization of the Jews*. NY: The Iversen-Ford Association, n.d.

1055.		_____(ed.). *Light for the World's Darkness (Proceedings from the Second New York Congress on Prophecy)*. New York: Loizeaux Brothers, 1944.

1056.		_____(ed.). *The Sure Word of Prophecy (Proceedings from the First New York Congress on Prophecy)*. New York: Fleming H. Revell, 1943.

1057.		Brooks, Keith L. *The Certain End, as Seen by the Prophet Daniel: A Fresh Examination of These Prophecies by the Cross-reference Method of Interpretation*. Los Angeles: American Prophetic League, 1942.

1058.		Brown, Arthur I. *The Eleventh 'Hour.'* Hoytville, OH: Fundamental Truth Publishers, 1940.

1059.		_____. *I Will Come Again*. Hoytville, OH: Fundamental Truth Publishers, 1947.

1060.		Brown, Charles E. *The Reign of Christ*. Anderson, IN: Gospel Trumpet Co., 1948.

1061.		Burton, Alfred H. *The Great Tribulation*. London: Advent Witness, Pickering & Inglis, 1940.

1062.		Chader, C. A. *God's Plan Through the Ages: An Evangelical Exposition Neither Adventistic nor Russellistic*. London: Marshall, Morgan & Scott, LTD and Grand Rapids, MI: Zondervan Publishing House, 1940.

1063.		Chafer, Lewis Sperry. *Systematic Theology* (vols. I-VIII). Dallas: Dallas Theological Seminary Press, 1948.

1064.		Cohn, Joseph H. *Will the Church Escape the Tribulation?* Findlay, OH: Fundamental Truth Publishers, n.d.; New York: American Board of Missions to the Jews, 1948.

1065.		Cooper, David L. *The Invading Forces of Russia and of the Antichrist Overthrown in Palestine*. Los Angeles: Biblical Research Society, n.d.

1066.　　＿＿＿. *Prophetic Fulfillments in Palestine Today.* Los Angeles: Biblical Research Society, 1940.

1067.　　＿＿＿. *The Seventy Weeks of Daniel.* Los Angeles: Biblical Research Society, 1941.

1068.　　＿＿＿. *When Gog's Armies Meet the Almighty: An Exposition of Ezekiel Thirty-Eight and Thirty-Nine.* Los Angeles: The Biblical Research Society, 1940.

1069.　　＿＿＿. *Why God's Interest is in the Jew.* Los Angeles: The Biblical Research Society, 1941.

1070.　　＿＿＿. *The World's Greatest Library Geographically Illustrated* [includes Prophecy Charts]. Los Angeles: The Biblical Research Society, 1942.

1071.　　Cottrell, Roy F. *Tomorrow in Prophecy: God's Preview of the World's Climax.* College Place, WA: Pub. by author, 1942.

1072.　　Davidson, David, engineer. *Through World Chaos to Cosmic Christ: Our Lord's Own Exposition of Prophecy.* London: The Covenant Publishing Company, LTD, 1944.

1073.　　Dawkins, David. *The Final Outcome of the Jew: The Key to All Prophecy and World History* (2nd ed., rev. and enlarged). Enumclaw, WA: Pub. by author, 1943.

1074.　　De Haan, M. R. *Daniel the Prophet; or 35 Simple Studies in the Book of Daniel.* Grand Rapids, MI: Zondervan Publishing Co., 1947.

1075.　　＿＿＿. *Revelation: 35 Simple Studies on the Major Themes in Revelation* (4th ed.). Grand Rapids, MI: Zondervan Publishing House, 1946.

1076.　　＿＿＿. *The Second Coming of Jesus.* Grand Rapids, MI: The Radio Bible Class of the Air, n.d.; Grand Rapids, MI: Zondervan Publishing House, 1944.

1077.   Falkenberg, Don R. *The Second Coming of Christ*. Columbus, OH: Bible Meditation League, 1948.

1078.   Farr, F. W. *Ten Reasons for Loving His Appearing*. Chicago: Bible Institute Colportage Association, n.d.

1079.   _____(ed.). *Timely Prophetic Considerations: Twelve Papers*. Los Angeles: American Prophetic League, 1940.

1080.   Farr, Frederic W, Howard W. Kellogg, & Keith Brooks. *Timely Prophetic Considerations*. Los Angeles: American Prophetic League, 1940.

1081.   Fletcher, George B. *The Millennium: What It Is Not and What It Is*. Swengel, PA: Bible Truth Depot, 1947.

1082.   Ford, W. Herschel. *Seven Simple Sermons on the Second Coming*. Grand Rapids, MI: Zondervan Publishing House, 1966, (1st ed., 1945).

1083.   _____. *Simple Sermons on Prophetic Themes*. Grand Rapids, MI: Zondervan Publishing House, n.d.

1084.   Franke, Elmer E. *The Rise and Fall of Nations in the Light of Bible Prophecy* (2nd ed.). People's Christian Bulletin, 1946.

1085.   Fraser, Alexander. *The Return of Christ in Glory: A Scriptural Study*. Scottdale, PA: Evangelical Fellowship, 1943.

1086.   Gaebelein, Arno C. *The History of the Scofield Reference Bible*. New York: Our Hope Publishing Co., 1943.

1087.   _____. *What Will Become of Europe?: World Darkness and Divine Light*. New York: Our Hope Publication Office, 1940.

1088.   _____. *Will There be a Millennium? When and How?: The Coming Reign of Christ in the Light of the Old and New Testaments*. New York: Our Hope Publication Office, 1943.

1089.   Gartenhaus, Jacob. *What of the Jews?* Atlanta: Home Mission Board of the Southern Baptist Convention, 1948.

1090.   Gilbert, Dan. *The Red Terror and Bible Prophecy.* Washington, D. C.: The Christian Press Bureau, 1944.

1091.   _____. *Russia's Next Move: In the Light of Prophecy.* Los Angeles: The Jewish Hope Publishing Co., n.d.

1092.   _____. *What Will Become of Germany in the Light of Bible Prophecy?* Los Angeles: The Jewish Hope Publishing Co., 1945.

1093.   _____. *Who Will Be the Antichrist?* Washington, D. C.: The Christian Press Bureau, 1945.

1094.   _____. *Will Russia Fight America?: The Question Considered in the Light of Bible Prophecy.* Los Angeles: The Jewish Hope Publishing Co., n.d.

1095.   Haimovitz, Charles. *Will Russia Clash with America?: The Question Considered in the Light of Bible Prophecy.* Los Angeles: The Jewish Hope Publishing Co., n.d.

1096.   Hamilton, Gavin. *The Great Tribulation.* New York: Loizeaux Brothers, Bible Truth Depot, 1941.

1097.   _____. *Is Armageddon Near?* Pub. by author, n.d.

1098.   _____. *Maranatha!: Highlight of the Twentieth Century.* New York: Loizeaux Brothers, Bible Truth Depot, 1943.

1099.   Harrison, Norman B. *The End: Rethinking the Revelation.* Minneapolis: The Harrison Service, 1941.

1100.   _____. *His Coming: Seven Significant Signs of the Times: Seven Reasons Why Christ **Must** Come Again.* Minneapolis: The Harrison Service, 1946.

1101.   _____. *His Sure Return.* Chicago: Bible Institute Colportage Association, 1926; Minneapolis: The Harrison Service, 1952.

1102.   Heward, Percy W. *The Holy Spirit's Two-fold Use of Millennial Prophecies.* London: The Sovereign Grace Advent Testimony, 1947.

1103.   Hill, G. W. *What Will Become of this Earth and the People Who are in It?* Amarillo, TX: Manney, 1943.

1104.   Hollenbeck, James C. *The Super Deceiver on the World Horizon: The Amazing Disclosure of the Most Mysterious Man of Destiny in the World Today* (3rd ed.). Los Angeles: Pub. by author, 1942.

1105.   Hough, Robert E. *The Christian After Death.* Chicago: Moody, 1947.

1106.   Ironside, H. A. *The Great Parenthesis: Timely Messages on the Interval Between the 69th and 70th Weeks of Daniel's Prophecy.* Grand Rapids, MI: Zondervan Publishing House, 1943.

1107.   _____. *The Lamp of Prophecy: Or, Signs of the Times.* Grand Rapids, MI: Zondervan Publishing House, 1940 .

1108.   Jacobsen, Henry. *The War We Can't Lose.* Victor Books, n.d.

1109.   Jessop, Harry E. *The Day of Wrath: A Study of Prophecy's Light on Today.* New York: Fleming H. Revell, Co., 1943.

1110.   Jones, Russell. *The Latter Days.* Grand Rapids, MI: Baker Book House, 1961 [1947].

1111.   Kelly, William. *The Prospects of the World According to the Scriptures* (new ed.). London: Hammond, 1946.

1112.   Lacey, Harry. *God and the Nations.* n.p., 1942.

1113.   Lacy, S. L. *The End of the World.* West Point, VA: Pub. by author, 1941.

1114.   Lang, George H. *Firstfruits and Harvest: A Study in Resur-rection and Rapture* (2nd ed.). Dorset, ENG: Pub. by author, 1946.

1115.   _____. *The Histories and Prophecies of Daniel.* London: The Paternoster Press, 1950.

1116.   _____. *Israel's National Future, the Testimony of the Word of God.* London: Paternoster Press, n.d.

1117.   _____. *The Revelation of Jesus Christ: Selected Studies.* London: Oliphants, 1945.

1118.   _____. *World Chaos: Its Root and Remedy; An Inquiry into the Deeper Reasons and Urgent Lessons.* London: Paternoster Press, 1948.

1119.   Leech, Norman A. *This is Your Destiny.* Los Angeles: DeVorss & Co., 1945.

1120.   Lindberg, Milton B. *The Jews and Armageddon: All Nations to Gather Against Jerusalem.* Chicago: Chicago Hebrew Mission, 1940.

1121.   _____. *A Modern Jonah on the Ship of Tarshish: Amazing Parallelism Between the Story of Jonah and the Prophetic Picture of End-time Events.* Chicago: Chicago Hebrew Mission, 1942.

1122.   Linder, Tom. *Timetable of Bible Prophecy and Strong Meat, Heb. 5:12.* Atlanta: Tom Linder Publishing Co., 1947.

1123.   Linton, John. *How Near is Christ's Coming?: Startling Prophetic Messages.* Westbrook Publishing Co., 1946.

1124.   _____. *Will Christ Come in This Generation?* San Antonio, TX: The Christian Jew Hour, n.d.

1125.   _____. *Will the Church Escape the Great Tribulation?* Ontario, CAN: Pub. by author, n.d.

1126.   Liss, Hellmuth M. *Babylon, Rome, Jerusalem: A Prophetic Study, Past - Present - Future.* Fundamentals, n.d.

1127.   Lockyer, Herbert. *Cameos of Prophecy: Are These the Last Days?* Grand Rapids, MI: Zondervan Publishing House, 1942.

1128.   _____. *The Immortality of Saints: A Handbook on the Hereafter for Christian Workers.* London: Pickering & Inglis, n.d.

1129.   _____. *Our Lord's Return.* Chicago: Bible Institute Colportage Association, 1935.

1130.   _____. *The Rapture of Saints.* London: Pickering & Inglis, n.d.

1131.   *Look Out! He is Coming!* Framingham, MA: Christian Workers Union, n.d.

1132.   Lowry, Cecil J. *The Coming Tribulation.* Grand Rapids, MI: Zondervan Publishing House, 1943.

1133.   Lundquist, H. L. *Why Study Prophecy?: An Appraisal of Its Dangers, An Appreciation of Its Benefits.* Chicago: Bible Institute Colportage Association, 1940.

1134.   MacArthur, Harry E., E. Mc Clelland Stuart, Britton Ross, & Keith L. Brooks. *The Rapture: Our Lord's Coming for His Church; or Papers on the Rapture.* Los Angeles: American Prophetic League, 1940.

1135.   Mawson, John T. *Jerusalem, the Coming Metropolis of the Earth: Her Sins, Sorrows, and Savior* (3rd ed.). Northern Counties Bible and Tract Depot, n.d.

1136.   McArthur, Harry H. (ed.). *The Rapture: Our Lord's Coming for His Church.* Los Angeles: American Prophetic League, 1940.

1137.   McClain, Alva J. *Daniel's Prophecy of the Seventy Weeks* (3rd ed.). Grand Rapids, MI: Zondervan Publishing House, 1940.

1138. McCrossan, Thomas J. *The Great Tribulation: Are We Now in it?* [and] *The Rapture: Who Will be Taken?* [and] *The Tribulation Church: Are They Church Members?* Seattle: Pub. by author, 1940.

1139. McPherson, Norman S. *Triumph Through Tribulation.* Otego, New York: Pub. by author, 1944.

1140. McWirter, James. *Is Christ Coming?* London: Methuen & Co. LTD, 1940.

1141. Miles, Frederic J. *Answers to Prophetic Questions.* Grand Rapids, MI: Zondervan Publishing House, 1943.

1142. _____. *The Horsemen are Riding.* London: Marshall, Morgan & Scott, 1947.

1143. _____. *Prophecy, Palestine and the Red Russian Menace.* Pub. by author, n.d.

1144. _____. *Prophecy, Past, Present and Prospective.* Grand Rapids, MI: Zondervan Publishing House, 1943.

1145. _____. *Russia and Palestine in Prophecy* (3rd ed.). Pub. by author, n.d.

1146. Nelson, Nels Lars. *The Second War in Heaven as Now Being Waged by Lucifer Through Hitler as a Dummy.* Independence, MO: Press of Zion's Printing and Publishing Co., 1941.

1147. Nichols, J. W. H. *The Star in the East: A Brief Prophetic Outline.* C. E. Johnston Co., n.d.

1148. Nixon, E. A. *The Last Day's Story of Daniel and the Revelation.* n.p., 1945.

1149. Payne, James. *Messiah's Kingdom Coming on the Earth: A Reply to the Mystic Interpretation of Scripture.* London: Sovereign Grace Advent Testimony, n.d.

1150.   _____. *The Millennial Temple of Solomon and Ezekiel.*
         London: n.p., 1947.

1151.   Pettingill, William L. *Light in Darkness: Simple Studies in God's
         Revealed Plan of the Ages.* Findlay, OH: Fundamental Truth
         Publishers, 1941.

1152.   _____. *Loving His Appearing and Other Prophetic Studies.*
         Findlay, OH: Fundamental Truth Publishers, 1943.

1153.   _____. *Nearing the End: Simple Studies Concerning the
         Second Coming of Christ and Related Events.* Chicago: Van
         Kampen Press, 1948.

1154.   Phillips, O. E. *Birth Pangs of a New Age.* Los Angeles: Biblical
         Research Society, 1941.

1155.   *The Prophetic Word in Crisis Days.* Findlay, OH: Dunham
         Publishing Co., n.d.

1156.   Raud, G. P. *Prophetic and Practical Light.* New York: American
         Bible Institute, 1943.

1157.   Reid, R. J. *Remarks on the Amillennialism and Kindred Teaching
         of Philip Mauro.* New York: Loizeaux Brothers, 1943.

1158.   Rice, John R. *Christ's Literal Reign on Earth from David's Throne
         at Jerusalem.* Wheaton, IL: Sword of the Lord, 1947.

1159.   _____. *The Coming Kingdom of Christ.* Dallas, TX: John R.
         Rice, n.d.; Wheaton, IL: Sword of the Lord, 1945.

1160.   _____. *Jewish Persecutions and Bible Prophecies.* Wheaton, IL:
         Sword of the Lord, n.d.

1161.   _____. *The Second Coming of Christ in Daniel.* Dallas: Pub.
         by author, n.d.

1162.   _____. *World-wide War and the Bible.* Wheaton, IL: Sword of
         the Lord, 1940.

1163.   Riggle, Herbert M. *Jesus is Coming Again.* Guthrie, OK: Faith Publishing House, 1943.

1164.   Rimmer, Harry. *The Coming King.* Grand Rapids, MI: Wm B. Eerdmans Publishing Co., 1941.

1165.   _____. *The Coming League and the Roman Dream.* Grand Rapids, MI: Wm B. Eerdmans Publishing Co., 1941.

1166.   _____. *The Coming War and the Rise of Russia.* Grand Rapids, MI: Wm B. Eerdmans Publishing Co., 1940.

1167.   _____. *Palestine, the Coming Storm Center.* Grand Rapids, MI: Wm B. Eerdmans Publishing Co., 1943.

1168.   _____. *The Shadow of Coming Events.* Grand Rapids, MI: Wm B. Eerdmans Publishing Co., 1950 [1946]. [Compilation of the four previous works]

1169.   Roberts, Oral. *The Drama of the End Time.* Franklin Springs, GA: Pentecostal Holiness Publishing House, 1941.

1170.   Robinson, William C. *Christ -- the Hope of Glory: Christological Eschatology* (2nd ed.). Grand Rapids, MI: Eerdmans, 1947.

1171.   Rose, George L. *The Antichrist: and the Man of Sin.* Glendale, CA: Rose Publishing Co., n.d.

1172.   _____. *The Beast: His Image, His Mark, His Name, and His Number.* Glendale, CA: Rose Publishing Co., n.d.

1173.   _____. *Tribulation Till Translation: A Harmonious Compendium of Prophecy and History of the Past, the Present, and the Future, Viewed from the Fundamental and the Posttribulation Rapture Standpoint.* Glendale, CA: Rose Publishing Co., 1943.

1174.   Smith, Frederick G. *Prophetic Lectures on Daniel and the Revelation.* Anderson, IN: Gospel Trumpet Co., 1941.

1175.   _____. *The Revelation Explained* (11th ed., thoroughly rev.). Anderson, IN: Gospel Trumpet Co., 1943.

1176.   Smith, Oswald J. *Prophecy: What Lies Ahead?* London: Marshall, Morgan & Scott, LTD, 1955, (1st ed.,1943).

1177.   Smith, Wilbur M. *The Atomic Age and the Word of God.* Chicago: Moody Press, 1945; Boston: W. A. Wilde, 1948.

1178.   _____. *55 Best Books on Prophecy.* Chicago: Moody Bible Institute, 1940.

1179.   _____. *Studies in Bible Prophecy.* Westfield, IN: Union Bible Seminary, n.d.

1180.   Spink, James F. *Will Hitler Obtain World Dominion?* New York: Loizeaux Brothers, 1942.

1181.   Spurgeon, Charles Hadden. *Spurgeon's Sermons on the Second Coming* (David O. Fuller, ed.). Grand Rapids, MI: Zondervan Publishing House, 1943.

1182.   Swain, Sam. *The Second Coming of Christ and the Great Tribulation: Will the Church Go Through the Tribulation?* Akron, OH: National Spiritual Defense Crusade, 1947.

1183.   Talbot, Louis T. *Is It Possible for Christ to Return in This Generation?* Glendale, CA: Church Press, 1942.

1184.   _____. *The Prophecies of Daniel.* Los Angeles: The Church of the Open Door, 1940.

1185.   _____. *The Prophecies of Daniel in the Light of Past, Present, and Future Events* (3rd ed.). Wheaton, IL: Van Kampen Press, 1954, (1st ed., 1940).

1186.   _____. *Russia: Her Invasion of Palestine in the Last Days and Her Final Destruction at the Return of Christ.* Los Angeles: Pub. by author, n.d.

1187.   Talbot, Louis T. and William W. Orr. *The New Nation of Israel and the Word of God: A Discussion Between Louis T. Talbot and William W. Orr Conducted Over the Bible Institute Radio Hour.* Los Angeles: Bible Institute of Los Angeles, 1948.

1188.   Talbot, Louis T. and Samuel H. Sutherland. *The Shape of Things to Come: Questions and Answers on Prophecy, as Given Over the Bible Institute Hour.* Los Angeles: Bible Institute of Los Angeles, n.d.

1189.   Tanner, W. F. *From Rome to Jerusalem.* Pub. by author, 1940.

1190.   Thiessen, Henry C. *Will the Church Pass Through the Tribulation?* Grand Rapids, MI: Zondervan Publishing House, 1940; (2nd ed.). New York: Loizeaux Brothers, 1941.

1191.   Trotter, William and Daniel T. Smith. *Eight Lectures on Prophecy* (new ed.). New York: Loizeaux Brothers, 1945.

1192.   _____. *Essays on Prophetic Interpretation.* Glasgow: R. L. Allan, n.d.; London: George Morrish, n.d.

1193.   _____. *Plain Papers on Prophetic Subjects.* Bible Institute Colportage Association, n.d.; (rev. ed., previously titled *Plain Papers on Prophetic and Other Subjects*). New York: Loizeaux Brothers, n.d.

1194.   Welch, Charles H. *Parable, Miracle and Sign of Matthew and John Considered Dispensationally.* Surrey, England: Leonard A. Canning, 1948.

1195.   Wells, Robert J. (ed.). *Prophetic Messages for Modern Times* (Messages from the Colonial Hills Bible Conference, March 19-26, 1944). East Point, GA: Colonial Hills Baptist Church, 1944.

1196.   Winrod, Gerald Burton. *Antichrist and the Atomic Bomb.* Wichita, KS: Defender Publishers, 1945.

1197.   Yuk, James. *Israel in the Holy Land Today and the Coming of Christ* (Catherine Smith, trans.). The American-European Fellowship for Christian Oneness and Evangelization, n.d.

SECTION SEVEN

THE COLD WAR PERIOD (PART 1), 1949-1957

The restoration of the Jews to Palestine and the establishment of a Jewish state in 1948 greatly boosted the credibility of dispensational premillennialism within the mainstream evangelical churches. But it was the expansion of evangelical and fundamentalist Protestantism into such mass media as radio and film production in the 1930s and 1940s and television in the 1950s and 1960s that provided premillennialists access to larger audiences and greater national exposure than even their most popular conferences had ever done.

Among the more popular Bible prophecy programs during the early Cold War era were: Theodore Epp's "Back to the Bible," which began broadcasting in 1939; M. R. DeHaan's "Radio Bible Class of the Air," which aired locally in Grand Rapids, Michigan, beginning in 1941, and then nationally by the 1950s; Louis Talbot's "Bible Institute Radio Hour," a ministry of BIOLA College which aired during the late 1940s and throughout the 1950s; and J. Vernon McGee's "Thru the Bible" program, which aired originally in Los Angeles in the 1950s and, afterwards, nationally until his death sometime in 1990 or 1991. (Incidentally, both Louis Talbot and J. Vernon McGee had served as ministers of Los Angeles's large independent fundamentalist congregation, The Church of the Open Door). In addition, the Moody Bible Institute of Chicago ran a series of popular Bible Study programs throughout this period over its own radio station, WMBI.

But while radio and television spread popular eschatology to audiences nationwide, Bible institutes and colleges remained the central network of premillennialist thought. These centers attracted ministers, missionaries, and laypeople, who then returned to their churches or went off to the mission fields deeply imbued with a dispensational premillennialist understanding of the Bible and a prophetic reading of world events. The three major centers of premillennialist thought during this period were the Bible Institute of Los Angeles or BIOLA College, Dallas Theological Seminary, and the Moody Bible Institute. The new generation of Bible prophecy scholars, whose popularity attracted students to these centers, included Charles Feinberg and Louis Talbot of BIOLA; Lewis Sperry Chafer and John Walvoord of Dallas; H. A. Ironside and Dwight Pentecost of Moody; and Wilbur Smith of Moody and, after 1947, of Fuller Seminary in Pasadena.

Their success, and the success of other lesser-known Bible teachers, stemmed from their ability to convince their readers and listeners that such events as the quick spread of communism, rising Arab nationalism, nuclear proliferation, and growing East-West tensions, were part of the endtimes scenario as outlined in the Bible.

1198.   Alderman, Paul Repton, Jr. *The Unfolding of the Ages: Prophecy Fulfilled, Prophecy Being Fulfilled, Prophecy to be Fulfilled.* Grand Rapids, MI: Zondervan Publishing House, 1954.

1199.   Angley, Ernest W. *Raptured.* Old Tappan, NJ: Fleming H. Revell, 1950.

1200.   Appelman, Hyman J. *Antichrist and the Jew, and the Valley of Dry Bones.* Grand Rapids, MI: Zondervan Publishing House, 1950.

1201.   _____. *The Atomic Bomb and the End of the World.* Grand Rapids, MI: Zondervan Publishing House, 1954.

1202.   Askwith, Charles. *A Recording of Prophecy.* London: Protestant Truth Society, 1949.

1203. Becker, Abraham A. *Entering the Covenant Week.* Freeman, SD: Pub. by author, 1953.

1204. _____. *Prophetic Definitions and Charts.* Freeman, SD: Pub. by author, 1954.

1205. Benson, Carman. *The Earth's Send.* Plainfield, NJ: Logos International, n.d.

1206. _____. *Jesus and Israel.* Plainfield, NJ: Logos International, n.d.

1207. Benson, Clarence H. *The Second Coming of Christ: Is It Near?* Birmingham, AL: Southeastern Bible School, 1951.

1208. Bezzant, R. and R. P. Pridham. *The Promise of Ezekiel's City.* Norwich, England: Simpkins, 1952.

1209. Bradbury, John W. (ed.). *Hastening the Day of God: Prophetic Messages.* Wheaton, IL: Van Kampen Press, 1953.

1210. _____. *Israel's Restoration.* New York: Iverson-Ford Associates, n.d.

1211. Brooks, Keith L. (ed.). *Prophetic Questions Answered.* Wheaton, IL: Van Kampen Press, 1951.

1212. Brown, Dennis J. *'Things Which Must Shortly Come to Pass.'* Riverside, CA: Pub. by author, 1954 .

1213. Browne, Frederic Z. *Visible Glory.* New York: Greenwich Book Publishers, 1957.

1214. Canney, Ella Mae. *God Speaks.* Glendale, CA: The Church Press, 1949.

1215. Cass, Charles. *All Eyes Are on Israel.* Los Angeles: Calvary Press, 1951.

1216. Cooper, David L. *Antichrist and the Worldwide Revival.* Los Angeles: Biblical Research Society, 1954.

1217. _____. *Grand March of Empire*. Los Angeles: Biblical Research Society, 1955.

1218. Culbertson, William. *The Relationship of the Doctrine of the Return of Christ to Practical Holiness*. Chicago: Moody Bible Institute, 1957.

1219. _____. *Christ the Hope of the World: The Promise of His Coming*. Chicago: Moody Bible Institute, 1954.

1220. Culbertson, William, et al. *Understanding the Times: Prophetic Messages Delivered at the Second International Congress on Prophecy, New York City*. Grand Rapids, MI: Zondervan Publishing House, 1956.

1221. Culver, Robert D. *Daniel and the Latter Days*. Chicago: Moody Press, 1954; Westwood, NJ: Fleming H. Revell, 1954.

1222. Dake, Finis Jennings. *One Hundred Prophetic Wonders from 1955 to Eternity*. Atlanta: Bible Research Foundation, n.d.

1223. _____. *The Rapture of the Church*. Atlanta: Bible Research Foundation, n.d.

1224. _____. *Revelation Expounded*. Atlanta: Bible Research Foundation, n.d.

1225. _____. *The Second Coming of Christ*. Atlanta: Bible Research Foundation, 1955.

1226. _____. *The Time of the Gentiles*. Atlanta: Bible Research Foundation, n.d.

1227. _____. *The Two Great Future World Empires*. Atlanta: Bible Research Foundation, n.d.

1228. _____. *Who are the Ten Virgins (Exposition of Matthew 24 and 25)*. Atlanta: Bible Research Foundation, n.d.

1229. _____. *Why Anti-Christ Will Never Come From the Vatican, Italy, Russia, Germany, China, Japan, India, the Americas, Africa, Europe, or From Hell.* Atlanta: Bible Research Foundation.

1230. _____. *Why Anti-Christ Will Never Conquer the World.* Atlanta: Bible Research Foundation, n.d.

1231. _____. *Why Anti-Christ Will Not Rule America or Be Worldwide Dictator.* Atlanta: Bible Research Foundation, n.d.

1232. _____. *Why Russia Will Never Conquer the World.* Atlanta: Bible Research Foundation, n.d.

1233. _____. *Why There Must Be Three More European, Asiatic and African Wars Before Christ Comes.* Atlanta: Bible Research Foundation, n.d.

1234. Davis, George T. B. *Bible Prophecies Fulfilled Today: Proving the Supernatural Inspiration of the Bible.* Philadelphia: The Million Testaments Campaigns, Inc., 1955.

1235. _____. *Israel Returns Home According to Prophecy.* Philadelphia: The Million Testaments Campaign, 1950.

1236. De Haan, M. R. *The Atomic Bomb in Prophecy: An Examination of Scripture Passages Dealing with the Devastation of the Earth in the Day of the Lord. Will It Be by Atomic Explosions?* Grand Rapids, MI: The Radio Bible Class, n.d.

1237. _____. *The Church and the Tribulation?: A Scriptural Answer to the Teachings of the Post-tribulation and Mid-tribulation Rapture.* Grand Rapids, MI: The Radio Bible Class, n.d.

1238. _____. *The Church, the Rapture, and the Tribulation: The Scriptural Answer to the Question, 'Will the Church Pass Through or Be Raptured Before the Tribulation?'* Grand Rapids, MI: The Radio Bible Class, n.d.

1239.   _____. *The First Rapture: A Study of the Life and Translation of Enoch as Recorded in Genesis 5, Hebrews 11, and Jude 14-15.* Grand Rapids, MI: The Radio Bible Class, n.d.

1240.   _____. *God's Miracle Nation: A Review of Some of the Bible Prophecies Concerning the Miraculous Preservation of Israel, with Emphasis on Their Return to Palestine.* Grand Rapids, MI: The Radio Bible Class, n.d.

1241.   _____. *The Jew and Palestine in Prophecy.* Grand Rapids, MI: The Radio Bible Class of the Air, 1950; Grand Rapids, MI: Zondervan Publishing House, 1950.

1242.   _____. *One Thousand Years of Peace on Earth: A Series of Four Messages on the Future Reign of Christ on Earth.* Grand Rapids, MI: The Radio Bible Class, n.d.

1243.   _____. *Palestine and the Middle East in Prophecy: Five Radio Sermons.* Grand Rapids, MI: The Radio Bible Class, n.d.

1244.   _____. *Palestine in History and in Prophecy: Five Expository Messages on the Scriptural Teaching of the Land of Palestine and the Future of the Nation of Israel.* Grand Rapids, MI: The Radio Bible Class, n.d.

1245.   _____. *The Rapture of the Church: Four Sermons.* Grand Rapids, MI: The Radio Bible Class, n.d.

1246.   _____. *The Return of the King, Revelation 22:20: A Bible Study Concerning the Certainty, Imminence, and Results of that Blessed Hope of Christ's Return.* Grand Rapids, MI: The Radio Bible Class, n.d.

1247.   _____. *Revelation.* Grand Rapids, MI: The Radio Bible Class of the Air, n.d.

1248.   _____. *Russia and the Final War: An Exposition of Prophecies of Ezekiel 38 and 39 Concerning the Fate of Russia in the Latter Days.* Grand Rapids, MI: The Radio Bible Class of the Air, n.d.

1249.   _____. *The Second Coming of Elijah: A Scriptural Comparison of the Ministries of John the Baptist and the Prophet Elijah in Relation to the First and Second Coming of Christ.* Grand Rapids, MI: The Radio Bible Class, n.d.

1250.   _____. *The Secret Rapture and the Secret of the Rapture: A Simple Study of the Scripture Teaching of 'That Blessed Hope.'* Grand Rapids, MI: The Radio Bible Class, n.d.

1251.   _____. *Signs of the Times.* Grand Rapids, MI: The Radio Bible Class of the Air., n.d.

1252.   _____. *Signs of the Times and Other Prophetic Messages.* Grand Rapids, MI: Zondervan, 1951.

1253.   _____. *The Time of Christ's Return; It is Later Than You Think: A Study of Some of the Signs of the Soon Return of Christ.* Grand Rapids, MI: The Radio Bible Class, n.d.

1254.   _____. *The United Nations in History and Prophecy: The Prophetic Significance of the Kingdom of Nimrod and the Tower of Babel.* Grand Rapids, MI: The Radio Bible Class, n.d.

1255.   _____. *Who Owns Palestine?: Five Messages.* Grand Rapids, MI: The Radio Bible Class, n.d.

1256.   DeLoach, Charles. *Seeds of Conflict.* Plainfield, NJ: Logos Publishing, n.d.

1257.   Derham, A. Morgan. *Shall These Things Be?: An Outline of Bible Teaching on the Return of Jesus Christ.* Chicago: InterVarsity Press, 1956.

1258.   Donham, Paul S. *The Beast and the Prophet.* Dallas: The Story Book Press, 1950.

1259.   Donn, F. S. *The Israel Way to Peace: A Study of Biblical Prophecy and the Twentieth Century.* New York: Exposition Press, 1957.

1260. Douty, Norman F. *Has Christ's Return Two Stages?* New York: Pageant Press, 1956.

1261. Eller, Vernard. *The Most Revealing Book of the Bible: Making Sense Out of Revelation.* Grand Rapids, MI: Eerdmans Publishing Co.

1262. English, E. Schuyler. *A Companion to the New Scofield Reference Bible.* New York: Oxford University Press, n.d.

1263. _____. *The Rapture* (2nd ed.) Neptune, NJ: Loizeaux Brothers, 1986, (1st ed., 1954).

1264. _____. *Re-thinking the Rapture: An Examination of What the Scriptures Teach as to the Time of the Translation of the Church in Relation to the Tribulation.* Travelers Rest, SC: Southern Bible Book House, 1954

1265. Epp, Theodore H. *Brief Outlines of Things to Come.* Chicago: Moody Press (Colportage Library, vol. 68), 1952.

1266. _____. *The Rise and Fall of Gentile Nations.* Lincoln, NE: Back to the Bible Publications, 1956.

1267. Erb, Paul. *The Alpha and the Omega: A Restatement of the Christian Hope in Christ's Coming.* Scottdale, PA: Herald Press, 1955.

1268. Evans, Robert L. *The Jew in the Plan of God.* New York: Loizeaux Brothers, 1950.

1269. _____. *Israel in the Last Days: The Olivet Discourse.* Altadena, CA: Emeth Publications, 1953.

1270. Feinberg, Charles. *Premillennialism or Amillennialism?* Wheaton, IL: Van Kampen Press, 1954.

1271. _____ (ed.). *Prophetic Truth Unfolding Today (Messages from the Fifth Congress on Prophecy).* Fleming H. Revell Co.

1272.   _____. *The Suez Canal in the Light of Prophecy*. Los Angeles: Bible Institute of Los Angeles, 1956.

1273.   Fisch, S. *Ezekiel*. London: Soncino Series, 1950.

1274.   Fison, J. E. *The Christian Hope: The Presence and the Parousia*. New York: Longmans, Green, 1954.

1275.   Fox, John S. *A Flood of Light Upon the Book of Revelation: Every Verse Simply Explained*. Somerset, England: The Open-Bible Kingdom Fellowship, 1953.

1276.   _____. *God's Great Week: The Story of the Ages from the Creation of Adamic Man Until the Rapidly-Approaching Millennial Reign on Earth of Jesus Christ*. Somerset, England: The Open-Bible Kingdom Fellowship, n.d., (3rd ed., 1953).

1277.   _____. *The Last Sign Post, or 1956-1958 and Beyond in Bible Prophecy*. Somerset, England: The Open-Bible Kingdom Fellowship, 1954.

1278.   _____. *Life, Death and the Resurrection, or Where are the Dead? A Vital Survey of the Scriptures Revealing Man's Destiny, His Resurrection and His Just Judgment to Come*. Somerset, England: The Open-Bible Kingdom Fellowship, 1950.

1279.   Fraser, Alexander. *The Return of Christ in Glory: Consolidating 'Is There But One Return of Christ?' and 'The Any Moment Return of Christ.'* Pittsburgh: The Evangelical Fellowship, 1950.

1280.   Fromow, George H. *New Testament Millennial Teaching*. London: Sovereign Grace Advent Testimony, n.d.

1281.   _____. *Will the Church Pass Through the Tribulation?* London: Sovereign Grace Advent Testimony, n.d.

1282.   Geraldi, Joseph. *Biblical Prophecies: A Look into the Future*. New York: Vantage Press, 1957.

1283. Gilbert, Dan. *The Mark of the Beast*. Washington, D. C.: Pub. by author, 1951.

1284. Gortner, L. Narver. *Are the Saints Scheduled to Go Through the Tribulation?* Springfield, MO: Gospel Publishing House, n.d.

1285. Graham, James R. *Watchman, What of the Night?* Berwyn, Ill: Men for Missions, n.d.; Minneapolis: Bethany Fellowship Press, n.d.; Los Angeles: Ambassadors for Christ, n.d.

1286. Hall, John G. *Dispensations of the Eternal Program of God*. Springfield, MO: Pub. by author, 1957.

1287. Hamilton, Frank. *The Bible and the Millennium*. Ventnor, NJ: Pub. by author, n.d.

1288. _____. *The New Testament and the Millennium*. Ventnor, NJ: Pub. by author, n.d.

1289. Hamilton, Gavin. *Maranatha*. Oak Park, IL: Pub. by author, n.d.

1290. _____. *The Rapture and the Great Tribulation*. Oak Park, IL: Pub. by author, 1957.

1291. Hayhoe, H. E. *Ten Scriptural Reasons by Which We Know the Church Will Not Go Through the Tribulation*. Oak Park, IL: Bible Truth Publishers, 1950.

1292. Hodges, Jesse W. *Christ's Kingdom and Coming; With an Analysis of Dispensationalism*. Grand Rapids, MI: Eerdmans Publishing Co., 1957.

1293. Hottel, William S. *The Dispensations of the Ages*. Cleveland: Union Gospel Press, 1953.

1294. *How B. W. Newton Learned Prophetic Truth*. London: Sovereign Grace Advent Testimony, 1957. [reprinted from *Watching and Waiting*]

1295.   Hull, William L. *The Fall and Rise of Israel*. Grand Rapids, MI: Zondervan, 1954.

1296.   _____. *Israel -- Key to Prophecy; The Story of Israel from the Regathering to the Millennium as Told by the Prophets*. Grand Rapids, MI: Zondervan Publishing Co., 1964 [1957].

1297.   Ironside, H. A. *Expository Notes on Ezekiel the Prophet*. New York: Loizeaux Brothers, 1949.

1298.   Jaggers, O. L. *The Atomic and Hydrogen Bombs in Bible Prophecy*. Los Angeles: Pub. by author, 1953.

1299.   Janeway, Jacob J. *Hope for the Jews: or The Jews Will Be Converted to the Christian Faith, and Settled and Reorganized as a Nation, in the Land of Palestine*. New Brunswick, NJ: J. Terhune and Son, 1953.

1300.   Janzen, Henry H. *A Brief Outline Study of the Seven Churches: Revelation Chapters Two and Three*. Canada: The Christian Press, LTD, 1949.

1301.   Jennings, F. C. *Studies in Revelation*. New York: Loizeaux Brothers, 1950.

1302.   Johnson, Carl. *Prophecy Made Plain for Times Like These*. Chicago: Moody Press.

1303.   Johnson, Marvin L. *Signs of the Times*. New York: Carlton Press, Inc., n.d.

1304.   Kingsbury, Frank H. *God's New Order* (Reprinted from *Watching and Waiting*, Oct.-Nov.-Dec., 1949). London: The Sovereign Grace Advent Testimony, n.d.

1305.   Ladd, George Eldon. *The Blessed Hope*. Grand Rapids, MI: Wm B. Eerdmans, 1956.

1306.   _____. *Crucial Questions about the Kingdom of God*. Grand Rapids, MI: Wm B. Eerdmans Publishing Co., 1952.

1307.   _____. *The Presence of the Future.* Grand Rapids, MI: William
            B. Eerdmans Publishing Co., n.d.

1308.   Laidlow, Robert Alexander. *Will the Church Go Through the Great
            Tribulation?* (reprinted ed.). New York: Loizeaux Brothers,
            n.d.

1309.   Langston, Earle L. *The Last Hour.* London and Worthing: Henry
            E. Walter LTD, 1951.

1310.   Lewis, William Rhodes and E. W. Rogers. *Who Will Go When
            the Lord Comes?: Select Rapture Theories Tested by Holy
            Scriptures.* Bath, England: Office of 'Echoes of Service', 1952.

1311.   Lincoln, William. *Lectures on the Book of Revelation.* New York:
            Fleming H. Revell, n.d.

1312.   Lockyer, Herbert. *The Bridegroom Cometh!* Grand Rapids, MI:
            Zondervan Publishing House, 1952.

1313.   _____. *The H-Bomb and the End of the Age* (2nd ed.). Grand
            Rapids, MI: Zondervan Publishing House, 1950.

1314.   _____. *Predictions of Things to Come.* Grand Rapids, MI:
            Zondervan Publishing House, 1952.

1315.   Lowry, Cecil J. *Whither Israeli? Mosaic Restorationism Examined.*
            Oakland, CA: Tabernacle Book Room (Pub. by author), 1955.

1316.   Luck, George C. *The Coming King.* Chicago: Moody Press, n.d.

1317.   Ludwigson, R. *Bible Prophecy Notes* (3rd ed.). Grand Rapids, MI:
            Zondervan Publishing House 1956.

1318.   Macartney, C. E. *Things Most Assuredly Believed.* n.p., n.d.

1319.   Meldau, Fred John. *The Seven Sevens of Prophetic Wonders: A
            Textbook on Some of the Unfulfilled Prophecies of the Bible.*
            Denver: Christian Victory, n.d.

1320. Miller, Harry Reigart. *The Millennium.* Chickasaw, AL: The Biblicist Press, 1957.

1321. Muller, Jac J. *When Christ Comes Again.* London: Marshall, Morgan & Scott, 1956.

1322. Naismith, Archie. *God's People and God's Purpose: or The Hope of Israel and the Church.* Kilmarnock, Scotland: John Ritchie, 1949.

1323. Newberry, Thomas. *The Expected One; or The Coming of the Son of God from Heaven and His Manifestation as Son of Man to Earth.* Kilmarnock, Scotland: John Ritchie, n.d.

1324. _____. *The Millennial Temple of Solomon and Ezekiel.* Glasglow: Pickering & Inglis, n.d.

1325. Newby, J. Edwin. *Chart Messages on the History and Prophecy of the Bible.* Berne, IN: Light and Hope Publications, 1951; Noblesville, IN: Pub. by author, 1970.

1326. Newell, Philip Rutherford. *Daniel: The Man Greatly Beloved, and His Prophecies.* Chicago: Moody Press, 1951.

1327. Nyquist, John G. *The Kingdom of the World in Prophecy.* New York: Pageant Press Inc., 1956.

1328. Ober, Douglas. *The Great World Crisis.* Wheaton, IL: Van Kampen Press, 1950.

1329. Owen, Frederick. *Abraham to the Middle-East Crisis.* Grand Rapids, MI: Eerdmans Publishing Co., 1957.

1330. Pache, Rene. *The Return of Christ* (Wm S. LaSor, trans.). Chicago: Moody Press, 1955.

1331. Peters, George N. H. *The Theocratic Kingdom of Our Lord Jesus, the Christ* (3 vols.). Grand Rapids, MI: Kregel Publications, 1952 and 1957.

1332.   Phillips, Ordis E. *The Kingdom of God.* Philadelphia: Hebrew
         Christian Fellowship, Inc., 1954.

1333.   _____. *Out of the Night.* Philadelphia: Hebrew Christian
         Fellowship, Inc., 1949.

1334.   Pieters, Albertus. *The Seed of Abraham.* Grand Rapids, MI: Wm.
         B. Eerdmans Publishing Co., 1950.

1335.   Pinch, E. Buckhurst. *The Approaching Crisis.* London: The
         Advent Testimony and Preparation Movement, 1953 .

1336.   _____. *The Return of the Lord Jesus Christ: A Concise
         Scriptural Survey.* London: Advent Testimony and Preparation
         Movement, n.d.; Chicago: Moody Press, 1957.

1337.   Pont, Charles E. *The World's Collision.* Boston: W. A. Wilde
         Co., 1956.

1338.   Price, Walter K. *Jesus' Prophetic Sermon.* Chicago: Moody Press,
         n.d.

1339.   Procter, W. C. *The Sure Word of Prophecy and Some Prophetic
         Psalms.* London: The Hilbert Publishing Co. LTD, n.d.

1340.   Reed, B. E. *Signs of Earth's Sunrise* (2nd ed.). Watertown, New
         York: Christian Book Service, 1950.

1341.   Reid, W. T. *Alarm and Admonition From the Prophet's Chamber.*
         Cincinnati: W. T. Reid, 1953.

1342.   Ritchie. J. M. *Messiah the Prince: A Study in Biblical Prophecy.*
         New York: Exposition Press, 1952.

1343.   Roberson, Lee. *Some Golden Daybreak: Sermons on the Second
         Coming of Christ.* Orlando, FL: Christ for the World
         Publishing, 1957.

1344.   _____ (ed.). *Will the Church Go Through the Great Tribulation?:
         A Fresh Examination.* London: Pickering & Inglis, 1955.

1345.   Ryrie, Charles C. *The Basis of the Premillennial Faith.* New York: Loizeaux Bros., 1953.

1346.   Smith, Oswald J. *The Voice of Prophecy.* London: Marshall, Morgan & Scott, 1954.

1347.   Smith, Wilbur M. *The Bible History of World Government, and a Forecast of its Future From Bible Prophecy.* Westfield, IN: Union Bible Seminary, Inc., 1955.

1348.   _____. *Egypt in Biblical Prophecy.* Boston: W. A. Wilde Co., 1957.

1349.   _____. *A Preliminary Bibliography for the Study of Biblical Prophecy.* Boston: W. A. Wilde Co., 1952.

1350.   _____. *The Second Advent of Christ.* Washington, D.C.: Christianity Today, n.d.

1351.   _____. *World Crises and the Prophetic Scriptures.* Chicago: Moody Press, 1950.

1352.   Spivey, Clark Dwight. *The Antichrist: Is the Pope Antichrist?* Anselmo, NE: Pub. by author, 1950.

1353.   Tennyson, Elwell Thomas. *The Time of the End.* Jefferson City, MO: Harvest Publishers, 1951.

1354.   Thomas, V. R. *End Time Shadows: God's Prophetic Word.* Burbank: Bread of Life Press, 1949.

1355.   Tidwell, W. M. *The Second Coming of Christ.* Kansas City, MO: Beacon Hill Press, 1951.

1356.   True, Jonathan. *Prophetic Papers.* Altoona, PA: Pub. by author, 1950.

1357.   Tulga, Chester E. *The Case for the Second Coming of Christ.* Chicago: Conservative Baptist Fellowship, 1951.

1358.   Unger, Merrill F. *Great Neglected Bible Prophecies.* Chicago:
         Scripture Press Foundation, 1955.

1359.   Van Gorder, John J. *ABC's of the Revelation.* Grand Rapids, MI:
         Zondervan Publishing Co., 1952.

1360.   Walvoord, John F. *The Rapture Question.* Findlay, OH: Dunham
         Publishing Co., 1957; (rev. and enlarged ed.). Grand Rapids,
         MI: Zondervan Publishing House, 1979.

1361.   _____. *The Return of the Lord.* Findlay, OH: Dunham
         Publishing Co., 1955; Grand Rapids, MI: Zondervan
         Publishing House, 1977.

1362.   _____. *The Revelation of Jesus Christ.* Findlay, OH: Dunham
         Publishing Co., 1957; Chicago: Moody Press, 1966 .

1363.   _____. *The Thessalonian Epistle.* Findlay, OH: Dunham
         Publishing Co., 1955.

1364.   Ward, Larry. *'...And There Will Be Famines.'* Grand Rapids, MI:
         Regal Publications.

1365.   Welch, Charles H. *Zion, the Overcomer, and the Millennium.*
         Surrey, ENG: The Berean Publishing Trust, 1956.

1366.   Weston, Frank S. *Pre- or Post- Millennialism: Does it Matter?*
         New York: American Board of Missions to the Jews, n.d.

1367.   White, F. H. *The Land, the City, and the Temple of Israel in the
         Millennium: Ezekiel 40-48.* London: Partridge, n.d.

1368.   Wilson, Paul. *A Defense of Dispensationalism.* Denver, CO:
         Wilson Foundation, n.d.

1369.   Wood, Leon J. *Is the Rapture Next?: An Answer to the Question,
         Will the Church Escape the Tribulation?* Grand Rapids, MI:
         Zondervan Publishing House, 1956.

1370.   Woods, John Purvis. *The Final Invasion of God.* Boston: W. A.
         Wilde Co., 1951.

1371. Woodson, Leslie H. *Population, Pollution and Prophecy.* New York: Fleming H. Revell Co., n.d.

1372. Wuest, Kenneth S. *Prophetic Light in the Present Darkness.* Grand Rapids, MI: Eerdmans, 1955; Grand Rapids, MI: Zondervan Publishing House, 1963.

1373. Young, Edward Joseph. *The Messianic Prophecies of Daniel.* Grand Rapids, MI: Eerdmans, 1954.

1374. _____. *The Prophecy of Daniel.* Grand Rapids, MI: Wm B. Eerdmans Publishing Co., 1949.

SECTION EIGHT

THE COLD WAR PERIOD (PART 2), 1958-1966

Tensions in the Middle East did not ease with time, as some had hoped, but were heightened. During the 1950s, relations between the Arab states and Israel grew more and more strained. Arab refusal to recognize the new State of Israel meant that a state of war existed between these peoples. Smoldering tensions in the Middle East did eventually flare up, resulting in crisis in the Suez region in 1956 and limited war between Egypt and Israel.

When the fighting ended and a cease-fire agreement was signed, Israel had taken firm control of the Sinai peninsula. For their part, Israel's only allies, Britain and France, gained control of the Suez Canal. For the Arabs, however, defeat proved divisive, as Egyptian president Gamal Nasser's vision of a united pan-Arab league was shattered. Rather than give the Arab League control over the Mideast region, as Nasser had hoped, this war and the later 1967 Six-Day War, changed the political and military configuration of the Middle East, establishing Israel, not Egypt, as the dominant power in the region.

Elsewhere in the world, Communism continued to spread. One dramatic example was in Cuba, where Communist guerrillas, led by Fidel Castro, successfully overthrew the repressive Batista regime in 1959. The fall of Cuba gave Communism its first toehold in the Americas, an event that created no small amount of fear among Americans, who saw marxist Cuba as another stepping stone toward the global spread of Communism.

Not surprisingly, the literature of this period greatly reflects these international developments as well as the uneasiness Americans felt as Cold War tensions intensified. Premillennialists' deep concern over the turn of world events is especially evident in their fear of communism and its threat to democratic American society.

The spread of Communism to the Americas prompted premillennialists to ask with greater frequency: "What role, if any, would the United States play in Last Days?" and "Is America destined for destruction or will America be spared the horrors of the Tribulation period?" The answer, wrote many premillennialists, is uncertain. Most could find no clear reference to the United States in the Bible's prophetic passages. America's key to survival, millennialists asserted, might be in its loyal support for Israel, God's chosen people.

But, as many millennialists mused, President Eisenhower had refused to commit U. S. troops in support of Israel during the Suez crisis, implying American support for the Arabs. Would America's tacit support of the Arabs and, its implied opposition to Israel incur God's wrath upon it? Perhaps, but America could still be forgiven this egregious error. If the United States were to voice whole-hearted support for Israel, they reasoned, perhaps the American nation might yet escape God's wrath.

The other literature of the period deals with standard prophecy themes.

1375.   Alderman, Paul Repton, Jr. *God's Spotlight on Tomorrow: Seven Sevens Concerning the Return of Christ.* New York: Loizeaux Brothers, 1960.

1376.   Armerding, Carl. *The Four and Twenty Elders.* New York: Loizeaux Brothers, n.d.

1377.   _____. *Signs of Christ's Coming -- As Son of Man.* Chicago: Moody Press, 1965; (rev. ed.). Chicago: Moody Press, 1971.

1378.   Barndollar, Walter. *The Validity of Dispensationalism.* Des Plaines, IL: Regular Baptist Press, 1964 and 1974.

1379.   Baughman, Ray E. *The Kingdom of God Visualized.* Chicago: Moody Press, n.d.

1380.   Bauman, Paul, Simon Forsberg, et al. *The Prophetic Word in Crisis Days: Prophetic Messages Delivered at the West Coast Prophetic Conference, Los Angeles.* Findlay, OH: Dunham Publishing Co., 1961.

1381.   Beshore, F. Kenton. *Five World-Shaking Events.* Los Angeles: Biblical Research Society, 1964.

1382.   _____. *What Are the Signs of the Last Days?* Los Angeles: Biblical Research Society, 1965.

1383.   Bloomfield, Arthur E. *All Things New: A Study of Revelation.* Minneapolis, MN: Bethany Fellowship, 1959.

1384.   _____. *The Changing Climate.* Minneapolis: Bethany Fellowship, 1956.

1385.   _____. *Signs of His Coming: A Study of the Olivet Discourse.* Minneapolis: Bethany Fellowship, 1962.

1386.   Branham, William M. *An Exposition of the Seven Church Ages.* Jeffersonville, IN: Branham Campaigns, n.d.

1387.   Britt, George L. *When Dust Shall Sing: The World Crisis in the Light of Biblical Prophecy.* Cleveland, TN: Pathway Press, 1958.

1388.   Brown, Arthur Copeland. *The Revelation Chronologically Arranged.* Golden, CO: Gospel Publications, 1965. [fold chart]

1389.   Cardey, Elmer L. *The Countdown of History.* Grand Rapids, MI: Baker Book House, 1962.

1390.   _____. *The Prophecy of Daniel.* n.p., n.d.

1391.   _____. *Unfolding the Revelation.* n.p., n.d.

1392.   Chater, E. H. *The Coming and Reign of Our Lord Jesus Christ* (3rd ed.). Denver, CO: Wilson Foundation, 1963.

1393.   *The Church and the End Times.* Los Angeles: The Bible Institute Hour, n.d.

1394.   Cooke, A. Ernest. *Fulfilled Prophecy: The Evidence of the Truth of the Bible Record.* Chicago: Moody Press, 1963.

1395.   Cox, Clyde C. *Apocalyptic Commentary.* Cleveland TN: Pathway Press, 1959.

1396.   Criswell, W. A. *Expository Sermons on Revelation* (5 vols). Grand Rapids, MI: Zondervan Publishing House, 1962.

1397.   Custance, Arthur C. *Some Striking Fulfilments of Prophecy.* Ottawa: Doorway Paper, 1962.

1398.   Dahl, Mikkel. *Tomorrow's Empire of the 'Beast' and His Number.* Toronto: Pub. by author, 1965.

1399.   Dahlin, John E. *Prophetic Truth for Today: Unveiling the End-time Events.* Minneapolis: Beacon Publications, 1961.

1400.   Darms, Anton. *The Jew Returns to Israel.* Grand Rapids, MI: Zondervan Publishing House, 1965.

1401.   De Haan, M. D. and M. R. De Haan. *Revelation.* Grand Rapids, MI: Zondervan Publishing House, n.d.

1402.   De Haan, M. R. *Coming Events in Prophecy.* Grand Rapids, MI: Zondervan Publishing House, 1962.

1403.   _____. *The Coming Golden Age: A Study of Bible Prophecies Dealing with the Restoration of the Earth at the Coming of Christ.* Grand Rapids, MI: The Radio Bible Class of the Air, n.d.

1404.   _____. *The Days of Noah, and Their Prophetic Message for Today.* Grand Rapids, MI: Zondervan Publishing Co., 1963.

1405.   Duff-Forbes, Lawrence. *Perils from the North.* Whittier, CA: Review, 1958.

1406. Epp, Theodore H. *God's Program for Israel: A Compact Do-It-Yourself Course.* Lincoln, NE: Back to the Bible Publications, 1962.

1407. _____. *Russia's Doom Prophesied in Ezekiel 38 and 39.* Lincoln, NE: Back to the Bible Publications, 1959.

1408. _____. *Why Must Jesus Come Again?* Lincoln, NE: Back to the Bible Publications, 1960.

1409. Feinberg, Charles L. (ed.). *Focus on Prophecy: Messages Delivered at the Congress on Prophecy...in Chicago.* Westwood, NJ: Fleming H. Revell Co., 1964.

1410. _____. *Isaac and Ishmael: Twentieth Century Version.* New York: American Board of Missions to the Jews, n.d.

1411. _____. *Israel in the Spotlight.* Chicago: Scripture Press, 1956; New York: American Board of Missions to the Jews, 1964.

1412. Fox, John S. *The Glorious Majesty of His Kingdom.* Somerset, ENG: The Open-Bible Kingdom Fellowship, 1958.

1413. Graham, Billy. *World Aflame.* New York: Doubleday, 1965.

1414. Hadjiantoniou, G. A. *The Postman of Patmos: Striking Messages of the Seven Letters to the Seven Churches.* Grand Rapids, MI: Zondervan Publishing House, 1961.

1415. Hadley, E. C. *Outline of Prophetic Events Soon to Come to Pass.* Danville, IL: Grace & Truth, n.d.

1416. Haldeman, I. M. *How to Study the Bible: The Second Coming, and Other Expositions.* Grand Rapids, MI: Baker Book House, 1963.

1417. Hall, John G. *Prophecy Marches On!* Springfield, MO: Pub. by author, 1963.

1418. Hamilton, Gavin. *Coming Kingdom Glories.* Oak Park, IL: Pub. by author, 1965.

1419. Harrison, William K. *Hope Triumphant: Studies on the Rapture of the Church.* Chicago: Moody Press, 1966.

1420. Hauff, Lewis. *Israel in Bible Prophecy.* n.p., n.d.

1421. Havner, Vance. *Repent or Else!* Westwood, NJ: Fleming H. Revell, 1958.

1422. Kac, Arthur W. *The Rebirth of the State of Israel -- Is it of God or of Men?* Chicago: Moody Press, 1958.

1423. Keller, F. P. *What Awaits You! The Great Plan. God Speaks to You For Your Welfare.* Berkeley: Immanuel Mission to Seamen, n.d.

1424. Kelley, Oscar A. *God's Ultimatum: The Great Day of Reckoning.* Oakhurst, CA: Pub. by author, 1961.

1425. Ketchum, Robert T. *Pre, Mid or Post Tribulation Rapture?* Chicago: Pub. by author, n.d.

1426. *The Kingdom of God.* Rochester, New York: Megiddo Mission Church, 1963.

1427. Knopf, Eugene. *When God Comes Down.* New York: Pageant Press Inc., 1959.

1428. Kuhlman, Paul and John I. Paton. *Outline Studies of Prophetic Truths.* Lincoln, NE: Back to the Bible Publishers, 1959.

1429. Ladd, George Eldon. *The Gospel of the Kingdom.* Grand Rapids, MI: Eerdmans, 1959.

1430. Lewis, Nettie Edell. *Lord of the Harvest: Gather the Wheat into my Barn.* New York: Exposition Press, 1959.

1431. Lindsay, J. Gordon. *The Antichrists Have Come!* Dallas: The Voice of Healing Publishing Co., 1958.

1432. _____. *Forty Signs of the Soon Coming of Christ.* Dallas: World Wide Revival, n.d.

1433. _____. *The Great Tribulation.* Dallas: World Wide Revival, n.d.

1434. _____. *Present World Events in the Light of Prophecy.* Dallas: World Wide Revival, n.d.

1435. _____. *Thunder Over Palestine or The Holy Land in Prophecy.* Dallas: World Wide Revival, n.d.

1436. _____. *The World Today in Prophecy.* Dallas: World Wide Revival, n.d.

1437. Linton, John. *Fifty Prophecies Fulfilled in One Day.* Wheaton, IL: Pub. by author, n.d.

1438. Logsdon, S. Franklin. *Profiles of Prophecy.* Wheaton, IL: Bowdon Publications, 1964.

1439. Longley, Arthur. *The Modern World in the Prophecies of Daniel.* Peterborough, ONT: The College Press, 1962.

1440. Lowman, G. E. *Prophecies for the Times* (booklet series). Baltimore: Baltimore Gospel Tabernacle, n.d.

1441. Manley, George T. *The Return of Christ.* London: InterVarsity Press, 1960.

1442. Martin, Alvin. *Fulfilled Prophecy in Israel Today. A Series of Prophetic Messages Delivered over Tabernacle Tidings, etc.* Moose Jaw, SK: Pub. by author, 1956.

1443. Mason, Clarence E., Jr. *Eschatology Including Ecclesiology.* Philadelphia: Philadelphia College of the Bible, 1964.

1444. McBirnie, W. S. *The Coming Decline and Fall of the Soviet Union.* Glendale, CA: Center for American Research and Education, n.d.

1445.   McClain, Alva J. *The Greatness of the Kingdom: An Inductive Study of the Kingdom of God as Set Forth in the Scriptures.* Grand Rapids, MI: Zondervan Publishing House, 1959.

1446.   McGee, J. Vernon. *Reveling Through Revelation, part 1.* Pasadena, CA: Thru the Bible Books, 1974, (1st ed., 1962).

1447.   _____. *Reveling Through Revelation, part 2.* Los Angeles: The Church of the Open Door, 1962.

1448.   Milton, John P. *Prophecy Interpreted: Essays in Old Testament Interpretation.* Minneapolis: Augsburg Publishers, 1960.

1449.   Montgomery, G. H. *I Predict: Things Which Must Shortly Come to Pass.* Wichita, KS: Mertmont Publishing Co., 1964.

1450.   Moody, Dale. *The Hope of Glory.* Grand Rapids, MI: W. B. Eerdmans Publishing Co., 1964.

1451.   Mount, Ralph H., Jr. *Babylon.* Mansfield, OH: Mount Publications, 1966, (2nd ed., 1986).

1452.   Murch, James DeForest, Clyde W. Taylor, John F. Walvoord, and John I. Paton. *The Coming World Church.* Lincoln, NE: Back to the Bible Broadcast, 1963.

1453.   Myers, John M. *The Trumpet Sounds.* New York: Pageant Press, 1965. [fiction]

1454.   Payne, J. Barton. *The Imminent Appearing of Christ.* Grand Rapids, MI: Wm B. Eerdmans, 1962.

1455.   Pentecost, J. Dwight. *Prophecy for Today: A Discussion of Major Themes of Prophecy.* Grand Rapids, MI: Zondervan Publishing House, 1961. [1980 edition has the subtitle: *The Middle East Crisis and the Future of the World*]

1456.   _____. *Things to Come: A Study in Biblical Eschatology.* Findlay, OH: Dunham Publishing Co., 1958 and 1965; Grand Rapids, MI: Zondervan Publishing House, 1976.

1457. Peterson, W. A. *In the Days to Come.* Sydney, AUS: W. A. Peterson, 1966.

1458. Radmacher, Earl D. *The Imminent Return of Christ.* Portland, OR: Western Conservative Baptist Seminary, 1964.

1459. Rasmussen, A. W. *The Last Chapter.* Living Books, n.d.

1460. Raud, Elsa. *Chapter and Verse: Bible Outlines in Doctrine, Christian Life, and Prophecy.* New York: Bible Christian Union, 1964.

1461. _____. *Introduction to Prophecy.* Findlay, OH: Dunham Publishing Co., 1960.

1462. Rissi, Matthias. *The Future of the World: An Exegetical Study of Revelation 19:11-22.* Naperville, IL: Allenson, 1966.

1463. Rogers, E. W. *Concerning the Future.* Chicago: Moody Press, 1962.

1464. Ryrie, Charles C. *Dispensationalism Today.* Chicago: Moody Press, 1965.

1465. Saloff-Astakhoff, N. I. *The Kingdom of God and the Kingdom of This World.* Pub. by author, 1964.

1466. Sauer, Erich. *From Eternity to Eternity.* Grand Rapids, MI: Eerdmans Publishing Co, n.d.

1467. Showers, Renald E. *What on Earth Is God Doing?* New York: Loizeaux Brothers, n.d.

1468. Spurgeon, Charles Hadden. *C. H. Spurgeon's Sermons on the Second Coming of Christ* (Charles C. Cook, ed.). London: Marshall, Morgan & Scott (The Kelvedon ed.), 1964.

1469. Stam, Cornelius R. *Man, His Nature and Destiny.* Chicago: Berean Bible Society, 1961.

1470. _____. *Things that Differ: The Fundamentals of Dispensa-
       tionalism.* Chicago: Berean Bible Society, 1959.

1471. Strauss, Lehman. *Armageddon.* Findlay, OH: Dunham Publishing
       Co., n.d.

1472. _____. *Christ's Literal Reign on Earth.* Findlay, OH: Dunham
       Publishing Co., n.d.

1473. _____. *Communism and Russia in Bible Prophecy.* Findlay,
       OH: Dunham Publishing Co., 1959.

1474. _____. *God's Plan for the Future.* Grand Rapids, MI:
       Zondervan Publishing House, 1965.

1475. *The Sure Word of Prophecy* (Senior Student). Chicago: Regular
       Baptist Press, July- September 1962.

1476. Stanton, Gerald. *Kept From the Hour: A Systematic Study of the
       Rapture in Bible Prophecy.* Grand Rapids, MI: Zondervan
       Publishing House, 1956.

1477. Strombeck, J. F. *First the Rapture* (3rd ed.). Moline, IL:
       Strombeck Agency, Inc., 1950 .

1478. Tatham, C. Ernest. *Bible Prophecy: Twelve Studies for Earnest
       Bible Students.* Oak Park, IL: Emmaus Bible School, 1964.

1479. Tenney, Merrill C. *The Glorious Destiny of the Believer*
       (Fundamentals of the Faith, no.6). Washington, D. C.:
       Christianity Today, n.d.

1480. _____. *Interpreting Revelation.* Grand Rapids, MI: Eerdmans
       Publishing Co, n.d.

1481. Torrance, T. F. *The Apocalypse Today.* Grand Rapids, MI:
       Eerdmans, 1959.

1482. Tracy, Edward H. *Babylon the Great is Fallen, is Fallen: A
       Reappraisal of Political Babylon and Preliminary*

Considerations which Appear to Demand It. San Francisco: Pub. by author, 1960.

1483. Tulga, Chester E. *Premillennialists and Their Critics.* Somerset, KY: Eastern Baptist Institute, 1961.

1484. Voss, Henry Daniel. *The Anti-Christ -- Christ Unmasked.* Tampa, FL: Voss Foundation, Inc., 1964.

1485. Walker, William H. *Will Russia Conquer the World?* Miami, FL: Miami Bible Institute, 1960.

1486. Wallace, R. B. *A Three-fold Cord: Creation, Revelation, Inspiration and the Purpose of the Ages.* Orange, CA: Ralph E. Welch Foundation, 1963.

1487. Walvoord, John F. *The Church in Prophecy.* Grand Rapids, MI: Zondervan Publishing House, 1964.

1488. _____. *Fifty Arguments for Pretribulation.* Minneapolis, MN: Central Conservative Baptist Seminary, n.d.

1489. _____. *Israel in Prophecy.* Grand Rapids, MI: Zondervan Publishing House, 1962.

1490. _____. *The Millennial Kingdom.* Findlay, OH: Dunham Publishing Co., 1959; (reprinted ed.). Grand Rapids: Zondervan Publishing House, 1976.

1491. _____. *The Prophetic Word in Crisis Days.* Findlay, OH: Dunham Publishing Co., 1961.

1492. Welch, Charles H. *An Alphabetical Analysis of Terms and Texts Used in the Study of 'Dispensational Truth'* (10 vols). Banstead: Berean Publishing Trust, 1957-1964.

1493. _____. *Dispensational Truth: or, The Place of Israel and the Church in the Purpose of the Ages* (3rd ed.). London: Berean Publishing Trust, 1959.

1494.   _____. *Just, and the Justifier: An Exposition of the Epistle to the Romans, Considered Doctrinally, Dispensationally and Practically, Together with Complete Structural Analysis.* London: Berean Publishing Trust, n.d.

1495.   Wood, A. Skevington. *Prophecy in the Space Age: Studies in Prophetic Themes.* Grand Rapids, MI: Zondervan Publishing House, 1963.

SECTION NINE

WAR AND PEACE
IN THE MIDDLE EAST, 1967-1978

The establishment of the state of Israel was, for the premillennialists, *the* prophetic sign heralding the imminent return of Christ. Once this event had taken place, millennialists diligently searched the Scriptures to map out the likely road events might take in the unfolding apocalyptic drama. Indeed, the persistent tensions in the Middle East and the occasional bloody skirmishes between Arabs and Israelis, continued to bolster the confidence of premillennial writers and spokespersons who responded to each new development, whether peaceful or militant, with a fresh series of prophetic speculations.

For example, when, during the 1967 Six-Day War, Israel reoccupied old Jerusalem, annexing it as well as the West Bank and Gaza Strip, the holy sites were once again in the possession of the Jews. Premillennialists saw this unexpected turn of affairs as an indisputable sign that things were shaping up for a restoration of the Jewish sacrificial system. That is, according to the millennialists, the possession of the ancient holy sites now made it possible for the Jews to rebuild their ancient temple, which had been destroyed by the Roman legions some nineteen hundred years earlier.

Millennialist writers of this period went to great lengths to show how a rebuilt temple fit into prophecy, including best-selling author Hal Lindsey, the most popular and influential prophecy writer since 1970. Lindsey, the author of *The Late Great Planet Earth*, which has sold 15 million copies since its publication, bases his enormous output of books on a popularized form of dispensational premillennial theology. In his books, Lindsey portrays the Hebrew prophets and Christian apostles as ancient seers whose visions were glimpses into the last decades of the twentieth century. Indeed, Lindsay speaks of St. John's Revelation as a first-century man's feeble attempt to describe his fascinating visionary encounter with the wonders and horrors of the postmodern world.

His simple and well-worn thesis is that the rebirth of the nation of Israel is a fulfillment of ancient prophecy and the sign that these are the Last Days. But Lindsey's success is due, in large part, to his ability to link together, in an exciting, convincing, and matter-of-fact way, chance incidents and random events within a unified prophetic framework. Indeed, for Lindsay, nothing is left to chance; all events are anticipated; all events fit into the prophetic pattern; history and Scripture point first to the rebirth of Israel in the Last Days and then to Armageddon.

Lindsey puts it this way in *The Late Great Planet Earth*: "To be specific about Israel's great significance as a sign of the time, there are three things that were to happen. First, the Jewish nation would be reborn in the land of Palestine. Secondly, the Jews would repossess Old Jerusalem and the sacred sites. Thirdly, they would rebuild their ancient temple of worship upon it historic site" (1970:50-1). Thus, to Lindsey, as well as to other millennialists of this period, the repossession of Old Jerusalem at the climax of the 1967 war was a divinely predestined event which, in Lindsey's words, "had to take place before the stage would be fully set" for Israel's part in this Last Days drama.

This point is also emphasized by another popular writer and conference speaker of this period, Tim LaHaye. In his book, *The Beginning of the End*, LaHaye, offering the same interpretation as Lindsey, contends that "the deep significance of the 1967 Six-Day War is seen in the prospect that at long last Israel can rebuild its Temple. This is not just a national yearning -- but a prophetic requirement of God's Word" (1972:50).

But the rebirth of Israel and the possible rebuilding of the ancient Jewish temple are important signs not merely because they fulfill the premillennialists' reading of the Bible, but because these events touch off a chain of events that end in the destruction of the world. In his sequel to *Late Great*, *The 1980's: Countdown to Armageddon*, Lindsey asserts: "In the Bible the reborn state of Israel is predicted as the center of the events that will lead to the last war of the world. Israel is literally the fuse of Armageddon -- a prophetic name for the last war" (1981:53). Scanning this work and others by Lindsey, one is struck by the fairly detailed chronology of events, even battle strategies, military tactics, and troop movements, that Lindsey lays out in his portrayal of the apocalyptic endtimes battle to be fought in the valley of Megiddo.

This popular millennialist bent toward mapping out battle strategies is not peculiar to Lindsey, however. Other millennialist authors, such as Charles Taylor, give equally detailed accounts of the Battle of Armageddon, as well as other conflicts they predict will take place just before and during the seven-year Tribulation period. Indeed, Taylor has a flare for the sensational, often reaching well beyond the text and into the realm of imagination. For example, it was Taylor who traveled to Palestine in the early 1980s to survey the buzzard population, believing that a marked increase in vultures would indicate the imminence of Armageddon. Such an increase, he told his listeners and viewers, would clear the way for the fulfillment of the prophecies in Ezekiel 39 and Revelation 19 which predicted that the birds will gather to prey on the flesh of the armies of Gog.

Similar to premillennialists' focus on Israel, there were other global developments during the 1960s, the 1970s, and the 1980s that sent up prophetic red flags for the millennialists, who connected those developments with political and economic life during the future Tribulation period. For example, the ecumenical church movement was seen by some premillennialists as a forerunner to the future demonic "world church" to be headed by an emissary of the Antichrist.

In addition, the organization of the International Monetary Fund and computerized banking services gave rise to the prediction that a one-world government was in the offing. The mark of the Beast (666), many believe, could refer to one's participation in the world economy; some speculated that even one's social security or credit card numbers could unwittingly mark a person for damnation. To warn fellow Christians, Salem Kirban, for instance, perused the pages of magazines and newpapers and combed through grocery store shelves in search of "666" combinations on company logos and product codes, reporting his findings in several of his books.

Still further, many viewed the European Common Market as the Revived Roman Empire of the Last Days, the empire from which the Antichrist would arise (Incidentally, while popes have remained popular candidates for the antichrist title, more recent antichrist nominees have included Henry Kissinger, King Juan Carlos of Spain, Ronald Reagan, and Mikhail Gorbachev. Currently, Saddam Hussein enjoys the spotlight as the "Man of Sin").

The literature listed below, and in the following section, represents an enormously vast and varied range of prophetic speculations within popular eschatological circles over the past twenty-five years. As in previous sections, the subject and scope of these writings range from highly sensational to fairly critical. After a fashion, one learns to discriminate between the reasoned and the ridiculous.

Still, one finds a noticeably more urgent timbre in premillennialist warnings. The Charismatic and Jesus Movements of the 1960s and 1970s with their emphasis on the emotions in worship and concern over demonic power may account for some of this added intensity as the turbulence of the 1960s focused the attention of Christian youth more keenly on a coming period of tribulation.

1496.   *The Amazing Prophecy Second Coming Bible*. Orange, CA: Amazing Prophecy, 1974. [reprint of the 1924 Biederwolf *Millennium Bible*]

1497.   Andersen, Loren E. *Prophecy and Antichrist, 666*. Fresno, CA: Pub. by author, 1976.

1498.   Anderson, Robert. *The Coming Prince: The Marvelous Prophecy of Daniel's Seventy Weeks Concerning the Antichrist*. Grand Rapids, MI: Kregel Publications, 1957, 1972, and 1975.

1499.   Armerding, Carl E. & W. Ward Gasque (eds.). *Dreams, Visions, and Oracles: The Layman's Guide to Biblical Prophecy*. Grand Rapids, MI: Baker Book House, 1977.

1500.   Baker, Charles F. *A Dispensational Theology*. Grand Rapids, MI: Grace Bible College Publications, 1971.

1501.   Barnhouse, Donald Grey. *Revelation: An Expository Commentary*. Grand Rapids, MI: Zondervan Publishing House, 1971.

1502.   Benson, John L. *The Future Reign of Christ on Planet Earth*. Denver, CO: B/P Publications, 1974.

1503.   _____. *Will the Real Anti-Christ Please Stand Up*. Denver, CO: B/P Publications, 1974.

1504. *The Bible and the Mideast Crisis.* Philadelphia: Eternity Magazine, 1967.

1505. *Bible Road Map.* Kerrville, TX: Herring Printing Co., 1971.

1506. Biederwolf, William E. *The Second Coming Bible.* Grand Rapids, MI: Baker Book House, 1977, (1st ed., 1924).

1507. Bloomfield, Arthur E. *Before the Last Battle: Armageddon.* Minneapolis: Bethany Fellowship Press, Inc., 1971.

1508. _____. *The End of Days.* Minneapolis: Bethany Fellowship Press, Inc.

1509. _____. *How to Recognize the Antichrist.* Minneapolis: Bethany Fellowship Press, Inc., 1975.

1510. _____. *The Last and Future World.* Grand Rapids, MI: Zondervan Publishing House, 1974.

1511. _____. *A Survey of Bible Prophecy.* Minneapolis: Bethany Fellowship, Inc., 1971.

1512. Boyer, James L. *Prophecy, Things to Come: A Study Guide.* Winona Lake, IN: BMH Books, 1974.

1513. Branham, William M. *The Revelation of the Seven Seals.* Tucson, AZ: Spoken Word Publications, 1967.

1514. Bratt, John H. *The Final Curtain: Studies in Eschatology.* Grand Rapids, MI: Baker Book House, 1978.

1515. Breese, Dave W. *The Five Horsemen.* Lincoln, NE: Back to the Bible Broadcast, 1975.

1516. _____. *What's Ahead?* Lincoln, NE: Back to the Bible Broadcast, 1974.

1517. Brubaker, Ray. *The Purpose of the Great Tribulation.* St. Petersburg, FL: Pub. by author, 1968.

1518.   Brunk, Menno J. *Fulfilled Prophecies*. Crockett, KY: Rod and
         Staff Publishing Co., 1971.

1519.   Burton, Alfred H. *The Future of Europe: Politically and
         Religiously, in the Light of Holy Scripture [and] Russia's
         Destiny: In the Light of Prophecy* (7th ed.). Oak Park, IL:
         Bible Truth Publishers, 1967.

1520.   Buxton, Clyde W. *Expect These Things*. Old Tappan, NJ:
         Fleming H. Revell Co., 1973.

1521.   Caldwell, William. *When the World Goes Boom*. Kisumu, Kenya:
         Evangel Publishing House, 1970.

1522.   Campbell, Donald K. *Daniel: Decoder of Dreams*. Wheaton, IL:
         Victor Books, 1977.

1523.   Cantelon, Willard. *The Day the Dollar Dies*. Plainfield, NJ: Logos
         Publishing, 1974.

1524.   Carter, James E. *What is to Come?* Nashville, TN: Broadman
         Press, 1975.

1525.   Chambers, Leon and Mildred Chambers. *Interpreting Satan-
         Antichrist: His World Empire*. Fairfax, AL: Pub. by author,
         1973.

1526.   Chilvers, Gordon. *The Shape of Things to Come -- Future Events
         in Prophecy*. Denver, CO: B/P Publications, 1974.

1527.   Clark, Doug. *America in Prophecy*. Orange, CA: Amazing
         Prophecy Center, n.d.

1528.   _____. *Anti-Christ's Temple*. Orange, CA: Amazing Prophecy
         Center, n.d.

1529.   _____. *The Chinese are Coming*. Orange, CA: Amazing
         Prophecy Center, n.d.

1530.   _____. *The Coming World Dictator: The Anti-christ*. Orange,
         CA: Amazing Prophecy Center, n.d.

1531. _____. *Doomsday in Prophecy.* Orange, CA: Amazing Prophecy Center, n.d.

1532. _____. *God's Next Move.* Orange, CA: Amazing Prophecy Center, n.d.

1533. _____. *Kissinger Giving U.S. to Russia?* Orange, CA: Amazing Prophecy Center, 1975.

1534. _____. *The Last World Government.* Orange, CA: Amazing Prophecy Center, n.d.

1535. _____. *Millions are Missing!* Orange, CA: Amazing Prophecy Center, n.d.

1536. _____. *The Next World War.* Orange, CA: Amazing Prophecy Center, n.d.

1537. _____. *Pollution in Prophecy.* Orange, CA: Amazing Prophecy Center, n.d.

1538. _____. *Prophecies of the 70's.* Orange, CA: Amazing Prophecy Center, n.d.

1539. _____. *Rapture.* Orange, CA: Amazing Prophecy Center, n.d.

1540. _____. *Silver and the Coming Crash.* Orange, CA: Amazing Prophecy Center, n.d.

1541. _____. *666: The Mark of the Beast.* Orange, CA: Amazing Prophecy Center, n.d.

1542. _____. *Watch the Jew.* Orange, CA: Amazing Prophecy Center, n.d.

1543. _____. *When Will the Church Be Raptured?* Orange, CA: Amazing Prophecy Center, n.d.

1544. _____. *Witchcraft in Prophecy.* Orange, CA: Amazing Prophecy Center, n.d.

1545. Clark, Douglas J. *Watch the Jewish Nation Rise and Tell the Time in Heaven and Earth.* Toronto: Anderson Brothers Printing, n.d.

1546. Clifford, David. *The Two Jerusalems in Prophecy.* Neptune, NJ: Loizeaux Brothers, 1978.

1547. Coder, S. Maxwell. *Israel's Destiny.* Chicago: Moody Press, 1978.

1548. Cohen, Gary G. *Civilization's Last Hurrah.* Chicago: Moody Press, n.d.

1549. _____. *The Horsemen Are Coming.* Chicago: Moody Press, 1974.

1550. _____. *Understanding Revelation: An Investigation of the Key Interpretational and Chronological Questions Which Surround the Book of Revelation.* Chicago: Moody Press, 1968; Collingswood, NJ: Christian Beacon Press, 1968.

1551. Cohen, Gary and Salem Kirban. *Revelation Visualized.* Chicago: Moody Press, n.d.

1552. Cribb, C. C. *From Now till Eternity: The Sequence of Prophetic Events.* Raleigh, NC: Manhattan, LTD, 1976.

1553. Criswell, W. A. *Welcome Back, Jesus!* Nashville: Broadman Press, 1976.

1554. _____. *What to Do Until Jesus Comes Back.* Nashville: Broadman Press, 1975.

1555. Crow, R. *Storm Over Israel: A Look at Israel, the Nations, and the Church as They will Appear at the End of the Age According to the Bible.* Bombay: Gospel Literature Service, 1968.

1556. Davis, Leo C. *The 'Seventy Weeks' Prophecy (of Daniel): Ancient Prophecy, Up-to-Date Fulfillment.* Bedford, IN: Pub. by author, 1974.

1557. Dayhoff, Irvin E. *The Majestic Hand in Bible Prophecy.* University Park, IA: Pub. by author, 1968.

1558. DeHaan, Richard W. *Israel and the Nations in Prophecy.* Grand Rapids, MI: Zondervan Publishing House, 1968, (revised ed., 1977).

1559. DeHaan, M. R. *Will the Church Go Through the Tribulation?* Grand Rapids, MI: The Radio Bible Class, 1967.

1560. Dennis, John. *Revelations about the Rapture.* Kansas City, MO: Any Moment Press, 1977.

1561. Dodrill, Rufus M. *Keep Your Eyes on the Sky.* Indianapolis: Pub. by Author, 1972.

1562. Douglas, Clyde E. *When All Hell Breaks Loose.* Phoenix, AZ: Tusayan Gospel Ministries, 1974.

1563. Douglas, John E., Sr. *Jerusalem and Israel in Bible Prophecy.* Dallas: World Missionary Evangelism, Inc., 1967.

1564. Duncan, M. Homer. *The Budding of the Fig Tree.* Lubbock, TX: The World-wide Missionary Crusader Inc., n.d.

1565. _____. *Doors of Hope in an Age of Despair.* Lubbock, TX: The World-wide Missionary Crusader Inc., n.d.

1566. _____. *His Glorious Appearing.* Lubbock, TX: The World-wide Missionary Crusader Inc., n.d.

1567. _____. *Israel: Past, Present, Future.* Lubbock, TX: The World-wide Missionary Crusader Inc., n.d.

1568. _____. *The Millennial Reign of Christ.* Lubbock, TX: The World-wide Missionary Crusader Inc., n.d.

1569. _____. *Outline of Things to Come.* Lubbock, TX: The World-wide Missionary Crusader Inc., n.d.

1570.   _____. *Prepare Now for the Second Coming of Christ.*
         Lubbock, TX: Missionary Crusaders, Inc., 1969.

1571.   _____. *Seventy-one Scriptural Signs That Indicate That Jesus
         is Coming Soon.* Lubbock, TX: The World-wide Missionary
         Crusader Inc., n.d.

1572.   Duty, Guy. *Escape from the Coming Tribulation: How to be
         Prepared for the Last Great Crisis of History.* Minneapolis:
         Bethany Fellowship, 1975.

1573.   Earle, Ralph. *What the Bible Says About the Second Coming.*
         Grand Rapids, MI: Baker Book House, 1970.

1574.   Eddleman, H. Leo (ed.). *Last Things: A Symposium of Prophetic
         Messages.* Grand Rapids, MI: Zondervan Publishing House,
         1969.

1575.   Ellison, Stanley A. *Biography of a Great Planet.* Wheaton, IL:
         Tyndale House Publishers, 1975.

1576.   Epp, Theodore H. *God's Program for Israel.* Lincoln, NE: Back to
         the Bible Correspondence School, 1976.

1577.   _____. *Practical Studies in Revelation.* Lincoln, NE: Back to
         the Bible Publications, 1969.

1578.   Erb, Paul. *Bible Prophecy: Questions and Answers.* Scottdale, PA:
         Herald Press, 1978.

1579.   Erickson, Millard. *Contemporary Options in Eschatology: A Study
         of the Millennium.* Grand Rapids, MI: Baker Book House,
         1977.

1580.   Esses, Michael (with Irene Harrell). *Next Visitor to Planet Earth.*
         Plainfield, NJ: Logos International, 1975.

1581.   Ezell, Douglas. *Revelations on Revelation: New Sound for Old
         Symbols.* Waco, TX: Word Books, 1977.

1582. Fackre, Gabriel J. *The Rainbow Sign: Christian Futurity.* Grand Rapids, MI: Eerdmans, 1969.

1583. Feinberg, Charles L. *Israel in the Spotlight* (rev. ed.). Chicago: Moody Press, 1975; (3rd. ed., entitled *Israel at the Center of History and Revelation*). Portland, OR: Multnomah Press, 1980.

1584. _____(ed.). *Jesus the King is Coming.* Chicago: Moody Press, 1975. [papers from the Seventh Congress on Prophecy, New York City, 1973, sponsored by the American Board of Missions to the Jews]

1585. _____(ed.). *Prophecy and the Seventies.* Chicago: Moody Press, 1971.

1586. Forseth, Marvin. *Israel's Destiny.* New Westminster, BC, Canada: Pub. by author, n.d.

1587. Fraley, Bob. *God Reveals the Identity of the 'Beast': Avoid Being Marked by the Beast.* Phoenix, AZ: Crane Publishing Co., 1978.

1588. Grant, Jim. *A Thief in the Night.* Chicago: Moody Press, 1973.

1589. Greene, Oliver B. *Bible Prophecy.* Greenville, SC: The Gospel Hour, Inc., 1970.

1590. _____. *The Second Coming of Jesus.* Greenville, SC: The Gospel Hour, Inc., 1971.

1591. _____. *Second Coming Truth.* Greenville, SC: The Gospel Hour, Inc., 1973.

1592. Gromacki, Robert G. *Are These the Last Days?* Old Tappan, NJ: Fleming H. Revell, Co., 1970; Shaumburg, IL: Regular Baptist Press, 1978.

1593. Gundry, Robert H. *The Church and the Tribulation.* Grand Rapids, MI: Zondervan Publishing House, 1973.

1594.   Halff, Charles. *Israel -- Nation of Destiny.* San Antonio, TX: The
         Christian Jew Foundation, 1974.

1595.   _____. *Palestine, the Jews, and the Return of Jesus.* San
         Antonio, TX: The Christian Jew Foundation, n.d.

1596.   _____. *Rapture: When and How?* San Antonio, TX: The
         Christian Jew Foundation, 1975.

1597.   Hall, John G. *God's Dispensational and Prophetic Plan.* Spring-
         field, MO: Pub. by author, 1972.

1598.   Han, Enoch. *The Prophecy Concerning the Restoration of the
         Jewish Nation.* Seoul: The Everlasting Gospel Association,
         n.d.

1599.   Hanson, Richard S. *The Future of the Great Planet Earth.*
         Minneapolis: Augsburg Publishers, 1972.

1600.   Helffrich, Reginald Boone. *Revelation 14:1-5: The 144,000
         Identified.* Live Oak, FL: Pub. by author, 1976.

1601.   Henry, Carl F. H. (ed.). *Prophecy in the Making (Proceedings from
         the Jerusalem Conference on Biblical Prophecy, Christian and
         Jewish).* Carol Stream, IL: Creation House, 1971.

1602.   Hiltgren, C. A. *God's Countdown in the 70's.* Los Angeles: Pub.
         by author, 1975.

1603.   Holloway, Cecil G. *Babylon.* Eastbourne, England: Prophetic
         Witness Publishing House, 1971.

1604.   Hooley, Robert. *Antichrist.* Denver: Liberty Publications, 1976.

1605.   _____. *Armageddon.* Denver: Liberty Publications, 1976.

1606.   _____. *Egypt: Trigger of Armageddon.* Denver: Liberty
         Publications, 1976.

1607. Horton, Stanley. *The Promise of His Coming: A New Testament Study of the Second Coming of Christ.* Springfield, MO: Gospel Publishing House, 1967.

1608. _____. *Welcome Back Jesus.* Springfield, MO: Gospel Publishing House, 1975. [reprint of previous title]

1609. Hoyt, Herman A. *Biblical Eschatology: Study Guide and Exams.* Chicago: Moody Press, 1974.

1610. _____. *The End Times.* Chicago: Moody Press, 1969.

1611. Huebner, R. A. *The Truth of the Pre-Tribulation Rapture Recovered: An Historical Sketch Including an Exposure of Past and Present Calumnies Employed in Attempts to Discredit it.* Millington, NJ: Present Truth Publishers, 1973.

1612. Humbard, Rex. *Why I Believe Jesus is Coming Soon.* Pasadena, CA: Compass Press, 1972.

1613. Hunting, Joseph H. *Israel -- A Modern Miracle* (2 vols). Melbourne: Pub. by author, 1969.

1614. _____. *'Israel My Son.'* Melbourne, AUS: The David Press, 1970.

1615. Hurst, William D. *Hooks in Their Jaws: A Premillennial Study of Bible Prophecy.* New York: Exposition Press, 1968.

1616. Inch, Morris A. *Understanding Bible Prophecy.* New York: Harper & Row, 1977.

1617. Jeremiah, James T. *Converging Signs in Biblical Prophecy* (2nd ed.). Cedarville, OH: Christian Educational Publications, 1974.

1618. Johnson, Carl G. *Prophecy Made Plain for Times Like These.* Chicago: Moody Press, 1972.

1619. Johnson, Miles Beardsley. *The Setting of the Stage.* San Luis Obispo, CA: Clarion Publications, 1975.

1620.   Jones, Russell B. *What, Where, and When is the Millennium?* Grand Rapids, MI: Baker Book House, 1975.

1621.   Josephson, Elmer A. *Israel: God's Key to World Redemption.* Hillsboro, KS: Bible Light Publications, 1974.

1622.   Kac, Arthur W. *The Death and Resurrection of Israel: A Message of Hope for a Time of Trouble.* Baltimore: King Brothers, 1969.

1623.   _____. *The Messianic Hope.* Grand Rapids, MI: Baker Book House, 1975.

1624.   Katterjohn, Arthur. *Lord, When?: Twenty-six Studies.* Carol Stream, IL: Creation House, 1976.

1625.   _____. *The Rapture -- When?* Wheaton, IL: Pub. by author, 1975.

1626.   Katterjohn, Arthur D. (with Mark Fackler). *The Tribulation People.* Carol Stream, IL: Creation House, 1975.

1627.   King, Geoffrey R. *The End of the World.* Eastbourne, ENG: Prophetic Witness Publishing House, 1971.

1628.   Kirban, Salem. *The Beginning of Sorrows.* Huntingdon Valley, PA: Salem Kirban Inc., 1972.

1629.   _____. *Charts on Revelation.* Huntingdon Valley, PA: Salem Kirban Inc., 1973.

1630.   _____. *Countdown to Rapture.* Huntingdon Valley, PA: Salem Kirban Inc.; Irvine, CA: Harvest House Publishers, 1977.

1631.   _____. *The Day Israel Dies.* Huntingdon Valley, PA: Salem Kirban Inc., 1975.

1632.   _____. *Day of Judgment : A Cantata of the Second Coming, the Tribulation Period and the Battle of Armageddon* (Words by Salem Kirban and Music by Janet C. Hutchinson). Huntingdon Valley, PA: Salem Kirban Inc., 1975.

1633. _____. *Guide to Survival: How the World Will End.* Huntingdon Valley, PA: Salem Kirban Inc.; Wheaton, IL: Tyndale House Publishers, 1968.

1634. _____. *I Predict.* Huntingdon Valley, PA: Salem Kirban Inc., 1971.

1635. _____. *Israel: Land of Peace, Land of Prophecy.* Huntingdon Valley, PA: Salem Kirban Inc., 1973.

1636. _____. *Kissinger, Man of Peace?* Huntingdon Valley, PA: Salem Kirban, Inc., 1974.

1637. _____. *1000* (A Novel). Iowa Falls, IA: Riverside Book and Bible House, 1973.

1638. _____. *Prophecy New Testament.* Huntingdon Valley, PA: Salem Kirban, Inc., 1973.

1639. _____. *Questions Frequently Asked Me on Prophecy.* Huntingdon Valley, PA: Salem Kirban Inc., 1972.

1640. _____. *Revelation Visualized.* Huntingdon Valley, PA: Salem Kirban Inc, n.d.

1641. _____. *The Rise of Antichrist.* Huntingdon Valley, PA: Salem Kirban, Inc., 1978; Chattanooga, TN: AMG Publishers, 1981.

1642. _____. *666.* Huntingdon Valley, PA: Salem Kirban Inc.; Wheaton, IL: Tyndale House Publishers, 1970.

1643. _____. *20 Reasons Why This Present Earth May Not Last Another 20 years.* Huntingdon Valley, PA: Salem Kirban, Inc., 1973.

1644. _____. *What in the World Will Happen Next?* Huntingdon Valley, PA: Salem Kirban, Inc., 1974.

1645.   Koch, Kurt E. *The Coming One: Israel in the Last Days.* Grand
        Rapids, MI: Kregel Publications, 1972.

1646.   _____. *Day X.* Grand Rapids, MI: Kregel Publications, 1971.

1647.   _____. *World Without Chance.* Grand Rapids, MI: Kregel
        Publications, 1974.

1648.   Krupp, Nate. *The Omega Generation?* Harrison, AR: New Leaf
        Press Inc., 1977.

1649.   Krutza, William J. *The Second Coming Bible Study Guide.* Grand
        Rapids, MI: Baker Book House, 1973.

1650.   Ladd, George Eldon. *A Commentary on the Revelation of John.*
        Grand Rapids, MI: Eerdmans, 1972.

1651.   _____. *The Last Things: An Eschatology for Laymen.* Grand
        Rapids, MI: Eerdmans, 1978.

1652.   LaHaye, Tim. *The Beginning of the End.* Wheaton, IL: Tyndale
        House Publisher, 1972.

1653.   _____. *Revelation Illustrated and Made Plain.* Family Life
        Seminars Publications, n.d.; (rev. ed.). Grand Rapids, MI:
        Zondervan Publishing House, 1975.

1654.   Levitt, Zola. *The Cairo Connection: Egypt in Prophecy.* Irvine,
        CA: Harvest House, 1978.

1655.   _____. *Israel in Agony.* Irvine, CA: Harvest House, 1975.

1656.   _____. *The Signs of the End.* Dallas: Pub. by author, 1978.

1657.   Lewis, W. Myrddin. *God's Ultimate.* Sussex, England: Prophetic
        Witness Publishing House, 1969.

1658.   Lightner, Robert P. *Prophecy in the Ring.* Chicago: Moody
        Press, n.d.

1659. 	Lindberg, Milton B. *Jacob's Trouble; A Nation in Distress: The Jewish Nation's Past, Present, and Future Foreshadowed in the Life Story of the Patriarch Jacob*. Chicago: American Messianic Fellowship, 1967, (1st ed., 1941).

1660. 	_____. *The Jew and Modern Israel*. Chicago: Moody Press, 1969.

1661. 	_____. *The State of Israel and the Jew Today in the Light of Prophecy*. Chicago: American Messianic Fellowship, 1968, (1st ed., 1930; previously titled *Palestine and the Jew*).

1662. 	Lindsay, J. Gordon. *The Antichrist and His Forerunner*. Dallas: Christ for the Nations, 1973.

1663. 	_____. *Forty-eight Signs in the Land of Israel of the Soon Coming of Christ*. Dallas: The Voice of Healing Publishing Co., 1968.

1664. 	Lindsey, Albert J. *Understanding Our Times: Daniel's Revelations*. Good News Agency, 1976.

1665. 	Lindsey, Hal. *Homo Sapiens: Extinction or Evacuation?* Grand Rapids, MI: Zondervan Publishing House, 1971.

1666. 	_____. *The Promise*. Irvine, CA: Harvest House Publishers, 1974; Eugene, OR: Harvest House Publishers, 1982.

1667. 	_____. *There's a New World Coming: 'A Prophetic Odyssey.'* Santa Ana, CA: Vision House Publishers, 1973; (updated ed.). Eugene, OR: Harvest House Publishers, 1984.

1668. 	_____. *The World's Final Hour: Evacuation or Extinction?* Grand Rapids, MI: Zondervan, 1976.

1669. 	Lindsey, Hal (with C. C. Carlson). *The Late Great Planet Earth*. Grand Rapids, MI: Zondervan, 1970.

1670. 	_____. *The Liberation of Planet Earth*. Grand Rapids, MI: Zondervan, 1974.

1671.   _____. *The Rapture: Truth or Consequences.* New York: Bantam Books, 1983.

1672.   _____. *Satan is Alive and Well on Planet Earth.* Grand Rapids, MI: Zondervan Publishing House, 1972.

1673.   _____. *The Terminal Generation.* Old Tappan, NJ: Fleming H. Revell, 1976; New York: Bantam Books, 1976.

1674.   Lockyer, Herbert. *The Church's Hope.* Eastbourne, ENG: Prophetic Witness Publishing House, 1971.

1675.   _____. *The Future of the Gentile Nations.* Eastbourne, ENG: Prophetic Witness Publishing House, 1971.

1676.   Logsdon, S. Franklin. *Is the U.S.A. in Prophecy?* Grand Rapids, MI: Zondervan Publishing House, 1968, (revised ed., 1974).

1677.   Lovett, C. S. *C. S. Lovett: Maranatha Man.* Baldwin Park, CA: Personal Christianity, 1978.

1678.   _____. *Jesus is Coming -- Get Ready Christian!* Baldwin Park, CA: Personal Christianity, 1969.

1679.   Lowe, William G. *Even So, Come, Lord Jesus: Twenty-eight Propositions to be Examined Before Abandoning Pretribulationism.* Narrowsburg, New York: Scripture Truth, 1973.

1680.   Ludwigson, Raymond. *A Survey of Bible Prophecy.* Grand Rapids, MI: Zondervan Publishing House, 1973.

1681.   MacDonald, John H. *The Great Tribulation.* Eastbourne, ENG: Prophetic Witness Publishing House, 1971.

1682.   MacPherson, Ian. *Dial the Future: A Book About the Second Coming of Christ.* Sussex, ENG: Prophetic Witness Publishing Co., 1975.

1683.   Mails, Thomas E. *The Vultures Gather; The Fig Tree Blooms.* Hayfield, MN: The Hayfield Publishing Co., 1972.

1684.   Malgo, Wim. *And Israel Shall Do Valiantly*. Hamilton, OH: The
         Midnight Call, Inc., n.d.

1685.   _____. *50 Questions Most Frequently Asked about the Second
         Coming*. Hamilton, OH: The Midnight Call, Inc., n.d.

1686.   _____. *The Great Mystery of the Rapture*. Hamilton, OH: The
         Midnight Call, Inc., n.d.

1687.   _____. *Israel's God Does not Lie*. Hamilton, OH: The
         Midnight Call, Inc., n.d.

1688.   _____. *1000 Years Peace: A Utopia?* Hamilton, OH: The
         Midnight Call, Inc., 1974.

1689.   _____. *The Rapture*. Hamilton, OH: The Midnight Call, Inc.,
         n.d.

1690.   Mason, Clarence E., Jr. *Prophetic Problems with Alternate
         Solutions*. Chicago: Moody Press, 1973.

1691.   Massegee, Charles. *Five Minutes till Midnight*. Ranger, TX:
         Lighthouse Publications, 1974.

1692.   Mauro, Philip. *The Seventy Weeks and the Great Tribulation: A
         Study of the Last Two Visions of Daniel and of the Olivet
         Discourse of the Lord Jesus Christ* (rev. ed.). Swengel, PA:
         Reiner, 1975.

1693.   Maybin, W. J. *The Second Advent*. Eastbourne, ENG: Prophetic
         Witness Publishing House, 1971.

1694.   McBirnie, W. S. *The Antichrist*. Dallas: Acclaimed Books, 1978.

1695.   McCall, Thomas S. (ed.). *America in History and Bible Prophecy:
         Bicentennial Congress on Prophecy*. Chicago: Moody Press,
         1976.

1696.   McCall, Thomas S., and Zola Levitt (ed). *America: In History and
         Bible Prophecy*. Chicago: Moody Press, 1976.

1697. McCall, Thomas S., and Zola Levitt. *The Coming Russian Invasion of Israel.* Chicago: Moody Press, 1974 and 1976.

1698. _____. *Israel and Tomorrow's Temple.* Chicago: Moody Press, 1973.

1699. _____. *Raptured.* Irvine, CA: Harvest House Publishers, 1975.

1700. _____. *Satan in the Sanctuary: Predictions and Preparations Concerning the Third Temple in Jerusalem.* Chicago: Moody Press, 1973.

1701. McClain, Alva J. *The Greatness of the Kingdom.* Chicago: Moody Press, 1968.

1702. _____. *The Jewish Problem and Its Divine Solution.* Winona Lake, IN: BMH Books, 1972, (1st ed., 1944).

1703. McGee, J. Vernon. *Reasoning Through Romans* (2 vols; 2nd ed.). Pasadena: Thru the Bible Books, 1973.

1704. _____. *World Dominion: Whose Will It Be? (The Time of the Gentiles), Daniel 2.* Pasadena, CA: Thru the Bible Books, n.d.

1705. McKeever, Jim. *Christians Will Go Through the Tribulation: How to Prepare for It.* Medford, OR: Alpha Omega Publishing Co., 1978.

1706. McMillan, Sim I. *Discern These Times.* Old Tappan, NJ: Fleming H. Revell Co., 1971.

1707. McNicol, John. *Interpreting Prophecy.* Eastbourne, England: Prophetic Witness Publishing House, 1971.

1708. McPherson, Aimee Semple. *Lost and Restored: The Dispensation of the Holy Spirit from the Coming of the Lord to His Coming Descension.* Los Angeles: Foursquare Bookshop, 1976.

1709.   McQuaid, Elwood. *...It Is No Dream!; Bible Prophecy: Fact or Fanaticism?* W. Collingswood, NJ: The Spearhead Press, 1978.

1710.   _____. *The Suffering and the Glory of Israel.* Fincastle, VA: Scripture Truth Book Co., 1973.

1711.   Meyer, Nathan M. *From Now to Eternity: Sermons from the Book of Revelation Presenting the Future History of the World.* Winona Lake, IN: BMH Books, 1976.

1712.   Miller, C. Leslie. *Goodbye, World.* Glendale, CA: Regal Books, 1972.

1713.   Nee, Watchman. *The Orthodoxy of the Church (Revelation 2-3).* Los Angeles: Stream, 1970.

1714.   Neighbor, Ralph W., and Gerald L. Stover. *Planet Earth: On the Brink of Eternity.* Elyria, OH: Morning Sunshine Publications, 1973.

1715.   Odle, Joe T. *Is Christ Coming Soon?* Nashville, TN: Broadman Press, 1971.

1716.   Olson, Arnold T. *Inside Jerusalem: City of Destiny.* Glendale, CA: Regal Books, 1968.

1717.   Onstad, Esther. *Courage for Today, Hope for Tomorrow: A Study of Revelation.* Minneapolis: Augsburg Publishing House, 1974.

1718.   Orr, William W. *The Coming King.* Wheaton, IL: Victor Books, 1974.

1719.   Otis, George. *The Ghost of Hagar.* Van Nuys, CA: Time-Light Books, 1974.

1720.   *Palestine and the Bible.* Bakersfield, CA: Conservative Viewpoint, n.d.

1721.   Park, Oscar. *Prophecy of Revelation*. Santa Barbara, CA: Miracles Today, 1976.

1722.   Park, Ronald J. *The Coming Crisis*. Eastbourne, ENG: Prophetic Witness Publishing House, 1971.

1723.   Payne, J. Barton. *Biblical Prophecy for Today*. New York: Harper & Row, 1974; Grand Rapids, MI: Baker Book House,1978.

1724.   _____. *Encyclopedia of Biblical Prophecy: The Complete Guide to Scriptural Predictions and Their Fulfillment*. New York: Harper & Row, 1973.

1725.   _____. *The Prophecy Map of World History*. New York: Harper & Row, 1974.

1726.   _____. *Revelation in Sequence: The Book Chronologically Arranged and Annotated*. Westchester, IL: Lithocolor Press, 1972.

1727.   Pentecost, J. Dwight. *Will Man Survive? Prophecy You Can Understand*. Chicago: Moody Press, 1971; (with subtitle *The Bible Looks at Man's Future*). Grand Rapids, MI: Lamplighter (Zondervan), 1990.

1728.   Petrie, Arthur. *The Regathering of Israel*. New York: American Board of Missions to the Jews, Inc., 1967.

1729.   Phillips, Bob. *The Great Future Escape: A Prophetic Revelation*. Santa Ana, CA: Vision House Publishers, 1973.

1730.   _____. *When the Earth Quakes*. Wheaton, IL: Key Publications, 1973.

1731.   Phillips, John. *Only God Can Prophesy!* Wheaton, IL: Harold Shaw Publishers, 1975.

1732.   Plueger, Aaron Luther. *Things to Come for Planet Earth: What the Bible Says about the Last Times*. St. Louis: Concordia Publishing House, 1977.

1733. Price, Walter K. *The Coming Antichrist*. Chicago: Moody Press, 1974.

1734. _____. *In the Final Days*. Chicago: Moody Press, 1977.

1735. _____. *Next Year in Jerusalem*. Chicago: Moody Press, 1975.

1736. Rice, John R. *Five Parables Illustrating Christ's Second Coming*. Murfreesboro, TN: Sword of the Lord Publishers, 1975.

1737. Roberts, Oral. *God's Timetable for the End of Time*. Tulsa, OK: Heliotrope Publishers, 1969.

1738. Ryrie, Charles C. *The Bible and Tomorrow's News: A New Look at Prophecy*. Wheaton, IL: Scripture Press Publications, 1969; Wheaton, IL: Victor Books, 1973.

1739. _____. *The Living End*. Old Tappan, NJ: Fleming H. Revell, 1976.

1740. _____. *Warnings to the Churches*. London: The Banner of Truth Trust, 1967.

1741. Ryrie, Charles C. (ed.). *The Ryrie Study Bible*. Chicago: Moody Press, 1978.

1742. Saxe, Raymond Hyman. *Israel's Future Triumph: An Exposition of Zechariah 12-14*. Ann Arbor, MI: Grace Bible Publications, 1978.

1743. Schafer, Raymond. *After the Rapture: Life in the New World*. Santa Ana, CA: Vision House, 1977.

1744. *The Second Coming Bible*. Grand Rapids, MI: Baker Book House, 1972.

1745. Sharrit, John T. *Soon-Coming World Shaking Events: As Foretold by God Almighty*. Phoenix, AZ: Christian Missionary Society, 1978.

1746.   Smith, Chuck. *Snatched Away!* Costa Mesa: Maranatha House Publishers, 1976; Costa Mesa, CA: The Word for Today, 1980.

1747.   _____. *The Soon to be Revealed Antichrist.* Costa Mesa: Maranatha House Publishers, 1976; Costa Mesa, CA: The Word for Today, 1979.

1748.   Smith, Wilbur M. *Egypt and Israel Coming Together?* Wheaton, IL: Tyndale House, 1978. [reprint of *Egypt in Biblical Prophecy,* 1957]

1749.   _____. *Israel, the Bible, and the Middle East.* Glendale, CA: G/L Publications, 1967.

1750.   _____. *Israeli / Arab Conflict and the Bible.* Glendale, CA: G/L Publications, 1967.

1751.   _____. *You Can Know the Future.* Glendale, CA: G/L Publications, 1971.

1752.   Sproule, John A. *A Revised Review of 'The Church and the Tribulation' by Robert H. Gundry.* Grace Theological Seminary, 1974; Birmingham, AL: Southeastern Bible College, 1974.

1753.   Stedman, Ray C. *What on Earth's Going to Happen?* Glendale, CA: Regal Books, 1970.

1754.   Straughan, Alfred D., Jr. *God's Coming Wrath: A Study of the Creational Phenomena of the Tribulation in the Book of Revelation.* New York: Carlton Press, 1971.

1755.   Strauss, Lehman. *Daniel.* Neptune, NJ: Loizeaux Bros., 1969.

1756.   _____. *The End of the Present World.* Grand Rapids, MI: Zondervan Publishing House, 1969, (1st ed., 1967).

1757.   Strother, Lydia R. and Claude L. Strother. *Prepare for Armageddon: Survival in the Nuclear Age.* Glendale, CA: Lee Press, 1969.

1758. Tatford, Frederick A. *The Common Market and Prophecy.* England: Green and Co., 1968.

1759. _____. *Daniel's Seventy Weeks.* Eastbourne, England: Prophetic Witness Publishing House, 1971.

1760. _____. *Five Minutes to Midnight.* London and Eastbourne: Victory Press, 1970.

1761. _____. *God's Program of the Ages.* Grand Rapids, MI: Kregel Publications, 1967.

1762. _____. *Israel and Her Future.* Eastbourne, England: Prophetic Witness Publishing House, n.d.

1763. _____. *The Jew and Prophecy.* England: Green and Co., n.d.; Eastbourne, England: Bible and Advent Testimony Movement, n.d.

1764. _____. *Outline of Events.* Eastbourne, England: Prophetic Witness Publishing House, n.d.

1765. _____. *The Patmos Letters.* Eastbourne, England: Prophetic Witness Publishing House, 1969.

1766. _____. *Russia and Prophecy.* Eastbourne, England: Prophetic Witness Publishing House, 1968.

1767. _____. *Will There be a Millennium?* Eastbourne, England: Prophetic Witness Publishing House, 1969.

1768. Taylor, Charles R. *Get All Excited: Jesus Is Coming Soon.* Redondo Beach, CA: Today in Bible Prophecy, Inc., 1974.

1769. _____. *Those Who Remain.* Redondo Beach, CA: Today in Bible Prophecy, 1980, (1st ed., 1976).

1770. _____. *World War III and the Destiny of America.* Redondo Beach, CA: Today in Bible Prophecy, Inc., 1971.

1771.   The Time of the End: 'Blow the Trumpet in Zion' (rev. and
         enlarged ed.). Winnipeg, CAN: Bible Research Council, 1969.

1772.   Tracy, Edward H. The United States in Prophecy. San Francisco:
         Convale, 1969.

1773.   Unger, Merrill F. Beyond the Crystal Ball. Chicago: Moody
         Press, 1973.

1774.   Vines, Jerry. 'I Shall Return' -- Jesus. Wheaton, IL: Victor Books,
         1977.

1775.   Walker, Paul L. Knowing the Future. Cleveland, TN: Pathway
         Press, 1976.

1776.   Walker, William H. Will Russia Conquer the World? (rev. ed.).
         Dalton, GA: Span Publications, 1978.

1777.   Walvoord, John F. The Blessed Hope and the Tribulation: A
         Biblical and Historical Study of Posttribulationism. Grand
         Rapids, MI: Zondervan Publishing House, 1976.

1778.   _____. Matthew: Thy Kingdom Come. Chicago: Moody Press,
         1974.

1779.   _____. The Nations in Prophecy. Grand Rapids, MI: Zondervan
         Publishing House, 1967.

1780.   _____. The Rapture Question. Grand Rapids, MI: Zondervan
         Publishing House, 1973 (revised and enlarged ed., 1979).

1781.   Walvoord, John F. & John E. Walvoord. Armageddon: Oil and the
         Middle East Crisis. Grand Rapids, MI: Zondervan Publishing
         House, 1974.

1782.   Ward, C. M. Favorite Sermons From Revelation. Springfield,
         MO: Revivaltime, 1978.

1783.   _____. What You Should Know About Prophecy. Springfield,
         MO: Gospel Publishing House, 1975.

1784. Webber, David and Noah W. Hutchings. *Signs of the Second Coming*. Oklahoma City: The Southwest Radio Church, 1977.

1785. *When is Jesus Coming Again: Leading Authorities and Their Views (Hal Lindsey and others)*. Carol Stream, IL: Creation House, 1974.

1786. White, John Wesley. *Re-entry: Striking Parallels Between Today's News Events and Christ's Second Coming*. Grand Rapids, MI: Zondervan Publishing House, 1970; Minneapolis: World Wide Publications, 1971.

1787. _____. *W W III*. Grand Rapids, MI: Zondervan Publishing House, 1977.

1788. Wilkerson, David (ed.). *David Wilkerson Presents the End Times New Testament*. Chappaqua, NY: Chosen Books; Old Tappan, NJ: Revell, 1975.

1789. _____. *The Vision*. New York: Pillar Books, 1974; New York: Spire Books, 1975.

1790. Wilkerson, David (with Kathryn Kullman, Hal Lindsey, W. A. Criswell, & Pat Boone). *Jesus Christ Solid Rock: The Return of Christ*. Grand Rapids, MI: Zondervan Publishing House, 1973.

1791. Willis, Charles D. *End of Days: 1971-2001: An Eschatological Study*. New York: Exposition Press, 1972.

1792. Wilson, Clifford A. and John Weldon. *Approaching the Decade of Shock*. San Diego: Master Books, 1978.

1793. Winkler, Wendell (ed.). *Premillennialism, True or False?* Fort Worth, TX: Winkler Publications, 1978.

1794. Witty, Robert G. *Signs of the Second Coming*. Nashville: Broadman Press, 1969.

1795. Wolf, Richard. *Israel, Act III*. Wheaton, IL: Tyndale House, 1967.

1796.   Wood, A. Skevington. *Signs of the Times: Biblical Prophecy and Current Events.* Grand Rapids, MI: Baker Book House, 1970.

1797.   Wood, Leon James. *The Bible and Future Events: An Introductory Survey of Last-day Events.* Grand Rapids, MI: Zondervan Publishing House, 1973.

1798.   Woodbridge, Charles J. *Bible Prophecy: Arranged as a Correspondence Course.* Chicago: Moody Press, 1967.

1799.   Woodrow, Ralph. *Great Prophecies of the Bible.* Riverside, CA: Ralph Woodrow Evangelistic Association, 1971.

1800.   Woodson, Leslie H. *Population, Pollution and Prophecy.* Old Tappan, NJ: Fleming H. Revell Co., 1973.

1801.   Yacovsky, F. Jacob. *The Missing 200 Years: God's Timetable.* Fern Parks, FL: Sar Sholem of Jerusalem, 1978.

1802.   Yerby, R. B. *Up, Up, and Away: The Glorious Kingdom and Coming of Jesus Christ.* Swengel, PA: Reiner Publications, 1976.

1803.   Zoller, John E. *The Second Coming of Christ and the Coming Ages.* New Era, MI: Christ for Everyone, 1968.

SECTION TEN

PEACE AND WAR
IN THE MIDDLE EAST, 1979-1992

For the sake of convenience and ease of reading, I have divided the contemporary literature of popular eschatology into two sections, placing the divide at 1978 and 1979, when Egypt and Israel signed the Peace Accords. As with the above sections, the dividing points are largely arbitrary and should not be taken as definitive (I suppose one could argue against my rationale and reasonably make a case for another date, but I see no point quibbling over so capricious a thing "date-setting.").

Even so, there is one important reason for dividing the literature in the late 1970s: the year 1988. Millennialists have long believed that Jesus' saying, "Truly I say to you, this generation will not pass away until all these things take place" (Matthew 24:34), should be understood to mean that within a generation after the rebirth of Israel as a nation, the rapture of the church and the seven-year Tribulation period would take place. Nineteen eighty-eight marked the fortieth anniversary of the state of Israel. Accordingly, the 1980s saw a noticeable rise in the publication of books and pamphlets giving frenzied discussions of this approaching date.

Some millennialists, such as Charles Taylor, Chuck Smith, and Colin Deal confidently preached that the rapture would occur sometime before the end of 1981. In his revisions to *Will Christ Return by 1988?*, Colin Deal predicted that 1982 would be the rapture year. Others, including Edgar Whisenant, argued for 1988 as the year of the rapture. As these and other dates came and went, some premillennialists began to fear that perhaps their mid-tribulation, or worse, their post-tribulation brothers and sisters, such as George Ladd and Robert Gundry, had been right all along.

Undaunted by these and other embarrassing miscalculations, some dispensationalist authors and lecturers have looked to the approach of the third millennium and the year 1999 as the *terminus ad quem* of human history. Henry Hall, for example, offered 1991 as the year to watch for both the rapture and the beginning of the seven-year Tribulation. More recently, premillennialists, such as Chicago-based Maranatha Missions and the Mission for the Coming Days headquartered in New York City, have confidently predicted October 1992 as the send-off date for Christians. In a recently published tract by Maranatha Missions, these premillennialists calculate that an average Biblical generation from Abraham to the time of Jesus was fifty-one years. As their reckoning goes, 1948 plus 51 years for a generation minus 7 years for the Tribulation equals 1992. In a tract from MCD, the writers argue that as God created the world in six days, so humankind has been allotted six days or 6,000 years. From the time of Adam to that of Christ was 4,000 years, they write, leaving only 2,000 years until the consummation of human history (cf., Deal 1981:166). Consequently, the end of all things will occur by December 31, 1999.

But these are the more extreme examples. For obvious reasons, most premillennialists shy away from setting specific dates for either the rapture or the Tribulation period, content to leave these matters in the hands of God. Even so, in many of the works listed below, one can certainly detect this roller-coaster ride of dispensational premillennialist date-setting activity throughout this period.

1804.   Ankerberg, John, and John Weldon. *One World: Biblical Prophecy and the New World Order.* Chicago: Moody Press, 1991.

1805.   Anstey, B. *The Church Will Not Go Through the Tribulation.* Vancouver, BC: Pub. by author, 1980

1806.   _____. *Outline of Prophetic Events: Chronologically Arranged from the Rapture to the Eternal State.* Vancouver, BC: Pub. by author, 1987.

1807. Austin, E. L. C. *God and the Russians*. Glendale, CA: Heaven & Home Hour, 1982.

1808. Baker, William W. *Theft of a Nation*. Las Vegas, NV: Defenders Publications, 1982.

1809. Barnhart, David R. *Israel, Land of Promise and Prophecy*. Eagan, MN: Abiding Word Publications, 1988.

1810. Barsoum, F. *Coming Mideast Wars in Prophecy*. Dallas: International Bible Association, 1980.

1811. Bates, Leon. *Projection for Survival*. Dallas: Bible Believers' Evangelistic Association, 1979.

1812. Baxter, Trvin, Jr. *A Message for the President*. Richmond, IN: Endtime, Inc., 1986.

1813. Beechick, Allen. *The Pre-Tribulation Rapture*. Denver: Accent Books, 1981.

1814. Benson, John L. *What's the World Coming To?* Shaumburg, IL: Regular Baptist Press, 1979.

1815. Best. W. E. *Christ's Kingdom is Future* (vols 3 & 4). Houston, TX: South Belt Assembly of Christ, 1992.

1816. Blackstone, William E. *Jesus Is Coming: God's Hope for a Restless Word* (updated ed.). Grand Rapids, MI: Kregel Publications, 1989.

1817. Bonck, Allen. *America the Daughter of Babylon: The Prophetic Story of America's Future*. Chicester, ENG: New Wine Press, 1989.

1818. Branson, Roy. *The End of the World* (2 vols). Lancaster, CA: Landmark Publications, 1988.

1819. Bray, John L. *The Origins of the Pre-Tribulation Rapture Teaching: also My Trip to Communist Romania*. Lakeland, FL: John L. Bray Ministry, 1982.

1820.   _____. *The Coming of Christ in First and Second Thessalonians*. Lakeland, FL: John L. Bray Ministry, n.d.

1821.   _____. *The Great Tribulation?* Lakeland, FL: John L. Bray Ministry, n.d.

1822.   _____. *Israel in Bible Prophecy*. Lakeland, FL: John L. Bray Ministry, 1983.

1823.   _____. *The Last Days and the Second Coming of Christ*. Lakeland, FL: John L. Bray Ministry, n.d.

1824.   _____. *The Midnight Cry*. Lakeland, FL: John L. Bray Ministry, n.d.

1825.   _____. *The Millennium: The Big Question*. Lakeland FL: John L. Bray Ministry, 1984.

1826.   _____. *The Rapture of the Saints*. Lakeland, FL: John L. Bray Ministry, n.d.

1827.   _____. *The Second Coming of Christ and Related Events*. Lakeland FL: John L. Bray Ministry, 1985.

1828.   Brooke, Tal. *When the World Will Be as One: The Coming New World Order in the New Age*. Eugene, OR: Harvest House Publishers, 1989.

1829.   Camping, Harold. *The Fig Tree: An Analysis of the Future of National Israel*. Oakland, CA: Family Stations, Inc., 1983.

1830.   _____. *The Seventy Weeks of Daniel Nine*. Oakland, CA: Family Stations, Inc., n.d.

1831.   _____. *When is the Rapture?* Oakland, CA: Family Stations, Inc., 1979.

1832.   Carr, Marc A. *Last Sands in the Hour Glass: Revelation Explored*. New Wilmington, PA: Son Rise Books, 1988.

1833.   Ceperley, Gordon G. *A Promised Land for a Chosen People.* Langhorne, PA: Philadelphia College of the Bible, 1979.

1834.   Chakmakjian, Hagop A. *In Quest of Justice and Peace in the Middle East: The Palestinian Conflict in Biblical Perspective.* New York: Vantage Press, 1980.

1835.   Chapman, Colin G. *Whose Promised Land?* (rev. ed.). Oxford, England: Lion Publishing, 1989.

1836.   Chitwood, Arlen L. *Israel and the Land.* Norman, OK: Lamp Broadcast, Inc., 1979.

1837.   _____. *Mysteries of the Kingdom.* Norman, OK: Lamp Broadcast, Inc., 1980.

1838.   Church, J. R. *Guardians of the Grail...And the Men Who Plan to Rule the World.* Oklahoma City: Prophecy Publications, 1989.

1839.   _____. *Hidden Prophecies in the Psalms.* Oklahoma City: Prophecy Publications, 1986 (rev. ed., 1990).

1840.   Clark, Doug. *The Coming Oil War: Predictions of Things to Come.* Irvine, CA: Harvest House Publishers, 1980.

1841.   Cook, W. Robert. *The Theology of John.* Chicago: Moody Press, 1979.

1842.   Corfield, Virginia. *Sow the Wind.* Covina, CA: The Provident Press, 1979.

1843.   Cumbey, Constance. *The Hidden Dangers of the Rainbow: The New Age Movement and Our Coming Age of Barbarism* (rev. ed.). Lafayette, LA: Huntington House, 1983.

1844.   Dahl, Mikkel. *'The Day After' Portraying in Narrative Form Startling Events on the Near Horizon.* Windsor, ONT: Dawn of Truth, n.d.

1845.   Dake, Finis Jennings. *The Rapture and the Second Coming of Christ.* Lawrenceville, GA: Dake Bible Sales, 1987, (1st ed., 1977).

1846.   _____. *Revelation Expounded; or Eternal Mysteries Simplified: One Hundred Ten Prophetic Future Wonders from 1950 to Eternity* (enlarged ed.). Lawrenceville, GA: Dake Bible Sales, 1987.

1847.   Davidson, Elishua. *Islam, Israel and the Last Days.* Eugene, OR: Harvest House Publishers, 1991.

1848.   Deal, Colin Hoyle. *Armageddon and the 21st Century.* Rutherford College, NC: End Time Ministry, 1988.

1849.   _____. *Christ Returns by 1988: 101 Reasons Why.* Rutherford College, NC: Pub. by author, 1979.

1850.   _____. *Will Christ Return by 1988?: 101 Reasons Why.* Rutherford College, NC: End-Times News, 1988.

1851.   Colin Deal End-Times News Tape Ministry. Rutherford College, NC.

        Cassette Tape Titles include:

1852.   _____. 'The Antichrist: From Earth or Outer Space?'

1853.   _____. 'The End-Time Alignment of Nations'

1854.   _____. 'Five Biblical Reasons Why Christ Will Return by 1988'

1855.   _____. 'Goliath and Big Foot in Bible Prophecy'

1856.   _____. 'Great Heavenly Signs (Matthew 24)'

1857.   _____. 'Rapture: Before, During, or After Tribulation?'

1858.   _____. 'The Russian War (WW III)'

1859.   _____. 'The Temple Under Construction'

1860.   Dumbrell, William J. *The End of the Beginning: Revelation 21-22 and the Old Testament*. Homebush West, NSW, AUS: Lancer Books, 1985.

1861.   Dyer, Charles H. (with Angela Elwell Hunt). *The Rise of Babylon: Sign of the End Times*. Wheaton, IL: Tyndale House Publishers, 1991.

1862.   Egner, David. *Israel, Act III*. Grand Rapids, MI: Radio Bible Class, 1979.

1863.   Ellison, Stanley A. *Who Owns the Land?: The Arab-Israeli Conflict*. Portland, OR: Multnomah Press, 1991.

1864.   Evans, Mike. *Israel: America's Key to Survival*. Bedford, TX: Bedford Books, 1983.

1865.   _____. *JerUSAlem, D. C. (David's Capital)*. Bedford, TX: Bedford Books, 1984.

1866.   _____. *The Return*. Nashville: Thomas Nelson Publishers, 1986.

1867.   Ewert, David. *And Then Comes the End*. Scottdale, PA: Herald Press, 1980.

1868.   Epp, Theodore H. *The Third Temple*. Lincoln, NE: Back to the Bible Broadcast, 1985.

1869.   Falwell, Jerry. *Nuclear War and the Second Coming of Jesus*. Lynchburg, VA: The Old Time Gospel Hour, 1983.

1870.   Feinberg, Charles L. *A Commentary on Revelation: The Grand Finale*. Winona Lake, IN: BMH Books, 1985.

1871.   _____. *Israel at the Center of History and Revelation* (3rd ed.). Portland, OR: Multnomah Press, 1980.

1872.   _____. *Millennialism, the Two Major Views: The Premillen-
         nial and Amillennial Systems of Biblical Interpretation
         Analyzed and Compared* (3rd ed., enlarged). Chicago: Moody
         Press, 1980; Winona Lake, IN: BMH Books, 1985.

1873.   Finger, Thomas N. *Christian Theology: An Eschatological
         Approach.* Nashville: Thomas Nelson Publishers, 1985;
         Scottdale, PA: Herald Press, 1989.

1874.   Goetz, William R. *Apocalypse Next.* Beaverlodge, AL, Canada:
         Horizon Books, 1980.

1875.   Goldberg, Louis. *Turbulence Over the Middle East: Israel and the
         Nations in Confrontation and the Coming Kingdom of Peace
         on Earth.* Neptune, NJ: Loizeaux Brothers, 1982.

1876.   Graham, Billy. *Approaching Hoofbeats: The Four Horsemen of the
         Apocalypse.* Waco, TX: Word Books, 1983.

1877.   _____. *Till Armageddon.* Waco, TX: Word Books, 1981.

1878.   Green, Joel B. *How to Read Prophecy.* Downers Grove, IL:
         InterVarsity Press, 1984.

1879.   Gundry, Robert H. *God in Control: An Exposition of the
         Prophecies of Daniel.* West Sussex: H. E. Walter, 1980.

1880.   Hailey, Homer. *Revelation: An Introduction and Commentary.*
         Grand Rapids, MI: Baker Books House, 1979.

1881.   Hall, R. Henry. *AD 1991: The Genesis of Holocaust.* Las Vegas:
         Spirit of Prophecy, n.d.

1882.   _____. *Ominous Portents of the Parousia of Christ.* Las Vegas,
         NV: Hall Publishing Co., 1984.

1883.   Hess, Tom. *Let My People Go: The Struggle of the Jewish
         People to Return to Israel* (2nd ed.). Washington, D.C.:
         Progressive Vision, 1988.

1884. Hirschmann, Maria Anne. *Will the East Wind Blow?: Hansi Reports on the Middle East.* Huntington Beach, CA: Hansi Ministries, S.P.A.R.C. Publishing Co., 1979.

1885. Hocking, David L. *The Coming World Leader: Understanding the Book of Revelation.* La Mirada, CA: Biola Hour Ministries, 1988; Portland, OR: Multnomah Press, 1988.

1886. _____. *The Final Holocaust -- Will Anyone Survive?* La Mirada, CA: Biola Hour Ministries, 1987.

1887. _____. *The Vision of Heaven: Revelation 4-6.* La Mirada, CA: Biola Hour Ministries, 1988.

1888. _____. *Why Jesus Came (Luke 19:28-24:54)* [and] *Prophecy.* La Mirada, CA: Biola Hour Ministries, 1987.

1889. Hook, Jack D. *Babylon the Great is Falling.* Waterloo, IA: Blessed Hope Publications, 1984.

1890. House, H. Wayne. *Dominion Theology, Blessing or Curse?: An Analysis of Christian Reconstruction.* Portland, OR: Multnomah Press, 1988.

1891. Houston, Graham. *Prophecy, A Gift for Today?* Downers Grove, IL: InterVarsity Press, 1989. [Published in Britain as *Prophecy Now*]

1892. Hubbard, David Allen. *The Second Coming: What Will Happen When Jesus Returns?* Downers Grove, IL: InterVarsity Press, 1984.

1893. Hunt, Dave. *Global Peace and the Rise of Antichrist.* Eugene, OR: Harvest House Publishers, 1990.

1894. _____. *Peace, Prosperity, and the Coming Holocaust.* Eugene, OR: Harvest House Publishers, 1983.

1895. _____. *Whatever Happened to Heaven.* Eugene, OR: Harvest House Publishers, 1988.

1896.   Ironside, H. A. and F. C. Ottman. *Studies in Biblical Prophecy*.
         Minneapolis, MN: Klock & Klock, 1983. [special edition,
         combining Ironside's *The Great Parenthesis* (1962), and
         Ottman's *God's Oath* (1911)]

1897.   James, Edgar C. *Arabs, Oil, and Armageddon*. Chicago: Moody
         Press, 1991, (1st ed., 1977).

1898.   _____. *Armageddon*. Chicago: Moody Press, 1981.

1899.   _____. *Armageddon and the New World Order* (rev. and
         updated). Chicago: Moody Press, 1991. [rev. ed. of previous
         title]

1900.   Jeffrey, Grant R. *Armageddon: Appointment with Destiny*. New
         York: Bantam Books, 1988.

1901.   _____. *Messiah: War in the Middle East and the Road to
         Armageddon*. Toronto: Frontier Research Publications, 1991.

1902.   Jeremiah, David (with C.C. Carlson). *Escape the Coming Night:
         The Bright Hope of Revelation*. Dallas, TX: Word Books,
         1990.

1903.   Johnson, Alan F. *Revelation: Bible Study Commentary*. Grand
         Rapids, MI: Zondervan Publishing House, 1983.

1904.   Johnson, Miles Beardsley. *The Faith of a Little Child*. San Luis
         Obispo, CA: Clarion Publications, 1982.

1905.   Jones, Russell Bradley. *The Great Tribulation*. Grand Rapids, MI:
         Baker Book House, 1980. [previously published]

1906.   Juster, Dan and Keith Intrater. *Israel, the Church, and the Last
         Days*. Shippensburg, PA: Destiny Image Publishers, 1990.

1907.   Kaiser, Walter C., Jr. *Back Toward the Future: Hints for
         Interpreting Biblical Prophecy*. Grand Rapids, MI: Baker Book
         House, 1989.

1908.   Karleen, Paul S. *The Pre-Wrath Rapture of the Church: Is It Biblical?* Langhorne, PA: BF Press, 1991.

1909.   Kac, Arthur W. *The Spiritual Dilemma of the Jewish People: Its Cause and Cure* (2nd ed.). Grand Rapids, MI: Baker Book House, 1983, (1st ed., 1963).

1910.   Kimball, William R. *The Rapture -- A Question of Timing.* n.p., n.d.

1911.   _____. *What the Bible Says About the Great Tribulation.* Joplin, MO: College Press, 1983; Grand Rapids, MI: Baker Book House, 1984.

1912.   Kirban, Salem. *Satan's Mark Exposed: 666.* Huntingdon Valley, PA: Salem Kirban Inc.; Chattanooga, TN: AMG Publishers, 1981.

1913.   Lalonde, Peter. *One World Under Antichrist.* Eugene, OR: Harvest House Publishers, 1991.

1914.   Lambert, Lance. *The Uniqueness of Israel.* Eastbourne, ENG: Kingsway Publications, 1980.

1915.   LaSor, William Sanford. *The Truth About Armageddon: What the Bible Says About the End Times.* San Francisco: Harper & Row, 1982; Grand Rapids, MI: Baker Book House, 1982.

1916.   Levitt, Zola. *Glory: The Future of the Believers.* Dallas: Pub. by author, 1979.

1917.   _____. *The Second Coming.* Dallas: Pub. by author, 1979.

1918.   Lewis, Arthur E. *The Dark Side of the Millennium: The Problem of Evil in Revelation 20:1-10.* Grand Rapids, MI: Baker Book House, 1980.

1919.   Lewis, David Allen. *Magog 1982 Cancelled: Did Israel Prevent the Third World War?* Harrison, AR: New Leaf Press, 1982.

1920.   _____. *Prophecy 2000* (3rd ed., expanded). Green Forest, AR: New Leaf Press, 1990.

1921.   _____. *Smashing the Gates of Hell in the Last Days*. Green Forest, AR: New Leaf Press, 1991.

1922.   Lewis, David A. and Robert Shreckhise. *UFO: End-Time Delusion* (2nd ed.). Green Forest, AR: New Leaf Press, 1992.

1923.   Lightner, Robert P. *The Last Days Handbook*. Nashville, TN: Thomas Nelson Publishers, 1990. [an expanded version of *Prophecy in the Ring*]

1924.   Lightle, Steve (with Eberhard Mühlen and Katie Fortune). *Exodus II: Let My People Go*. Kingwood, TX: Hunter Books, 1983.

1925.   Lindsell, Harold. *The Gathering Storm: World Events and the Return of Christ*. Wheaton, IL: Tyndale House Publishers, 1980.

1926.   Lindsey, Hal. *Combat Faith*. New York: Bantam Books, 1986.

1927.   _____. *The 1980's: Countdown to Armageddon*. King of Prussia, PA: Westgate Press, Inc., 1980.

1928.   _____. *A Prophetic Walk Through the Holy Land*. Eugene, OR: Harvest House Publishers, 1983.

1929.   _____. *The Road to Holocaust*. New York: Bantam Books, 1989.

1930.   Lindsted, Rob. *The Next Move: Current Events in Bible Prophecy*. Wichita, KS: Bible Truth, 1985 and 1987.

1931.   Loane, Marcus L. *They Overcame: An Exposition of the First Three Chapters of Revelation*. Grand Rapids, MI: Baker Book House, 1981, (1st ed., 1971).

1932.   Lovett, C. S. *Latest Word on the Last Days*. Baldwin Park, CA: Personal Christianity, 1980.

1933.   Lundstrom, Lowell. *The Wind Whispers Warning*. Sisseton, SD: Lowell Lundstrom Ministries, 1979.

1934.   Lutzer, Erwin W. *Coming to Grips with the Antichrist's New Age Roots*. Chicago: Moody Press, 1990.

1935.   _____. *Coming to Grips with the Role of Europe in Prophecy*. Chicago: Moody Press, 1990.

1936.   MacArthur, John Jr. *The Future of Israel*. Chicago: Moody Press, 1991.

1937.   _____. *The Return and Reign of Jesus Christ*. Chicago: Moody Press, 1988.

1938.   _____. *The Second Coming of the Lord Jesus Christ* (David Sper, ed.). Panorama City, CA: Word of Grace Communications, 1981.

1939.   _____. *Signs of Christ's Return*. Chicago: Moody Press, 1987.

1940.   MacDonald, Ken and Agnes. *The Second Coming: Tough Questions Answered*. Newcomerstown, OH: Berean Publications, 1991.

1941.   MacNaughtan, K. A. (ed.). *The Covenants and the Promises*. Victoria, AUS: The David Press, 1980.

1942.   MacWilliams, E. J. *The Last Days of God's Church*. Eau Gallie, FL: Harbour House, 1991.

1943.   Mains, David R. *The Rise of the Religion of Anti-christism*. Grand Rapids, MI: Zondervan Publishing House, 1985.

1944.   Manhattan, Avro. *The Vatican - Moscow - Washington Alliance*. Chino, CA: Chick Publications, 1986.

1945.   Marrs, Texe W. *Dark Secrets of the New Age: Satan's Plan for a One World Religion*. Westchester, IL: Crossway Books, 1987.

1946.   _____. *Mega Forces: Signs and Wonders of the Coming Chaos*. Austin, TX: Living Truth Publishers, 1988. [originally entitled *Rush to Armageddon*]

1947.   _____. *Millennium: Peace, Promises, and the Day They Take Our Money Away*. Austin, TX: Living Truth Publishers, 1990.

1948.   _____. *Mystery Mark of the New Age: Satan's Design for World Domination*. Westchester, IL: Crossway Books, 1988.

1949.   _____. *Ravaged By The New Age: Satan's Plan to Destroy Our Kids*. Austin, TX: Living Truth Publications, 1989.

1950.   _____. *Rush to Armageddon*. Wheaton, IL: Tyndale Books, 1987.

1951.   Martin, Ralph. *The Return of the Lord*. Ann Arbor, MI: Servant Books, 1983.

1952.   Mayhue, Richard L. *Snatched Before the Storm!: A Case for Pretribulationism*. Winona Lake, IN: BMH Books, 1980.

1953.   McGee, J. Vernon. *The Best of J. Vernon McGee* (vol 1). Nashville: Thomas Nelson Publishers, 1988.

1954.   _____. *He Is Coming Again*. Pasadena, CA: Thru the Bible Books, 1988.

1955.   McKeever, Jim. *How You Can Be Prepared*. Medford, OR: Alpha Omega Publishing Co., 1980.

1956.   _____. *Now You Can Understand the Book of Revelation*. Medford, OR: Alpha Omega Publishing Co., 1980.

1957.   _____. *The Rapture Book: Victory in the End Times*. Medford, OR: Alpha Omega Publishing Co., 1987.

1958.   Meacham, Wesley. *Troubled Waters: Prophecy from a Layman's Point of View*. Tulsa, OK: Calaar Publications, 1984.

1959.   Meresco, Donald. *New Light on the Rapture.* New York: Bible Light, 1980.

1960.   Meyer, Nathan M. *The Patmos Prediction.* Oklahoma City, OK: Prophecy Publications, 1989.

1961.   *Millennium Superworld.* Rochester, New York: Megiddo Mission Church, 1980.

1962.   Miller, E. J. *The Final Battle* (rev. ed.). Chicester, England: New Wine Press, 1987.

1963.   Millhoen, Quilliam B. *Wars and Rumors of Wars.* Fairfax, VA: King David Publishing Co., 1983.

1964.   Milne, Bruce. *What the Bible Teaches About the End of the World.* Wheaton, IL: Tyndale, 1979.

1965.   Nee, Watchman. *Aids to 'Revelation.'* New York: Christian Fellowship Publishers, 1983.

1966.   Noe, John. *The Apocalypse Conspiracy: Why the World May Not End as Soon as You Think and What You Should Be Doing in the Meantime.* Brentwood, TN: Wolgemuth & Hyatt, 1991.

1967.   Otis, George, Jr. *The Last of the Giants: Lifting the Veil on Islam and the End Times.* Tarrytown, NY: Fleming H. Revell, 1991.

1968.   Pentecost, J. Dwight. *Prophecy for Today: God's Purpose and Plan for Our Future* (rev. ed.). Grand Rapids, MI: Discovery House Publishers, 1989.

1969.   _____. *Thy Kingdom Come.* Wheaton, IL: Victor Books, 1990.

1970.   Pike, Theodore W. *Israel, Our Duty -- Our Dilemma.* Oregon City, OR: Big Sky Press, 1984.

1971.   Poland, Larry W. *How to Prepare for the Coming Persecution.* San Bernardino, CA: Here's Life Publishers, 1990.

1972.   Powell, Ivor. *What in the World Will Happen Next?* Grand Rapids: Kregel Publications, 1985.

1973.   Prince, Derek. *The Last Word on the Middle East.* Lincoln, VA: Chosen Books, 1982.

1974.   Pruit, Robert J. *And Then Shall the End Come.* Cleveland, TN: White Wing Publishing House, n.d.

1975.   Reiter, Richard R., et al. *The Rapture: Pre-, Mid-, or Post-Tribulation?* Grand Rapids, MI: Academic Books, Zondervan Publishing House, 1984.

1976.   Relfe, Mary Stewart. *The New Money System: 666.* Montgomery, AL: Ministries Inc., 1981.

1977.   Richards, Larry. *Tomorrow Today.* Wheaton, IL: Victor Books, 1986.

1978.   Rioux, Norman H. *From Here to Armageddon.* Pub. by Author, 1986.

1979.   Robertson, Pat. *The New Millennium.* Dallas, TX: Word Books, 1990.

1980.   _____. *The New World Order.* Dallas, TX: Word Books, 1991.

1981.   _____. *The Secret Kingdom.* New York: Bantam Books, 1984.

1982.   Rosen, Moishe (with Bob Massie). *Beyond the Gulf War: Overture to Armageddon.* San Bernardino, CA: Here's Life Publishers, 1991.

1983.   Rosenthal, Marvin J. *The Pre-Wrath Rapture of the Church.* Nashville: Thomas Nelson, 1990.

1984.   Rumble, Dale. *Crucible of the Future: A Prophetic Look Into the Nineties.* Shippensburg, PA: Destiny Image Publishers, 1989.

1985.   Russ, Mike. *The Battle for Planet Earth: From Abraham to Armageddon.* New York: Ballantine Books, 1981.

1986.   Ryrie, Charles C. *The Final Countdown*. Wheaton, IL: Victor Books, 1982. [rev. & updated version of *The Bible and Tomorrow's News*]

1987.   _____. *What You Should Know About the Rapture.* Chicago: Moody Press, 1981.

1988.   Sanders, J. Oswald. *Certainties of Christ's Second Coming*. Manila: O. M. F. Publishers, 1977; Eastbourne, ENG: Kingsway, 1983.

1989.   Sheppa, Milton A. *Is 'The Tribulation Period' Real?* Longview, WA: Pub. by author, 1989.

1990.   Shorrosh, Anis. *Jesus, Prophecy, and the Middle East*. Nashville: Thomas Nelson, 1982.

1991.   Showers, Renald E. *The Most High God.* West Collingswood, NJ: Friends of Israel, 1982.

1992.   Skolfield, E. H. *Hidden Beast*. Fort Myers, FL: Fish House, 1989.

1993.   Smith, Chuck. *End Times: A Report on Future Survival.* Costa Mesa: Maranatha House Publishers, 1978; Costa Mesa, CA: The Word for Today, 1980.

1994.   _____. *The Final Curtain.* Costa Mesa, CA: The Word for Today, 1984.

1995.   _____. *Future Survival.* Costa Mesa, CA: The Word for Today, 1980.

1996.   _____. *The Tribulation and the Church.* Costa Mesa, CA: The Word for Today, 1980.

1997.   _____. *What the World is Coming To.* Costa Mesa, CA: The Word for Today, 1980.

1998.   _____ (with Dave Wimbash). *Dateline Earth: Countdown to Eternity*. Old Tappan, NJ: Chosen Books, 1989.

1999.   Spillman, James R. *Omega Cometh: How to Live in the Last Days*. Old Tappan, NJ: Fleming H. Revell, 1979.

2000.   Sproule, John A. *In Defense of Pretribulationism*. Winona Lake, IN: BMH Books, 1980. [rev. ed. of *A Revised Review of 'The Church and the Tribulation'* by Robert H. Gundry.]

2001.   Strauss, Lehman. *God's Prophetic Calendar*. Neptune, NJ: Loizeaux Brothers, 1987.

2002.   *A Study of Premillennialism*. Fairmont, IN: Guardian of Truth Foundation, 1982.

2003.   Swaggart, Jimmy. *Armageddon: The Future of Planet Earth*. Baton Rouge, LA: Jimmy Swaggart Ministries, 1987.

2004.   _____. *Four Conditions for Being Included in the Rapture*. Baton Rouge, LA: Jimmy Swaggart Ministries, 1981.

2005.   _____. *The Future of Planet Earth*. Baton Rouge, LA: Jimmy Swaggart Ministries, 1982.

2006.   _____. *The Great White Throne Judgment*. Baton Rouge, LA: Jimmy Swaggart Ministries, 1979.

2007.   _____. *Will the Church Go Through the Great Tribulation Period?* Baton Rouge, LA: Jimmy Swaggart Ministries, 1981.

2008.   Sweeting, George. *Your Future*. Chicago: Moody Press, 1984.

2009.   Tan, Paul Lee. *The Interpretation of Prophecy*. Winona Lake, IN: BMH Books, 1974; Rockville, MD: Assurance Publishers, 1988.

2010.   _____. *Jesus Is Coming: Major Themes in Bible Prophecy*. Rockville, MD: Assurance Publishers, 1982.

2011. Tanner, Don, and George Johnson. *Cities in Space: Our Incredible Future...Science Fiction or Scientific Fact?* Irvine, CA: Harvest House Publishers, 1979.

2012. Ted. *The Climax.* St. Petersburg, FL: The Gospel Truth, 1982.

2013. *These Things Shall Be: The Coming of Elijah, The Second Advent of Christ, the First Judgment, Armageddon, The Millennial Reign of Christ, The Second Judgment, Eternity.* Rochester, New York: The Megiddo Church, 1983.

2014. Toussaint, Stanley D., and Charles H. Dyer (eds.). *Essays in Honor of J. Dwight Pentecost.* Chicago: Moody Press, 1986.

2015. *The United States of Europe.* St. Petersburg, FL: Gos's News Behind the News, n.d.

2016. Vanderbreggen, Cornelius, Jr. *The Promise of His Coming* (3rd ed.). Hiawassee, GA: The Reapers' Fellowship, Inc., 1985.

2017. Vander Lugt, Herbert. *Israel: Key to World Peace.* Grand Rapids, MI: Radio Bible Class, 1981.

2018. _____. *Perhaps Today!: The Rapture of the Church.* Grand Rapids, MI: Radio Bible Class, 1984.

2019. _____. *There's a New Day Coming: A Survey of Endtime Events.* Grand Rapids, MI: Radio Bible Class, 1983.

2020. Van Impe, Jack. *America, Israel, Russia, and World War III.* Royal Oak, MI: Jack Van Impe Ministries, 1984.

2021. _____. *11:59... And Counting!* Nashville: Thomas Nelson Publishers, 1987.

2022. _____. *Israel's Final Holocaust.* Nashville: Thomas Nelson Publishers, 1979; Royal Oak, MI: Jack Van Impe Ministries, 1983.

2023. _____. *Revelation Revealed: Verse By Verse.* Royal Oak, MI: Jack Van Impe Ministries, 1982.

2024.   _____. *Signs of the Times*. Royal Oak, MI: Jack Van Impe
         Ministries, 1979.

2025.   Vigeveno, H. S. *In the Eye of the Apocalypse: Understanding the
         Revelation, God's Message of Hope for the End Times*.
         Ventura, CA: Regal Books, 1990.

2026.   Walvoord, John F. *Armageddon: Oil and the Middle East Crisis*
         (rev. ed.). Grand Rapids, MI: Zondervan Publishing House,
         1990.

2027.   _____. *Major Bible Prophecies: 37 Crucial Prophecies that
         Affect You Today*. Grand Rapids, MI: Zondervan Publishing
         House, 1991.

2028.   _____. *Prophecy Knowledge Handbook*. Wheaton, IL: Victor
         Books, 1990.

2029.   Wead, Doug, David Lewis, and Hal Donaldson. *Where is the Lost
         Ark?* Indianapolis: Bethany House Publishers, 1982.

2030.   Webber, David. *The Image of the Ages: Iraq / Babylon...
         Armageddon*. Lafayette, LA: Huntington House, 1991.

2031.   Webber, David & Noah W. Hutchings. *Computers and the Beast of
         Revelation*. Shreveport, LA: Huntington House, 1986.

2032.   Whisenant, Edgar C. *88 Reasons Why the Rapture Will Be in
         1988* (new expanded edition with, *On Borrowed Time*).
         Nashville, TN: World Bible Society, 1988, (1st ed., 1979).

2033.   _____. *The Final Shout: Rapture Report 1989*. Nashville, TN:
         World Bible Society, 1989.

2034.   White, John Wesley. *Arming for Armageddon*. Milford, MI: Mott
         Media, Inc., 1983.

2035.   _____. *Thinking the Unthinkable: Are All the Pieces in Place?*
         Lake Mary, FL: Creation House, 1992.

2036. Willmington, H. L. *The King Is Coming: An Outline Study of the Last Days* (rev. and expanded ed.). Wheaton, IL: Tyndale House Publishers, 1988.

2037. Wilson, Clifford A. *1980's: Decade of Shock.* San Diego: Master Books, 1980.

2038. Wilson, James Larkin. *No More Babies: End of the Human Race.* Houston, TX: Pub. by author, 1991.

2039. Yoho, Walter Allan. *The Blazing Torch of Prophecy.* Winston-Salem, NC: Piedmont Bible College Press, 1989.

2040. Youssef, Michael. *Earth King.* Westchester, IL: Crossway Book, 1988.

SECTION ELEVEN

AMILLENNIAL, POST-MILLENNIAL AND ANTI-PREMILLENNIAL WORKS

For the purposes of comparison, this section comprises selected works that fall outside the main circles of premillennialism or that in some way take exception with some current of popular eschatological thought.

2041. Adams, Jay E. *The Time is at Hand.* Nutley, NJ: Presbyterian and Reformed Publishing Co., 1966 and 1970. [A revised and corrected edition of '*I Will Tell You a Mystery*']

2042. Allis, Oswald T. (ed.). *An Examination of Several Scripture Prophecies Which the Reverend M. W. Hath Applyed to the Times After the Coming of the Messiah.* London: R. Burrough and J. Baker, 1707. [reprinted]

2043. _____. *Prophecy and the Church: An Examination of the Claim of Dispensationalists that the Christian Church is a mystery parenthesis which interrupts the fulfilment to Israel of the Kingdom prophecies of the Old Testament.* Philadelphia: The Presbyterian and Reformed Publishing Co., 1945.

2044.   Bacchiocchi, Samuele. *Hal Lindsey's Prophetic Jigsaw Puzzle: Five Predictions that Failed!* Berrien Springs, MI: Biblical Perspectives, 1985.

2045.   Baker, Nelson B. *What is the World Coming To?: A Study for Laymen of the Last Things.* Philadelphia: Westminster Press, 1965.

2046.   Baldinger, Albert H. *Sermons on Revelation.* New York: George H. Doran Co., 1924.

2047.   Berkhof, Louis. *The Second Coming of Christ.* Grand Rapids, MI: Wm B. Eerdmans, 1953.

2048.   Berkouwer, G. C. *The Return of Christ.* Grand Rapids, MI: Eerdmans Publishing Co., 1972.

2049.   Boersma, T. *Is the Bible a Jigsaw Puzzle: An Evaluation of Hal Lindsey's Writings.* St. Catherine, ONT: Paideia Press, 1978.

2050.   Boettner, Loraine. *The Millennium.* Philadelphia: Presbyterian and Reformed Publishing Co., 1957 and 1964, (rev. ed., 1984).

2051.   Campbell, Roderick. *Israel and the New Covenant.* Philadelphia: Presbyterian and Reformed Publishing Co., 1954.

2052.   Carver, Everett I. *When Jesus Comes Again.* Phillipsburg, NJ: Presbyterian and Reformed Publishing Co., 1979.

2053.   Chilton, David. *The Great Tribulation.* Ft. Worth, TX: Dominion Press, 1987.

2054.   _____. *Paradise Restored: A Biblical Theology of Dominion.* Tyler, TX: Reconstruction Press, 1985.

2055.   Cox, William E. *Amillennialism Today.* Philadelphia: Presbyterian & Reformed Publishing Co., 1966.

2056.   _____. *Biblical Studies in Final Things.* Nutley, NJ: Presbyterian & Reformed Publishing Co., 1977.

2057. _____. *An Examination of Dispensationalism.* Philadelphia: Presbyterian & Reformed Publishing Co., 1974 [1963].

2058. _____. *In These Last Days.* Philadelphia: Presbyterian & Reformed Publishing Co., 1964.

2059. _____. *The Millennium, With an Exposition of Revelation Twenty.* Philadelphia: Presbyterian & Reformed Publishing Co., 1964.

2060. _____. *Why I Left Scofieldism.* Phillipsburg, NJ: Presbyterian & Reformed Publishing Co., 1978.

2061. Davis, John Jefferson. *Christ's Victorious Kingdom: Post-millennialism Reconsidered.* Grand Rapids, MI: Baker Book House, 1986.

2062. DeCaro, Louis A. *Israel Today: Fulfillment of Prophecy?* Grand Rapids, MI: Baker Book House, 1974.

2063. Fuller, Daniel P. *Gospel and Law: Contrast or Continuum?: The Hermeneutics of Dispensationalism and Covenant Theology.* Grand Rapids, MI: Eerdmans, 1980.

2064. Gentry, Kenneth L. *The Beast of Revelation.* Tyler, TX: Institute for Christian Economics, 1989.

2065. _____. *Before Jerusalem Fell; Dating the Book of Revelation: An Exegetical and Historical Argument for a Pre-A.D. 70 Composition.* Tyler, TX: Institute for Christian Economics, 1989.

2066. _____. *The Greatness of the Great Commission: The Christian Enterprise in a Fallen World.* Tyler, TX: Institute for Christian Economics, 1990.

2067. Gettys, Joseph Miller. *How to Study the Revelation* (rev. ed.). Greenwood, SC: Attic Press, 1973.

2068. Graebner, Theodore. *War in the Light of Prophecy: Was it Foretold? A Reply to Modern Chiliasm.* St. Louis: Concordia

Publishing House, 1941. [rev. version of *Prophecy and the War*]

2069.   Grimsrud, Ted. *Triumph of the Lamb: A Self-Study Guide to the Book of Revelation.* Scottdale, PA: Herald Press, 1987.

2070.   Halsell, Grace. *Prophecy and Politics: Militant Evangelists on the Road to Nuclear War.* Brooklyn, NY: Lawrence Hill Books, 1986.

2071.   _____. *Prophecy and Politics: Secret Alliance Between Israel and U. S. Christian Right.* Brooklyn, NY: Lawrence Hill Books, 1989.

2072.   Hamilton, Floyd E. *The Basis of Millennial Faith.* Grand Rapids, MI: Eerdmans Publishing Co., 1942, 1948, and 1952.

2073.   _____. *Will the Church Escape the Great Tribulation?* (3rd ed.). New York: Loizeaux Bros., Bible Truth Depot, 1944.

2074.   Hendricksen, William. *And So All Israel Shall Be Saved.* Grand Rapids, MI: Baker Book House, 1945.

2075.   _____. *Israel and the Bible.* Grand Rapids, MI: Baker Book House, 1968.

2076.   _____. *Israel in Prophecy.* Grand Rapids, MI: Baker Book House, 1968. [reprint of *Israel and the Bible*]

2077.   _____. *Lectures on the Last Things.* Grand Rapids, MI: Baker Book House, 1951.

2078.   _____. *More Than Conquerors.* Grand Rapids, MI: Baker Book House, 1956.

2079.   Hoekema, Anthony A. *The Bible and the Future.* Grand Rapids, MI: Eerdmans, 1979.

2080.   Horton, Thomas C. *These Pre-Millennialists: Who Are They?* Los Angeles: Pub. by author, 1921.

2081. Hoven, Victor Emanuel. *The Purpose and Progress in Prophecy.* Eugene, OR: EBU Press, 1930.

2082. Hughes, Philip Edgcombe. *The Book of Revelation.* London: InterVarsity Press; Grand Rapids, MI: Eerdmans Publishing Co., 1990.

2083. _____. *Interpreting Prophecy.* Grand Rapids, MI: Wm B. Eerdmans Publishing Co., 1976.

2084. Hulse, Erroll. *The Restoration of Israel.* Worthing, ENG.: Henry E. Walter LTD, 1968.

2085. Jewett, Robert. *Jesus Against the Rapture: Seven Unexpected Prophecies.* Philadelphia: Westminster Press, 1979.

2086. Kempin, Albert J. *Why the Millennial Doctrine Is Not Biblical.* Anderson, IN: Gospel Trumpet Company, n.d.

2087. Kik, J. Marcellus. *The Eschatology of Victory.* Nutley, New York: The Presbyterian and Reformed Publishing Co., 1971.

2088. _____. *Matthew Twenty-four: An Exposition.* Swengel, PA: Bible Truth Expositors, 1948.

2089. _____. *Revelation Twenty: An Exposition.* Philadelphia: Presbyterian and Reformed Publishing Co., 1955.

2090. König, Adrio. *The Eclipse of Christ in Eschatology: Toward a Christ-centered Approach.* Grand Rapids, MI: W. B. Eerdmans Publishing Co., 1989.

2091. Kromminga, Diedrich H. *The Millennium: Its Nature, Function, and Relation to the Consummation of the World.* Grand Rapids, MI: Eerdmans, 1948.

2092. _____. *The Millennium in the Church: Studies in the History of Christian Chiliasm.* Grand Rapids, MI: Eerdmans, 1943 and 1945.

2093.   Lehman, Chester K. *The Fulfillment of Prophecy*. Scottdale, PA: Herold Press, 1971.

2094.   Limburg, James. *The Prophets and the Powerless*. Atlanta: John Knox Press, 1977.

2095.   Mains, George Preston. *Premillennialism: Non-Scriptural, Non-Historic, Non-Scientific, Non-Philosophical*. New York: The Abingdon Press, 1920.

2096.   Mathews, Shailer. *Will Christ Come Again?* Chicago: American Institute of Sacred Literature, 1917.

2097.   MacPherson, Dave. *The Great Rapture Hoax*. Fletcher, NC: New Puritan Library, 1983.

2098.   _____. *The Incredible Cover-Up*. Medford, OR: Omega Publications, 1975. [combines rev. and updated editions of *The Unbelievable Pre-Trib Origin* and *The Late Great Pre-Trib Rapture*]

2099.   _____. *The Late Great Pre-Trib Rapture*. Kansas City, MO: Heart of America Bible Society, 1974.

2100.   _____. *The Unbelievable Pre-Trib Origin: The Recent Discovery of a Well-known Theory's Beginning -- and Its Incredible Cover-up*. Kansas City, MO: Heart of America Bible Society, 1973.

2101.   McKnight, R. J. G. *The Second Coming of Christ: Is it Premillennial?* Wilkensburg, PA: Pub. by author, 1915. [a critique of W. E. B. 's *Jesus Is Coming*]

2102.   Miladin, George C. *Is This Really the End? A Reformed Analysis of the Late Great Planet Earth*. Cherry Hill, NJ: Mack Publishing Co., 1973.

2103.   Morris, S. L. *The Drama of Christianity: An Interpretation of the Book of Revelation*. Grand Rapids, MI: Baker Book House, 1982. [reprint of 1928 edition]

2104. Murray, George L. *Millennial Studies: A Search for Truth*. Grand Rapids, MI: Baker Book House, 1948.

2105. North, Gary. *Millennialism and Social Theory*. Tyler, TX: Institute for Christian Economics, 1990.

2106. Rall, Harris F. *Modern Premillennialism and the Christian Hope*. New York: Abingdon, 1920.

2107. Robertson, John A. T. *Jesus and His Coming*. Philadelphia: Westminster Press, 1979.

2108. Sisco, Paul E. *Scofield or the Scriptures: A Comparison of Certain Notes by C. I. Scofield with the Holy Bible*. Alden, NY: Pub. by author, n.d.

2109. Tanner, Jacob. *The Thousand Years Not Pre-millennial*. Minneapolis: Augsburg Publishing House, 1934.

2110. Schlissel, Steve, and David Brown. *Hal Lindsey and the Restoration of the Jews.* Edmonton, AB: Still Waters Revival Books, 1990.

2111. Standfield, James M. *Christ's Second Coming: The Pre-millennial View Shown to be Untrue From the Standpoint of the Scriptures*. Pub. by author, n.d.

2112. Summers, Ray. *Worthy is the Lamb*. Nashville: Broadman Press, 1951.

2113. Van Dyken, Peter L. *Premillennialism: An Absurd and Fantastic Illusion*. Ripon, CA: n.p., n.d.

2114. Wilson, H. Speed. *Rapture!; Prophecy or Heresy: Will Biblical Christians Be Removed from the Earth to Heaven?* Canton, OH: Daring Publishing Group, 1989.

2115. Zens, Jon. *Dispensationalism: A Reformed Inquiry into its Leading Figures and Features*. Nutley, NJ: Presbyterian and Reformed Publishing Co., 1978.

SECTION TWELVE

SELECTED
JOURNALS AND PERIODICALS

2116. *Bibliotheca Sacra* (1934 - pres., beginning with vol. 91); Publisher: Dallas Theological Seminary (formerly Evangelical Theological College).

2117. *Christian Beacon* (1936 - pres., beginning with vol. 1); Editor: Carl McIntire; Publisher: Christian Beacon, Collingswood, NJ.

2118. *The Christian Fundamentalist* (1927-1932, 6 vols.); Editor: William Bell Riley; Publisher: World's Christian Fundamentals Association, Minneapolis.

2119. *Christian Herald* (1901 - pres., beginning with vol. 25) Current Publisher: Christian Herald Association, Chappaqua, NY.

2120. *Christian Herald and Signs of Our Times* (1878 - 1901, 24 vols.) Published in New York (Previously *Signs of Our Times*)

2121. *Christian Workers Magazine* (1910-1920, vols. 11-20); Publisher: Moody Bible Institute, Chicago.

2122. *Christianity Today* (1956 - pres., beginning with vol. 1); First Editor: Carl F. H. Henry; Originally Published in Washington

D. C.; Current Publisher: Christianity Today, Inc., Carol Stream, IL.

2123. *Eternity* (1950-1989, 40 vols.); Publisher: Foundation for Christian Living, Philadelphia.

2124. *The King's Business* (1910-1970, 61 vols.); Long-time Editor: Keith L. Brooks. Publisher: Bible Institute of Los Angeles.

2125. *Moody [Bible Institute] Monthly* (1920 - pres., beginning with vol. 21); Publisher: Moody Bible Institute, Chicago (previously *Christian Workers Magazine*).

2126. *Our Hope: A Testimony for our Lord Jesus Christ* (1894-1957, 64 vols.); Main Editor: Arno C. Gaebelein; Publisher: Arno C. Gaebelein, Inc., New York.

2127. *Prophetic Times* (1863-1874, 12 vols); Editor: Joseph Seiss; Published in Philadelphia.

2128. *Revelation* (1931-1950, 20 vols.); Main Editor: Donald Grey Barnhouse; Publisher: American Bible Conference Association, Philadelphia.

2129. *Signs of Our Times* (1867-1875, 9 vols.); Editor: Michael P. Baxter; Published in London.

2130. *The Sunday School Times* (1859-1966, 108 vols.); Long-time Editor: Charles Trumbull, 1903-1941; Publisher: J. D. Wattles, Philadelphia.

2131. *Sword of the Lord* (1934 - pres., beginning with vol. 1); Editor: John R. Rice; Publisher: Sword of the Lord, Wheaton, IL, and Murfreesboro, TN.

2132. *Truth; or Testimony for Christ* (1874-1897, 24 vols.) Editor: James H. Brookes; Published in St. Louis.

2133. *Watchword* (1878-1897, 19 vols.); Editor: A. J. Gordon; Published in Boston.

2134. *Watchword and Truth* (1898-1921, 23 vols.); Editor: Robert Cameron; Published in Boston. [combines *Watchword* and *Truth*]

2135. *Waymarks in the Wilderness* (1864-1872, 10 vols.); Editor: James Inglis; Published in New York.

2136. *Winona Echoes* (1904-1948) Published as *Winona Review: Addresses Delivered at the Annual Bible Conference* sometime in 1902 or 1903, thereafter published as *Winona Echoes*; Printed in Winona Lake, IN, 1904-1938; Printed by Zondervan in Grand Rapids, MI, 1939-1948.

PART THREE

SELECTED BIOGRAPHICAL SKETCHES

American Protestant millennialism is not so much a movement as it is a loose collection of popular writers and conference speakers. This section lists brief biographical sketches of some of the more influential individuals in popular eschatological circles in the United States since the time of William Miller (1782-1849) and John Nelson Darby (1800-1882).

List of Biographical Sources

2137.   Bowden, Henry Warner. *Dictionary of American Religious Biography.* Westport, CT: Greenwood Press, 1977.

2138.   Burgess, Stanley M. and Gary B. McGee (eds.). *Dictionary of Pentecostal and Charismatic Movements.* Grand Rapids, MI: Zondervan Publishing House, 1988.

2139.   Dollar, George W. *A History of Fundamentalism in America.* Greenville, SC: Bob Jones University Press, 1973.

2140.   Elwell, Walter A. (ed.). *Evangelical Dictionary of Theology.* Grand Rapids, MI: Baker Book House, 1984.

2141.   Gartenhaus, Jacob. *Famous Hebrew Christians.* Grand Rapids, MI: Baker Book House, 1979.

2142.   Hammack, Mary L. *A Dictionary of Women in Church History.* Chicago: Moody Press, 1984.

2143.   Lippy, Charles H. (ed.). *Twentieth-Century Shapers of American Popular Religion.* Westport, CT: Greenwood Press, 1989.

2144.   Melton, J. Gordon. *Biographical Dictionary of American Cult and Sect Leaders.* New York: Garland Publishing, Inc., 1986.

2145.   _____. *Religious Leaders of America.* Detroit, MI: Gale Research Inc., 1991.

2146.   Moyer, Elgin. *Wycliffe Biographical Dictionary of the Church* (rev. & enlarged by Earle E. Cairns). Chicago: Moody Press, 1982.

2147.   Reid, Daniel G., Robert D. Linder, Bruce L. Shelley, and Harry S. Stout (eds.). *Dictionary of Christianity in America.* Downers Grove, IL: InterVarsity Press, 1990.

Biographical Sketches

Allis, Oswald T. (1880-1973) A professor at Westminster Seminary, 1929-1936. With J. Gresham Machen, Allis helped found Westminster Seminary, which was organized in 1929 by Machen in protest over Princeton Seminary's slide toward liberalism. Allis was later a contributing editor of *Christianity Today.* In his works on eschatology, Allis voiced strong support for Presbyterianism's traditional amillennialist position.

-----*Prophecy and the Church: An Examination of the Claim of Dispensationalists that the Christian Church is a mystery parenthesis which interrupts the fulfilment to Israel of the Kingdom prophecies of the Old Testament.* Philadelphia: The Presbyterian and Reformed Publishing Co., 1945.

Anderson, Sir Robert (1841-1918) A British barrister and member of the Plymouth Brethren. Anderson was born in Dublin and educated there at Trinity College. He embarked upon a law career in 1863. In 1868, Anderson was appointed to the Home Office Bureau as an advisor on Irish Affairs, serving until 1877, and again after 1880. Despite his duties, Anderson found time to study theology and preach lay sermons. Anderson supported the pre-tribulation rapture view, the theory that the "Church" would be taken from the earth *before* the Tribulation period of divine judgment. His most popular book, published in over twenty editions, was *The Coming Prince*, a premillennial treatise on the prophecies in the Book of Daniel as they relate to the Last Days.

-----*The Coming Prince.* London: Pickering & Inglis, n.d.

-----*The Coming Prince: The Marvelous Prophecy of Daniel's Seventy Weeks Concerning the Antichrist.* Grand Rapids, MI: Kregel Publications, 1957; (18th ed.). Grand Rapids, MI: Kregel Publications, 1972.

-----*The Coming Prince; or, The Seventy Weeks of Daniel, with an Answer to the Higher Criticism* (5th ed.). London: Hodder & Stoughton, 1895.

-----*Forgotten Truths.* London: James Nisbet & Company, 1913; (2nd ed.). London: James Nisbet & Co., 1914.

-----*Human Destiny* (6th ed.). New York: Gospel Publishing House, n.d.; (9th ed.). Glasgow: Pickering & Inglis, 1913.

-----*Unfulfilled Prophecy and "The Hope of the Church."* London: James Nisbet & Co., 1917; (2nd ed.). Glasgow: Pickering and Inglis, n.d.

Appelman, Hyman J. (b. 1902) An independent Jewish Christian evangelist. Appelman, a Ukrainian Jew, emigrated to the United States with his family in 1914. He studied at Northwestern and DePaul Universities, 1918-1921. From 1921 to 1925, Appelman worked as a lawyer in Chicago; exhaustion from overwork forced him to move west to Kansas City and then to Denver. During his convalescence, Appelman converted to Christianity. Still uncertain about the future and contemplating suicide, Appelman joined the Army. While serving his enlistment, Appelman recovered and was then confirmed in his Christian faith. Discharged from Army service in 1930, he was called as pastor of a Southern Baptist church in Lawton, Okla. He attended Southwestern Baptist Theological Seminary, 1930-1933, afterwards becoming Texas State Evangelist for the Southern Baptist Church, 1933-1942. Thereafter, Appelman became an independent evangelist traveling throughout the United States and taking occasional excursions abroad.

-----*Antichrist and the Jew, and the Valley of Dry Bones.* Grand Rapids, MI: Zondervan Publishing House, 1950.

-----*The Atomic Bomb and the End of the World.* Grand Rapids, MI: Zondervan Publishing House, 1954.

-----*The Battle of Armageddon.* Grand Rapids, MI: Zondervan Publishing House, 1942; Faith of Our Fathers Broadcast, 1944.

-----*The Jew in History and Destiny.* Grand Rapids, MI: Zondervan Publishing House, 1947.

Armerding, Carl (1883-?) A Plymouth Brethren missionary and minister. Armerding was briefly a missionary to Honduras and a minister in New Mexico. At the urging of Harry Ironside, Armerding joined the faculty of the Evangelical Theological Seminary (later Dallas Theological Seminary). While director of the Central American Mission, 1943-1963, Armerding taught for a time at Moody Bible Institute, 1943-1947, and later at Wheaton College, 1948-1962.

-----*The Four and Twenty Elders.* New York: Loizeaux Brothers, n.d.

-----*Signs of Christ's Coming -- As Son of Man.* Chicago: Moody Press, 1965; (rev. ed.). Chicago: Moody Press, 1971

-----, and W. Ward Gasque (eds.). *Dreams, Visions, and Oracles: The Layman's Guide to Biblical Prophecy.* Grand Rapids, MI: Baker Book House, 1977.

Baron, David (1855-1926) A Polish-born English missionary to the Jews. Baron was born in Suwalki, Poland, and educated in the Yeshiva. While still in his teens, he emigrated to Hull (in Yorkshire), England. On October 17, 1878, Baron converted to Christianity. He attended Harley House College to train as a missionary, finishing his course in 1881. In July 1881, Baron joined the Mildmay Mission to the Jews, a relationship lasting over twelve years. In 1883, Baron moved to London and then left the country as a missionary on the Western frontier of Russia, 1885-1889. Afterwards, Baron toured widely, visiting Palestine in 1891. In 1893, Baron joined the Hebrew Christian Testimony to Israel and served on its staff, writing books and tracts, until his death on October 28, 1926.

-----*The Ancient Scriptures and the Modern Jew.* 1900; (3rd ed.). London: Hodder & Stoughton, n.d.; (new ed.). Findlay, OH: Dunham Publishing Co., n.d.

-----*Israel's Inalienable Possession: The Gifts and the Calling of God Which are Without Repentance.* London: Morgan & Scott, n.d.

-----*The Jewish Problem: Its Solution; or Israel's Present and Future* (6th ed., carefully rev.). London: Morgan and Scott, n.d.

-----*The Visions and Prophecies of Zechariah.* London: Morgan & Scott, 1918.

Bauman, Louis S. (1875-1950) A Minister of the Grace Brethren Churches. An active member of the Brethren Church from youth, Bauman began to show strong interest in missionary work. He was a charter member of the Foreign Mission Society, 1900, and a member of its board of trustees, 1904, and its secretary from 1906 to near the end of his life. During this same period, Bauman's views on the millennium shifted towards premillennialism. After the death of his first wife, Bauman moved to Long Beach, California, where he formed a

Brethren congregation, a church he led from 1912 to 1947. He helped found Grace Theological Seminary, 1935, and the National Fellowship of Brethren Church, 1939 (now Grace Brethren Churches).

-----*God and Gog*. Long Beach, CA: Pub. by author, 1934.

-----*Light from Bible Prophecy: as Related to the Present Crisis*. New York: Fleming H. Revell Co., 1940.

-----*Russian Events in the Light of Biblical Prophecy*. New York: Fleming H. Revell Co., 1942.

-----*Shirts and Sheets: or Anti-Semitism, A Present-day Sign of the First Magnitude*. Long Beach, CA: Pub. by author, 1934.

-----*The Time of Jacob's Trouble.*Long Beach, CA: Pub. by author, 1938.

Beet, Joseph A. (1840-1924) An English Wesleyan minister and educator. After serving a number of churches from 1864-1885, Beet was professor of systematic theology at Wesleyan College, 1885-1905, and a member of the faculty of theology at the University of London, 1901-1905. Two of Beet's works, *The Last Things* and *The Immortality of the Soul*, were the occasion for much criticism by unsympathetic scholars.

-----*The Last Things.*London: Hodder & Stoughton, 1897; (3rd ed.). New York: Eaton and Mains; Cincinnati: Curts and Jennings, 1898.

-----*The Last Things in Few Words*. London: Hodder & Stoughton, 1913.

Biederwolf, William E. (1867-1939) A Presbyterian minister. Biederwolf attended Wabash College, Princeton University, and the University of Berlin. He served as a chaplain during the Spanish-American War, spending six months in Cuba. An itinerant evangelist and well-known Bible teacher, Biederwolf held revival meetings with Billy Sunday and J. Wilbur Chapman. He also participated at the Winona Lake Bible conferences serving as its director, 1922-1939. During this period, Biederwolf also served as head, and then as president, of the Winona Lake School of Theology. His most popular work, *The Millennium Bible,* has been reprinted several times.

-----*The Amazing Prophecy Second Coming Bible.* Orange, CA: Amazing Prophecy, 1974.

-----*The Millennium Bible (American Standard Bible).* Nashville: Thomas Nelson Co., 1924.

-----*The Millennium Bible: Being a Help to the Study of the Holy Scriptures in Their Testimony to the Second Coming of Our Lord and Saviour Jesus Christ.* Chicago: Glad Tidings Publishing Co., 1924.

-----*The Second Coming Bible.* Grand Rapids, MI: Baker Book House, 1977.

-----*The Second Coming of Christ.* Chicago: Glad Tidings Publishing Co., n.d.

Birks, Thomas Rawson (1810-1883) English evangelical and theologian. Birks served as minister at Kelshall in Herefordshire from 1844 until his appointment at Trinity Chapel, Cambridge, a post he held until 1877. He was appointed Professor of moral philosophy at Cambridge, 1872, and continued in that position until his death in 1883. For a period of twenty-one years, Rawson was also an honorary secretary of the Evangelical Alliance.

-----*First Elements of Sacred Prophecy.* n.p., 1844.

-----*The Four Prophetic Empires and the Kingdom of Messiah.* London: Seeley, 1844.

-----*The Mystery of Providence: or The Prophetic History of the Decline and Fall of the Roman Empire.* London: Nisbet, 1848.

-----*Outlines of Unfulfilled Prophecy: Being an Inquiry into the Scripture Testimony Respecting the "Good Things to Come."* London: Seeley, 1854.

-----*Thoughts on the Times and Seasons of Sacred Prophecy.* London: Hodder & Stoughton, 1880.

-----*The Two Later Visions of Daniel: Historically Explained.* London: Seeley, 1846.

Blackstone, William E. (1841-1935) A Methodist Episcopal layman. Blackstone was the author of *Jesus Is Coming!*, a popular exposition on the Second Coming of Christ and a defense of dispensational premillennialism. Blackstone became quite interested in the return of the Jews to Palestine and a future Jewish state. It was for this reason that he helped found the Chicago Hebrew Mission in 1889 and also worked to promote World Zionism in the United States and abroad. In 1891, Blackstone sent a letter to president Benjamin Harrison, requesting that the president push for an international conference on the condition of the Jews and their return to Palestine. Blackstone's *Jesus Is Coming!* (originally published in 1878) remains in print and still enjoys wide circulation today.

-----*The Heart of the Jewish Problem.* Chicago: Chicago Hebrew Mission, n.d.

-----*Jesus Is Coming!* New York: Fleming H. Revell, 1886; (re-rev. ed.). Christian and Missionary Alliance, 1908.

-----*Jesus Is Coming: God's Hope for a Restless Word* (updated ed.). Grand Rapids, MI: Kregel Publications, 1989.

-----*The Millennium: A Discussion of the Question, "Do the Scriptures Teach that There Is to Be a Millennium?"* New York: Fleming H. Revell Co., 1904.

-----*Satan: His Kingdom and Its Overthrow.* New York: Fleming H. Revell, 1900.

-----*The "Times of the Gentiles" and "The Time of the End."* n.p., n.d.

Blanchard, Charles A. (1848-1926) A Congregationalist minister and president of Wheaton College, 1882-1926. From 1913 until his death,

Blanchard was also president of the Chicago Hebrew Mission, founded by W.E. Blackstone in 1889.

-----*Light on the Last Days.* Chicago: Bible Institute Colportage Association, 1913.

-----*The World War and the Bible.* Chicago: Bible Institute Colportage Association, 1918.

Branham, William M. (1909-1965) A pentecostal minister and healer. Branham heard the voice of God at the age of seven. He began his tent ministry at the age of twenty-four. In 1937, Branham had a series of visions in which he saw the rise of Mussolini, Hitler, communism, the menace of technology, the decline of morality among women in the United States, and, last of all, the final destruction of America. Later, during a baptismal service in the Ohio River, Branham saw a bright light and heard a voice proclaim that just as John's ministry heralded the first coming of Christ, Branham's would herald the second advent. Branham's healing ministry began in 1946 after an angelic visitation. Soon after, his fame as a healer spread throughout pentecostal circles in the United States. The details of his healing ministry were recorded by Gordon Lindsay in the first issues of *The Voice of Healing* magazine.

-----*An Exposition of the Seven Church Ages.* Jeffersonville, IN: Branham Campaigns, n.d.

-----*The Revelation of the Seven Seals.* Tucson, AZ: Spoken Word Publications, 1967.

Brookes, James H. (1830-1897) A Presbyterian minister. A devoted follower of Darby, Brookes was editor of *The Truth or Testimony for Christ* from 1874 to 1897 and the author of numerous books and tracts. Brookes was also major figure in the early Prophetic conferences, popularizing the two-phase coming of Christ: first, *for* his saints at the rapture; second, *with* his saints at the judgment. Among his most famous students was C. I. Scofield.

-----*Bible Reading on the Second Coming.* Springfield, IL: Edwin A. Wilson, 1877.

-----*I Am Coming: A Setting Forth of the Second Coming of Our Lord Jesus Christ as Personal -- Private -- Premillennial* (7th ed., rev.). Glasgow: Pickering & Inglis, n.d.

-----*Israel and the Church.* St. Louis: Gospel Book and Tract Depository, n.d.

-----*Maranatha; or, The Lord Cometh.* St. Louis: Edward Brendell, 1878; (9th ed.). New York: Fleming H. Revell, 1889.

-----*Till He Come* [sic]. New York: Fleming H. Revell, 1895.

Brooks, Keith L. (1887-1954) A Baptist layman and professor at the Bible Institute of Los Angeles, 1917-1928. Brooks was also editor of *The King's Business* and *Prophecy Monthly.*

-----*The Age-end Prophecy of Our Lord: A Verse by Verse Comment on Matthew 24-25.* Los Angeles: American Prophetic League, n.d.

-----*The Certain End, as Seen by the Prophet Daniel: A Fresh Examination of These Prophecies by the Cross-reference Method of Interpretation.* Los Angeles: American Prophetic League, 1942.

-----*The Consummation: Vital Prophetic Truth.* Los Angeles: Brooks Publishers, n.d.

-----*Harvest of Iniquity: Impending World Events as Revealed in the Book of Revelation.* Los Angeles: Brooks Publications, 1933.

-----*The Jews and the Passion for Palestine in the Light of Prophecy.* Grand Rapids, MI: Zondervan Publishing House, 1937.

-----*Prophecies of Daniel and Revelation.* Los Angeles: BIOLA, 1925.

-----*Prophecy and the Tottering Nations.* Los Angeles: BIOLA, 1935.

-----*Prophetic Questions Answered.* Wheaton, IL: Van Kampen Press, 1951.

-----*Prophetic Text Book.* Los Angeles: BIOLA, 1933.

Brown, David (1803-1897) A Scottish Presbyterian minister, professor and president of Free Church College, Edinburgh. Brown was educated at Aberdeen University, graduating in 1821. After holding several pastorates, Brown was appointed a professor of Church history and apologetics at Free Church College, Aberdeen, 1857. In 1876, Brown became principal of the College and served in that post until his death in 1897 at 94. A well-known postmillennialist, his books have been reprinted often and remain popular among like-minded Reformed scholars.

-----*The Apocalypse: Its Structure and Primary Predictions.* New York: Christian Literature Co., 1891.

-----*Christ's Second Coming: Will It be Premillennial?* New York: Carter, 1856; (5th ed.). London: Hamilton, Adams & Co., 1859; (6th ed.). New York: Carter, 1876; (7th ed.). Edinburgh: T & T Clark, 1882.

-----*The Restoration of the Jews: The History, Principles, and Bearings of the Question.* n.p., .n.d.

Buswell, Oliver J., Jr. (1895-1980?) A Presbyterian minister. Buswell received graduate degrees from McCormick Seminary and New York University. After serving as a chaplain during the First World War, Buswell ministered to churches in Minnesota, Wisconsin, and New York. A fundamentalist and disciple of J. Gresham Machen, Buswell was dismissed from the ministry by the Presbyterian Church in 1936 for his support of an independent fundamentalist mission board. Buswell was president of Wheaton College, 1926-1939, and of the National Bible Institute (Shelton College), 1941-1955. For a time, Buswell was a colleague of Carl McIntire, an Orthodox Presbyterian, and served with several independent separatist Presbyterian churches.

-----*Unfulfilled Prophecies.* Grand Rapids, MI: Zondervan Publishing House, 1937.

Cameron, Robert (1845?-1922?) A Baptist minister and leader at the Niagara Bible Conferences. Cameron became known for his posttribulation rapture position within premillennialism. After the deaths of A. J. Gordon (1895) and James H. Brookes (1897) their respective journals *The Watchword* and *Truth* were merged by Cameron in 1898 to form *Watchword and Truth*. He edited this journal until his own death sometime early in the 1920s.

-----*The Doctrine of the Ages*. New York: Fleming H. Revell, 1896.

-----*Scriptural Truth About the Lord's Return*. New York: Fleming H. Revell, 1922.

Chafer, Lewis Sperry (1871-1952) A Presbyterian minister and educator. An itinerant Bible teacher and protegé of C. I. Scofield, Chafer was a member of the faculty of the Philadelphia School of the Bible, 1914-1923. In 1924, Chafer founded the Evangelical Theological College (later Dallas Theological Seminary) and was its president until his death. He was also a longtime editor of *Bibliotheca Sacra*, which he bought in 1934.

-----*Dispensations*. Dallas, TX: Dallas Theological Seminary Press, 1936.

-----*He That is Spiritual*. New York: Our Hope Publishing Co., 1918.

-----*The Kingdom in History and Prophecy*. New York: Fleming H. Revell, 1915; Philadelphia: The Sunday School Times, 1922; Chicago: Moody Press, 1936.

-----*Must We Dismiss the Millennium?* Crescent City, FL: Biblical Testimony League, 1922.

-----*Seven Major Biblical Signs of the Times*. Philadelphia: The Sunday School Times, 1919.

-----*Signs of the Times*. Chicago: Bible Institute Colportage Association, 1919.

-----*Systematic Theology* (vols I-VIII). Dallas: Dallas Theological Seminary Press, 1948.

Chapman, J. Wilbur (1859-1918) A Presbyterian minister and evangelist. Chapman became a full-time evangelist in 1893, working for a time with D. L. Moody. Chapman also helped Billy Sunday get his start in mass evangelism. With Sol Dickey, Chapman set up the Winona Lake Bible Conference center, which he then directed. He was elected moderator of the Presbyterian General Assembly in 1918 but died before completing his term.

-----*A Reason for My Hope.* New York: Our Hope, 1916.

Cooper, David L. (1886-1984) Founder and director of the Biblical Research Society. The major purpose of the Biblical Research Society, for which Cooper founded it in 1930, was to spread the Gospel to the Jews through the distribution of free literature. Cooper's works generally center on the endtimes prophecies that relate to the Jews and a revived Jewish state in Palestine. His books are still reprinted and circulated by the Biblical Research Society.

-----*Antichrist and the Worldwide Revival.* Los Angeles: Biblical Research Society, 1954.

-----*Future Events Revealed: An Exposition of the Olivet Discourse.* Los Angeles: Biblical Research Society, 1935.

-----*Grand March of Empire.* Los Angeles: Biblical Research Society, 1955.

-----*The Invading Forces of Russia and of the Antichrist Overthrown in Palestine.* Los Angeles: Biblical Research Society, n.d.

-----*Is the Jew Still First on God's Prophetic Program?: Vital Questions Answered.* Los Angeles: Biblical Research Society, 1935.

-----*May Christ Delay His Return 1000 Years?* Los Angeles: Biblical Research Society, n.d.

-----*Preparing for the World-wide Revival.* Los Angeles: Biblical Research Society, 1938.

-----*Prophetic Fulfillments in Palestine Today.* Los Angeles: Biblical Research Society, 1940.

-----*The Seventy Weeks of Daniel.* Los Angeles: Biblical Research Society, 1941.

-----*When Gog's Armies Meet the Almighty: An Exposition of Ezekiel Thirty-Eight and Thirty-Nine.* Los Angeles: The Biblical Research Society, 1940.

-----*Why God's Interest is in the Jew.* Los Angeles: The Biblical Research Society, 1941.

-----*The World's Greatest Library Geographically Illustrated* [includes Prophecy Charts]. Los Angeles: The Biblical Research Society, 1942.

Criswell, W. A. (b. 1909) A Southern Baptist minister. After graduating from Baylor University and Southern Baptist Seminary, Criswell pastored churches in Oklahoma. In 1944 he became the minister of the 7,000-member First Baptist Church in Dallas. Under his leadership, the First Baptist Church grew to over 26,000 by the mid-1980s. A colorfully outspoken individual, Criswell has denounced Catholics, Atheists, Communists, and Blacks, which may account for his appeal. A strong supporter of Israel, Criswell was awarded the Israeli Humanitarian Award by Israeli Prime Minister Menachem Begin in 1978.

-----*Expository Sermons on Revelation* (5 vols). Grand Rapids, MI: Zondervan Publishing House, 1962.

-----*Welcome Back, Jesus!* Nashville: Broadman Press, 1976.

-----*What to Do Until Jesus Comes Back.* Nashville: Broadman Press, 1975.

Cumming, John (1807-1881) A Scottish evangelical minister. From 1832 until late in his life, Cumming served as pastor of the National Scottish Church at Covent Garden, London. His popular style and anti-Catholic, anti-papal preaching created a measure of controversy, and with it, larger and larger crowds. Of his two hundred publications, his ones on prophetic themes were the most widely read, both in Britain and the United States.

-----*Apocalyptic Sketches: or, Lectures on the Seven Churches of Asia Minor.* London: Arthur Hall, Virtue & Co., 1851.

-----*The Destiny of Nations as Indicated in Prophecy.* London: Hurst and Blackett, 1864.

-----*The End: or The Proximate Signs of the Close of This Dispensation.* Boston: John P. Jewett, 1855.

-----*God in History.* New York: Lane and Scott, 1852.

-----*The Great Consummation: The Millennial Rest, or the World as it Will Be.* New York: Carleton, 1863.

-----*The Great Preparation: or Redemption Draweth Nigh.* New York: Rudd & Carleton, 1861.

-----*The Great Tribulation: or The Things Coming on the Earth.* New York: Rudd & Carleton, 1860.

-----*The Last Warning Cry: With Reasons for the Hope that is in Me.* New York: G.W. Carleton, 1867.

-----*Prophetic Studies: Lectures on the Book of Daniel.* Philadelphia: Lindsay and Blakiston, 1854.

-----*Signs of the Times: or The Present, Past, and Future.* Philadelphia: Lindsay and Blakiston, 1855.

-----*The Soundings of the Last Trumpet: or The Last Woe.* London: James Nisbet, 1867.

Darby, John Nelson (1800-1882) A Minister and leader of the Plymouth Brethren. Early in life, Darby became interested in prophecy and developed a dispensational theology of the Christian Scriptures. Beginning in the 1830s, Darby began traveling throughout the British

Isles, spreading his dispensational views. His lectures and writings gained some adherents as well as some converts to the separated Plymouth Brethren, of which Darby was a leader. His successes were short-lived, however, as disagreement over his doctrine of the secret rapture -- the removal of the saints from the earth before the Tribulation period -- and other positions led to a rift among the Plymouth Brethren in 1845. He traveled to America on six separate occasions, 1862-1877, winning many devoted disciples, including James H. Brookes. Darby was also a tireless exponent of ecclesiastical separatism.

-----*Collected Writings*, 34 vols and index. (William Kelly, ed.). London: G. Morrish, 1934.

-----*The Hopes of the Church of God, in Connection with the Destiny of the Jews and the Nations as Revealed in Prophecy: Eleven Lectures Delivered in Geneva, 1840* (new ed., rev.). London: Morrish, n.d.

-----*Lectures on the Second Coming.* London: G. Morrish, 1909.

-----*Notes on the Apocalypse.* London: G. Morrish, n.d.

-----*Notes on the Book of the Revelation.* London: W. H. Broom, 1876.

-----*The Restoration of the Jewish Nation (Matt. 24, 25).* London: Morrish, n.d.

-----*Will the Saints Be in the Tribulation?* New York: Loizeaux Brothers, n.d.

DeHaan, M. R. (1891-1965) Independent fundamentalist minister and radio preacher. DeHaan studied medicine at the University of Illinois at Chicago, graduating as class valedictorian in 1914. Seven years later, while convalescing after a near-fatal medical accident, DeHaan had a conversion experience. He then sold his practice and attended Western Theological Seminary, graduating in 1925. In 1929, DeHaan left the Reformed Church in America and became an independent fundamentalist minister. A heart attack and disagreement with his parishioners led to DeHaan's resignation from pastoral ministry in 1938. In 1941, he founded the Radio Bible Class of the Air in Grand Rapids, MI, a program that expanded nationally over the next two decades. At his death in 1965, DeHaan's son, Richard, took over the broadcast ministry.

-----*The Atomic Bomb in Prophecy: An Examination of Scripture Passages Dealing with the Devastation of the Earth in the Day of the Lord. Will It Be by Atomic Explosions?* Grand Rapids, MI: The Radio Bible Class, n.d.

-----*The Church and the Tribulation?: A Scriptural Answer to the Teachings of the Post-tribulation and Mid-tribulation Rapture.* Grand Rapids, MI: The Radio Bible Class, n.d.

-----*The Church, the Rapture, and the Tribulation: The Scriptural Answer to the Question, "Will the Church Pass Through or Be Raptured Before the Tribulation?"* Grand Rapids, MI: The Radio Bible Class, n.d.

-----*Coming Events in Prophecy.* Grand Rapids, MI: Zondervan Publishing House, 1962.

-----*The Coming Golden Age: A Study of Bible Prophecies Dealing with the Restoration of the Earth at the Coming of Christ.* Grand Rapids, MI: The Radio Bible Class of the Air, n.d.

-----*Daniel the Prophet; or 35 Simple Studies in the Book of Daniel.* Grand Rapids, MI: Zondervan Publishing Co., 1947.

-----*The Days of Noah, and Their Prophetic Message for Today.* Grand Rapids, MI: Zondervan Publishing Co., 1963.

-----*The First Rapture: A Study of the Life and Translation of Enoch as Recorded in Genesis 5, Hebrews 11, and Jude 14-15.* Grand Rapids, MI: The Radio Bible Class, n.d.

-----*God's Miracle Nation: A Review of Some of the Bible Prophecies Concerning the Miraculous Preservation of Israel, with Emphasis on Their Return to Palestine.* Grand Rapids, MI: The Radio Bible Class, n.d.

-----*The Jew and Palestine in Prophecy.* Grand Rapids, MI: The Radio Bible Class of the Air, 1950; Grand Rapids, MI: Zondervan Publishing House, 1950.

-----*One Thousand Years of Peace on Earth: A Series of Four Messages on the Future Reign of Christ on Earth.* Grand Rapids, MI: The Radio Bible Class, n.d.

-----*Palestine and the Middle East in Prophecy: Five Radio Sermons.* Grand Rapids, MI: The Radio Bible Class, n.d.

-----*Palestine in History and in Prophecy: Five Expository Messages on the Scriptural Teaching of the Land of Palestine and the Future of the Nation of Israel.* Grand Rapids, MI: The Radio Bible Class, n.d.

-----*The Rapture of the Church: Four Sermons.* Grand Rapids, MI: The Radio Bible Class, n.d.

-----*The Return of the King, Revelation 22:20: A Bible Study Concerning the Certainty, Imminence, and Results of that Blessed Hope of Christ's Return.* Grand Rapids, MI: The Radio Bible Class, n.d.

-----*Revelation.* Grand Rapids, MI: The Radio Bible Class of the Air., n.d.

-----*Revelation: 35 Simple Studies on the Major Themes in Revelation* (4th ed.). Grand Rapids, MI: Zondervan Publishing House, 1946.

-----*Russia and the Final War: An Exposition of Prophecies of Ezekiel 38 and 39 Concerning the Fate of Russia in the Latter Days.* Grand Rapids, MI: The Radio Bible Class of the Air, n.d.

-----*The Second Coming of Elijah: A Scriptural Comparison of the Ministries of John the Baptist and the Prophet Elijah in Relation to the First and Second Coming of Christ.* Grand Rapids, MI: The Radio Bible Class, n.d.

-----*The Second Coming of Jesus.* Grand Rapids, MI: The Radio Bible Class of the Air, n.d.; Grand Rapids, MI: Zondervan Publishing House, 1944.

-----*The Secret Rapture and the Secret of the Rapture: A Simple Study of the Scripture Teaching of "That Blessed Hope"*. Grand Rapids, MI: The Radio Bible Class, n.d.

-----*Signs of the Times*. Grand Rapids, MI: The Radio Bible Class of the Air., n.d.

-----*Signs of the Times and Other Prophetic Messages*. Grand Rapids, MI: Zondervan, 1951.

-----*The Time of Christ's Return; It is Later Than You Think: A Study of Some of the Signs of the Soon Return of Christ*. Grand Rapids, MI: The Radio Bible Class, n.d.

-----*The United Nations in History and Prophecy: The Prophetic Significance of the Kingdom of Nimrod and the Tower of Babel*. Grand Rapids, MI: The Radio Bible Class, n.d.

-----*Who Owns Palestine?: Five Messages*. Grand Rapids, MI: The Radio Bible Class, n.d.

-----*Will the Church Go Through the Tribulation?* Grand Rapids, MI: The Radio Bible Class, 1967.

Dixon, A. C. (1854-1925) A Baptist minister. A militant fundamentalist, Dixon crusaded against liquor and liberals. In 1893, Dixon joined D. L. Moody in Chicago to preach against the World's Parliament of Religions. Dixon later became minister of the Moody Church, serving from 1906 to 1911. While in Los Angeles for a conference, Dixon met Lyman Stewart, a wealthy oilman, and secured funding for the publication and distribution of *The Fundamentals: A Testimony to the Truth* (1910-1915), which Dixon edited, together with Reuben Torrey of BIOLA.

-----, et al. *Advent Testimony Addresses*. London: C. J. Thynne, 1918.

----- (ed.). *The Fundamentals: A Testimony to the Truth* (12 vols.). Los Angeles: BIOLA, 1917.

Drummond, Henry (1786-1860) Drummond was born in England and
educated at Oxford. He was among the first English clergy members and
lay leaders in Britain to study prophecy. Beginning in 1826, Drummond
hosted prophetic meetings at his estate, known as the Albury prophetic
conferences. His *Dialogues on Prophecy* (1827-1829) were his
impressionistic record of the first series of these meetings. The Albury
conferences were forerunners to the Niagara and Northfield conferences,
which adopted similar conference formats and expositional styles.
Originally an Anglican, Drummond left the Church of England in 1831
to join Edward Irving in founding the Catholic Apostlic Church
(Irvingite).

-----*A Defense of the Students of Prophecy.* London: James Nisbet,
1828.

-----(ed.). *Dialogues on Prophecy* (3 vols). London: James Nisbet,
1827-1829.

Drummond, Henry (1851-1897) A member of the Free Presbyterian
Church, Scotland. Drummond traveled widely and was for a time
associated with D. L. Moody and the Northfield conference, 1887.
However, his mild defense of the evolutionary process in *Natural Law
in the Spiritual World* (1883) and especially in *Ascent of Man* (1894),
created a stir among fundamentalists, however, who came to regard him
as an enemy of Bible truth.

-----*The City Without a Church.* New York: James Pott, 1893.

Epp, Theodore (1907-1985) A Mennonite minister and religious
broadcaster. Epp studied for a time at the Bible Institute of Los Angeles
and Southwestern Baptist Theological Seminary. From 1932 to 1936,
Epp pastored a Mennonite church in Oklahoma. From 1936 to 1938, he
worked in Kansas starting new churches. In 1939, Epp moved to
Lincoln, Nebraska, and began his "Back to the Bible" radio broadcasts.
His radio ministry soon gained widespread appeal, at one time airing
over 600 stations. Epp was also a founder of the National Religious
Broadcaster, 1944, an organization formed to coordinate programming
and set broadcasting standards for this booming parachurch industry.

-----*Brief Outlines of Things to Come.* Chicago: Moody Press (Colportage Library, vol. 68), 1952.

-----*God's Program for Israel.* Lincoln, NE: Back to the Bible Correspondence School, 1976.

-----*God's Program for Israel: A Compact Do-It-Yourself Course.* Lincoln, NE: Back to the Bible Publications, 1962.

-----*Practical Studies in Revelation.* Lincoln, NE: Back to the Bible Publications, 1969.

-----*The Rise and Fall of Gentile Nations.* Lincoln, NE: Back to the Bible Publications, 1956.

-----*Russia's Doom Prophesied in Ezekiel 38 and 39.* Lincoln, NE: Back to the Bible Publications, 1959.

-----*The Third Temple.* Lincoln, NE: Back to the Bible Broadcast, 1985.

-----*Why Must Jesus Come Again?* Lincoln, NE: Back to the Bible Publications, 1960.

Erdman, Charles R. (1866-1960) A Presbyterian minister and educator. From 1890-1905, Erdman served churches in Pennsylvania. He became a professor of practical theology at Princeton Seminary in 1905, a post he held until his retirement. In 1925, at the height of the Modernist controversy, Erdman, a moderate fundamentalist, was moderator of the General Assembly. He was among only a handful of conservatives who gained the respect of both liberals and fundamentalists during this bitter conflict. Erdman was also president of the Presbyterian Board of Foreign Missions, 1928-1940.

-----*The Return of Christ.* New York: George H. Doran Co., 1922.

Erdman, William J. (1834-1923) A Presbyterian minister and an army chaplain during the Civil War. He was an itinerant evangelist from 1888-1920 and a Niagara Prophecy Conference participant. He was minister of Moody's Chicago Avenue Church, 1875-1878, and was one of the founders of the Moody Bible Institute, 1889. Erdman was also one of the consulting editors of *The Scofield Reference Bible* (1909).

----- *The Parousia of Christ, a Period of Time: or When Will the Church be Translated?* Illinois: Gospel Publishing Co., n.d.

-----*The Return of Christ.* Germantown, PA: n.p., 1913.

Evans, William (1870-1950) A Presbyterian minister and conference speaker. Born in England, Evans attended the Moody Bible Institute, becoming its first graduate in 1892. He received degrees from the Chicago Lutheran Seminary and later from Chicago Theological Seminary. He directed the Moody Bible Correspondence courses for nearly fifteen years before becoming dean of the Bible Institute of Los Angeles in 1915. After 1918, Evans became an itinerant Bible teacher, directing Bible conferences throughout the United States and Canada until his death in 1950 .

-----*Christ's Last Message to His Church: An Exposition of the Seven Letters of Revelation I-III.* New York: Fleming H. Revell, 1926.

-----*The Coming King: The World's Next Great Crisis.* New York: Fleming H. Revell Co., 1923.

Faber, George S. (1773-1843) A minister in the Church of England. Faber was among the first of the English divines to revive interest in the study of prophecy and the Last Days.

-----*A Dissertation on the Prophecies that have been Fulfilled, Are Now Fulfilling, or will Hereafter be Fulfilled, Relative to the Great Period of 1260 Years; the Papal and Mohammedan Apostasies; the Tyrannical Reign of Anti-Christ..; and the Restoration of the Jews* (2 vols., 2nd American ed.). New York: Duckinck & Ward 1811.

-----*Eight Dissertations on Certain Connected Prophetical Passages of Holy Scripture: Bearing, More or Less, Upon the Promise of a Mighty Deliverer.* London: Seeley, Burnside and Seeley, 1845.

-----*A General and Connected View of Prophecies Relative to the Conversion, Restoration, Union and Future Glory, of the House of*

Judah and Israel: The Progress and Final Overthrow, or the Antichristian Confederacy in the Land of Palestine; and the Ultimate Diffusion of Christianity (2nd ed., rev. and corrected). London: F. C. and J. Rivington, 1809.

-----*Napoleon III, the Man of Prophecy; or The Revival of the French Emperorship Anticipated from the Necessity of Prophecy.* New York: D. Appleton, 1859.

-----*The Sacred Calendar of Prophecy: or A Dissertation on the Prophecies which treat of the Grand Period of Seven Times, and especially of its Second Moiety, or the Latter Three Times and a Half.* London: C. & J. Rivington, 1828.

Falwell, Jerry (b. 1933) A fundamentalist Baptist minister and televangelist. Falwell was born a twin in Lynchburg, VA. Through the influence of the radio ministry of Charles E. Fuller, Falwell converted to Christianity in 1952. After his conversion, Falwell attended the Baptist Bible College in Springfield, MO, 1952-1956. Returning to his hometown of Lynchburg, Falwell founded the Thomas Road Baptist Church. With his church's membership growing, Falwell expanded his ministry to include radio and television. In 1971, Falwell founded Liberty Baptist College. By the 1980s, the membership of the Thomas Road Baptist Church had grown to nearly 20,000. In 1979, Falwell founded the Moral Majority, an organization that opposed civil rights legislation, abortion rights, and the teaching of evolution in the public schools. The Moral Majority sought to replace courses in biological evolution and sex education with prayer and Bible reading. Falwell resigned from the leadership of the Moral Majority in 1987 to devote more time to his church's ministries. The Moral Majority was dissolved in 1989.

-----*Nuclear War and the Second Coming of Jesus.* Lynchburg, VA: The Old Time Gospel Hour, 1983.

Feinberg, Charles L. (b. 1909) A Cumberland Presbyterian minister. Professor at Dallas Theological Seminary, 1934-1948, and Old Testament professor and dean at Talbot Seminary at Biola College from 1948 until his retirement.

-----*A Commentary on Revelation: The Grand Finale.* Winona Lake, IN: BMH Books, 1985.

-----(ed.). *Focus on Prophecy: Messages Delivered at the Congress on Prophecy...in Chicago.* Westwood, NJ: Fleming H. Revell Co., 1964.

-----*Isaac and Ishmael: Twentieth Century Version.* New York: American Board of Missions to the Jews, n.d.

-----*Israel at the Center of History and Revelation* (3rd ed.). Portland, OR: Multnomah Press, 1980.

-----*Israel in the Last Days: The Olivet Discourse.* Altadena, CA: Emeth Publications, 1953.

-----*Israel in the Spotlight.* Chicago: Scripture Press, 1956; New York: American Board of Missions to the Jews, 1964; (rev. ed.). Chicago: Moody Press, 1975.

-----(ed.). *Jesus the King is Coming.* Chicago: Moody Press, 1975.

-----*Millennialism, the Two Major Views: The Premillennial and Amillennial Systems of Biblical Interpretation Analyzed and Compared* (3rd ed., enlarged). Chicago: Moody Press, 1980.

-----*Premillennialism or Amillennialism?* (2nd ed., enlarged). Wheaton, IL: Van Kampen Press, 1954.

-----*Premillennialism or Amillennialism?: The Premillennial and Amillennial Systems of Interpretation Analyzed and Compared.* Grand Rapids, MI: Zondervan Publishing House, 1936.

-----(ed.). *Prophecy and the Seventies.* Chicago: Moody Press, 1971.

-----(ed.). *Prophetic Truth Unfolding Today (Messages from the Fifth Congress on Prophecy).* Fleming H. Revell Co.

-----*The Suez Canal in the Light of Prophecy.* Los Angeles: Bible Institute of Los Angeles, 1956.

Frost, Henry W. (1858-1945) A Presbyterian minister and missionary. Frost was graduated from Princeton University, 1880. After a brief career in the oil industry, Frost established the Overseas Missionary Fellowship, the American branch of the China Inland Mission, 1889. Frost served as its first secretary, 1889-1893, and as its coordinating director in Philadelphia, 1893-1919. He was ordained a Presbyterian minister, 1904. A prolific author, Frost was a popular speaker at Bible and Prophecy conferences throughout the United States. He was also one of the contributors to *The Fundamentals* (1910-1915), the multi-volume statement on Protestant fundamentalism.

-----*Matthew Twenty-Four and the Revelation*. New York: Oxford University Press, 1924.

-----*The Second Coming of Christ*. Grand Rapids, MI: Wm B. Eerdmans Publishing Co., 1934.

Gaebelein, Arno C. (1861-1945) A Methodist minister and German immigrant. Gaebelein was director of Hope of Israel Mission, 1894-1899, an organization that supported Christian missionary activity among the Jews. A prolific writer, Gaebelein authored over forty books and was editor of *Our Hope* magazine from 1894 until his death in 1945.

-----*As it Was -- So Shall it Be*. New York: Our Hope Publication Office, 1937.

-----*The Conflict of the Ages: The Mystery of Lawlessness, Its Origin, Historic Development and Coming Defeat*. New York: Our Hope; London: Pickering & Inglis, 1933.

-----*Fulfilled Prophecy: A Potent Argument for the Inspiration of the Bible*. New York: Our Hope Publication Office, n.d.

-----*The Harmony of the Prophetic Word: A Key to Old Testament Prophecy Concerning Things to Come*. New York: Fleming H. Revell, 1907.

-----*Hath God Cast Away His People?* New York: Gospel Publishing House, 1905.

-----*The History of the Scofield Reference Bible.* New York: Our Hope Publishing Co., 1943.

-----*The Hope of the Ages: The Messianic Hope in Revelation, in History, and in Realization.* New York: Our Hope Publication Office, 1938.

-----*Hopeless -- Yet There is Hope: A Study in World Conditions and Their Solution.* New York: Our Hope Publication Office; London: Pickering & Inglis, 1935.

----- *If Christ Should Return -- What?* New York: Our Hope, n.d.

-----*The Jewish Question.* New York: Our Hope, 1912.

-----*The League of Nations in the Light of Prophecy.* New York: Our Hope Publication Office, 1920.

-----*Maranatha Bells: The Blessed Hope in Prose and Poetry.* New York: Arno Gaebelein, Inc., 1935.

-----*Meat in Due Season: Sermons, Discourses and Expositions of the Word of Prophecy.* New York: A. C. Gaebelein, Inc., n.d.; New York: Our Hope Publication Office, 1933.

-----*Our Age and Its End* [bound with C. I. Scofield's *Lectures on Prophecy*]. New York: Our Hope, n.d.

-----*The Prophet Daniel: A Key to the Visions and Prophecies of the Book of Daniel.* Los Angeles: Bible House of Los Angeles, 1911.

-----*The Prophet Ezekiel.* New York: Our Hope Publication Office, 1918.

-----*The Return of the Lord: What the New Testament Teaches About the Second Coming of Christ.* New York: Our Hope Publication Office 1925.

-----*The Revelation.* New York: Loizeaux Brothers, n.d.

-----*Studies in Prophecy*. New York: Our Hope Publication Office, 1918.

----- *"Things to Come."* New York: Our Hope Publication Office, n.d.

-----*The Unfinished Symphony*. New York: Our Hope, n.d.

----- *Will There be a Millennium? When and How?: The Coming Reign of Christ in the Light of the Old and New Testaments*. New York: Our Hope Publication Office, 1943.

-----*What Will Become of Europe?: World Darkness and Divine Light*. New York: Our Hope, 1940.

-----*World Prospects; How Is It All Going to End? A Study in Sacred Prophecy and Present Day World Conditions*. New York: Our Hope; London: Pickering & Inglis, 1934.

-----*The Work of Christ: Past, Present and Future*. New York: Our Hope Publication Office, 1913.

Gartenhaus, Jacob (1896-1984) A Jewish Christian evangelist. After converting to Christianity in 1916, Gartenhaus attended the Moody Bible Institute and the Southern Baptist Seminary in Louisville, KY. In 1921, Gartenhaus was appointed by the Home Missions Board of the Southern Baptist Church to its Jewish department, serving until it was dissolved in 1949. In 1951, Gartenhaus and his wife, Lillian (1903-1992), founded the International Board of Jewish Missions, an organization that promotes Jewish missions among the churches. During his long ministry, Gartenhaus placed special emphasis on the Second Coming of Christ, a theme promoted through publication of a number of tracts, booklets, and through his organization's news letter, *The Everlasting Nation*. An early work by Gartenhaus, *Winning Jews to Christ*, was well received by evangelical Protestants, quickly becoming a standard text in the field of Jewish evangelization.

-----*The Jew and Jesus Christ*. Nashville: Southern Baptist Convention, 1934.

-----*The Rebirth of a Nation: Zionism in History and Prophecy.* Nashville: Broadman Press, 1936.

-----*What of the Jews?* Atlanta: Home Mission Board of the Southern Baptist Convention, 1948.

Gilbert, Dan (1911-1962) A Baptist minister. Gilbert was sometime secretary of the World's Christian Fundamentals Association. He was also a noted conference speaker and the author of a number of books, many of which focused on endtimes themes.

-----*The Mark of the Beast.* Washington, D. C.: Pub. by author, 1951.

-----*The Red Terror and Bible Prophecy.* Washington, D. C.: The Christian Press Bureau, 1944.

-----*What Will Become of Germany in the Light of Bible Prophecy?* Los Angeles: The Jewish Hope Publishing Co., 1945.

-----*Who Will Be the Antichrist?* Washington, D. C.: The Christian Press Bureau, 1945.

-----*Will Russia Fight America?: The Question Considered in the Light of Bible Prophecy.* Los Angeles: The Jewish Hope Publishing Co., n.d.

Gordon, Adoniram Judson (1836-1895) A Baptist minister. Gordon served as member and then chair of the executive committee of the American Baptist Missionary Board, 1871-1894. Spurred by his premillennial beliefs, Gordon founded the Boston Missionary Training School (later Gordon College and Divinity School), 1889. Gordon was long associated with D. L. Moody, holding joint meetings and participating at summer conferences with him. Gordon was also one of the founders of the early prophetic conference movement, attending the Niagara Bible conferences and the American Bible and Prophetic conference. He was also editor of *Watchword* from 1878 until his death in 1895.

-----*Ecce Venit: Behold He Cometh.* New York: Fleming H. Revell, 1889.

Graham, Billy (b. 1918) A Baptist. Graham is perhaps the best-known and most widely traveled evangelist of the twentieth century. At the death of William Bell Riley, Graham became president of Northwestern Schools, 1947-1951. After successful evangelistic crusades in Los Angeles and New York in the late 1940s, he founded the Billy Graham Crusades (later Billy Graham Ministries). Graham remains moderate in his views on Bible prophecy and the endtimes, as witnessed by his books on the subject, *Till Armageddon* (1981) and *Approaching Hoofbeats* (1983). The evangelistic messages of his earliest crusades, however, give evidence of his earlier dispensational premillennial convictions.

-----*Approaching Hoofbeats: The Four Horsemen of the Apocalypse.* Waco, TX: Word Books, 1983.

-----*Till Armageddon.* Waco, TX: Word Books, 1981.

-----*World Aflame.* New York: Doubleday & Co., 1965.

Grant, F. W. (1834-1902) A Plymouth Brethren leader. While serving as a priest in the Church of Canada, Grant was won over to the Brethren through their literature in the 1860s. Moving to Plainfield, NJ, Grant became an author and lecturer. Differences with the exclusive ecclesiology of John Nelson Darby led to Grant's dismissal from the Plymouth Brethren in 1884. With the help of the Loizeaux brothers, who published materials sympathetic to dispensational eschatology, Grant formed his own group. His most influential work was *The Numerical Bible*, which posited the existence of replicating numerical patterns in the Bible, for instance, repeating uses of the numbers "seven" and "twelve" in the Old and New Testaments.

-----*The Hope of the Morning Star; with a Review of Objections to an Immediate Expectation of the Coming of the Lord and the Taking Away of the Saints to Meet Him Before the Closing Tribulation.* New York: Loizeaux Brothers, n.d.

-----*Lessons of the Ages.* New York: Loizeaux Brothers, n.d.

-----*The Numerical Bible.* New York: Loizeaux Brothers, n.d.

-----*The Numerical Structure of Scripture.* New York: Loizeaux Brothers, n.d.; Swengel, PA: Bible Truth Depot, 1887.

-----*The Prophetic History of the Church.* New York: Loizeaux Brothers, 1902.

-----*The Revelation of Christ.* New York: Loizeaux Brothers, n.d.

Gray, James M. (1851-1935) A minister of the Protestant Episcopal Church and an independent evangelist. Gray was dean and president of the Moody Bible Institute from 1904 until his retirement in 1934. A leading fundamentalist spokesperson and dispensational writer, Gray was a frequent participant at prophecy conferences. He was also one of the consulting editors of *The Scofield Reference Bible* (1909), and a contributor to *The Fundamentals* (1910-1915).

-----*The Audacity of Unbelief, and Other Papers.* Chicago: The Bible Institute Colportage Association, n.d.

-----*Great Epochs of Sacred History, and The Shadows They Cast.* Chicago: The Bible Institute Colportage Association, 1910.

-----, et al. *How I Came to Believe in Our Lord's Return and Why I Believe the Lord's Return is Near.* Chicago: Bible Institute Colportage Association, 1935.

-----*My Faith in Jesus Christ.* Chicago: Bible Institute Colportage Association, 1927.

-----*The Present Darkness and the Coming Light.* Chicago: The Bible Institute Colportage Association, n.d.

-----*Prophecy and the Lord's Return: A Collection of Popular Articles and Addresses.* New York: Fleming H. Revell, 1917.

-----*Satan and the Saints; or The Present Darkness and the Coming Light.* New York: Fleming H. Revell Co., 1909; Edinburgh: Oliphant, Anderson and Ferrier, n.d.

-----*The Second Coming of Christ; The Meaning, Period, and Order of Events [and] How I Came to Believe in the Lord's Return.* Chicago: The Bible Institute Colportage Association, n.d.

-----*Studying the Second Coming for Yourself* (Christian Faith Series # 6). Chicago: The Bible Institute Colportage Association, n.d.

----- *A Text-Book on Prophecy.* New York: Fleming H. Revell Co., 1918.

Greene, Oliver B. (b. 1915) A Baptist evangelist. After twenty-five years as a tent preacher, Greene turned to radio. His program, "The Gospel Hour," is heard nationwide.

-----*Bible Prophecy.* Greenville, SC: The Gospel Hour, Inc., 1970.

-----*The Second Coming of Jesus.* Greenville, SC: The Gospel Hour, Inc., 1971.

----- *Second Coming Truth.* Greenville, SC: The Gospel Hour, Inc., 1973.

Guinness, H. Grattan (1835-1910) An English layman and supporter of foreign missions. He founded and directed the East London Institute for Home and Foreign Missions, 1873-1910, an organization that trained thousands of missionaries throughout this period. He was also co-founder of the Livingston Inland Mission, 1880. Guinness was best known in the United States for his works on prophetic themes.

-----*The Approaching End of the Age, Viewed in the Light of History, Prophecy, and Science.* 1878; New York: A. C. Armstrong, 1881; London: Hodder & Stoughton, 1884; (rev. ed. by E. H. Horne). London: Marshall, Morgan & Scott, 1918.

-----*History Unveiling Prophecy; or Time as an Interpreter.* New York: Fleming H. Revell, 1905.

-----*Key to the Apocalypse: or The Seven Interpretations of Symbolic Prophecy.* London: Hodder & Stoughton, 1899.

-----*The Last Hour of Gentile World Rule; Showing From the Word of God that the Sands Have Nearly All Run Out of the Hour-Glass of Gentile World Rule, etc.* Toronto: A. Sims, n.d.

-----*Romanism and the Reformation from the Standpoint of Prophecy.* A. C. Armstrong, 1887; Arnold Publishing Co., 1890.

-----, and Mrs. Guinness. *Light for the Last Days: A Study in Chronological Prophecy.* London: Marshall, Morgan & Scott, LTD, 1917 [1886].

Gundry, Robert H. (b. 1933?) A professor since 1962 at Westmont College in Santa Barbara. Gundry is one of the first major evangelical writers to hold the posttribulation rapture view since George E. Ladd had revived this view in the 1950s. His book, *The Church and the Tribulation* (1973), gave renewed credibility to the posttribulation rapture position among premillennial evangelicals.

-----*The Church and the Tribulation.* Grand Rapids, MI: Zondervan Publishing House, 1973.

-----*God in Control: An Exposition of the Prophecies of Daniel.* West Sussex: H. E. Walter, 1980.

Haldeman, I. M. (1845-1933) A Baptist minister. He was pastor of the First Baptist Church of New York City from 1884 until his death. During his long tenure, Haldeman established himself as one of America's premier pulpit ministers. A conservative, he disagreed strongly with fellow Baptists Harry Emerson Fosdick and Walter Rauschenbusch over social and theological issues. Because of his enormous output of books and articles on prophecy and related themes, Haldeman was called "the dispensationalist pastor" by those who admired him.

-----*The Coming of Christ, Both Pre-Millennial and Imminent.* New York: C. C. Cook, 1906.

-----*The Coming of Christ: Is the Millennium to Come Before Christ?* New York: Pub. by author, n.d.

-----*The Coming of Christ: The Two-fold Coming and the Immediacy.* New York: Pub. by author, n.d.

-----*A Dispensational Key to the Holy Scriptures.* Philadelphia: Philadelphia School of the Bible, 1915.

-----*The History of the Doctrine of Our Lord's Return.* New York: First Baptist Church, n.d.

-----*How to Study the Bible: The Second Coming and Other Expositions.* New York: C. C. Cook, 1904.

-----*Is the Coming of Christ Before or After the Millennium?* New York: C. C. Cook, 1917.

-----*The Judgment Seat of Christ.* New York: C. C. Cook, 1917.

-----*The Kingdom of God: What Is It? -- When Is It? -- Where Is It?* New York: C. C. Cook, 1931.

-----*Professor Shailer Mathews's Burlesque on the Second Coming.* New York: Pub. by author, 1918.

-----*A Review of Mr. Philip Mauro's Book "The Gospel of the Kingdom": A Defence of Dispensational Truth and the Scofield Bible.* New York: F. E. Fitch, 1931.

-----*The Second Coming of Christ: In Relation to Doctrine, to Promise, and to Exhortation.* New York: Charles C. Cook, 1917.

-----*The Signs of the Times.* Philadelphia: Philadelphia School of the Bible, 1919 [1910].

-----*Ten Sermons on the Second Coming.* New York: Fleming H. Revell, Co., 1916; (2nd ed.). Philadelphia: Philadelphia School of the Bible, 1917.

-----*This Hour Not the Hour of Peace.* New York: Charles C. Cook, 1915.

-----*The Thousand Years and After.* New York: Charles C. Cook, 1917.

-----*Why I Preach the Second Coming.* New York: Fleming H. Revell, Co., 1919.

Hubbard, David A. (b. 1928) An American Baptist minister. Professor at Westmont College, 1957-1963, and president of Fuller Seminary since 1963. Hubbard plans to retire as president of Fuller in 1993.

-----*The Second Coming: What Will Happen When Jesus Returns?* Downers Grove, IL: InterVarsity Press, 1984.

Ironside, Harry A. (1876-1951) A minister of the Plymouth Brethren Churches. From his conversion at age fourteen until he was twenty, Ironside preached for the Salvation Army and was soon nicknamed "the boy preacher from Los Angeles." After joining the Plymouth Brethren in 1896, Ironside was for 34 years a Bible conference speaker and itinerant preacher. He was a visiting professor at Dallas Theological Seminary, 1925-1943 and pastor of the Moody Memorial Church, 1930-1948. A prolific writer, he authored over 60 works, including Bible commentaries, many of which remain in print.

-----*Expository Notes on Ezekiel the Prophet.* New York: Loizeaux Brothers, 1949.

-----*Four Golden Hours at Kingsway Hall, London.* London: Marshall, Morgan & Scott, LTD, 1939.

-----*The Great Parenthesis: Timely Messages on the Interval Between the 69th and 70th Weeks of Daniel's Prophecy.* Grand Rapids, MI: Zondervan Publishing House, 1943.

-----*The Lamp of Prophecy: or, Signs of the Times.* Grand Rapids, MI: Zondervan Publishing House, 1940.

-----*Lectures on Daniel the Prophet.* New York: Loizeaux Brothers, n.d.

-----*Lectures on the Revelation.* New York: Loizeaux Brothers, n.d.

-----*Looking Backward Over a Third of a Century of Prophetic Fulfilment.* New York: Loizeaux Brothers, n.d.

-----*The Midnight Cry!* Western Book and Tract Co., n.d.; New York: Loizeaux Brothers, 1928.

-----*The Mysteries of God.* New York: Loizeaux Brothers, n.d.

-----*Not Wrath, But Rapture: or Will the Church Participate in the Great Tribulation?* New York: Loizeaux Brothers, n.d.

-----*Setting the Stage for the Last Act of the Great World Drama.* New York: Loizeaux Brothers, n.d.

-----*Wrongly Dividing the Word of Truth: Ultra-dispensationalism Examined in the Light of Holy Scripture* (3rd ed.). Oakland, CA: Western Book & Tract, 1938.

-----, and F. C. Ottman. *Studies in Biblical Prophecy.* Minneapolis, MN: Klock & Klock, 1983.

Kellogg, Samuel H. (1839-1899) A Presbyterian minister and missionary to India. Kellogg attended Williams College, 1856, and graduated from Princeton University, 1861, and Princeton Seminary, 1864. From 1864-1876, Kellogg was a missionary to India, teaching at the Theological School in Allahabad. He published a grammar of the Hindi language, 1875. The death of his wife prompted Kellogg's return to the States in 1876. He was a professor at Western Seminary in Allegheny, PA, 1877-1885. He served a pastorate in Toronto, 1886-1892, after which he returned to India in 1892, where he died in 1899. During his fifteen-year furlough from missionary work, Kellogg became well-known among dispensational premillennialists, becoming both a leader as well as a regular speaker at the Niagara Bible Conferences.

-----*An Abridgement of The Jews; or Prediction and Fulfillment, an Argument for the Times. With a Supplementary Chapter by Henry S. Nesbitt.* Madras: Milton Stewart Evangelistic Funds, 1927.

-----*A-millennialism; How Does It Differ from Premillennial Views?:*
A Fresh Examination of Prophecy as it Bears Upon the A-millennial
Position. Los Angeles: American Prophetic League, 1939.

-----*Are Premillennialists Right?* (new ed.). New York: Fleming H.
Revell Co., 1923.

-----*The Jews: or, Prediction and Fulfillment, an Argument for the*
Times. New York: Anson D. F. Randolph & Co., 1883.

Kelly, William (1821-1906) A Plymouth Brethren minister. Kelly was
graduated from Trinity College, Dublin. He was a protegé of John
Nelson Darby, editing the latter's collected works. Kelly was also editor
of *Bible Treasury,* 1856-1906.

-----*Babylon and the Beast.* London: W. H. Broom, n.d.

-----*Christ's Coming Again, Chiefly on the Heavenly Side.* London: T.
Weston, 1904.

-----*The Coming of the Lord* (new ed.). London: F. E. Race, 1919.

-----*The Day of the Lord: 2 Thess. ii. 1,2* (new ed.). London: F. E.
Race, 1919.

-----*Elements of Prophecy.* London: G. Morrish, 1876.

-----*Lectures on the Second Coming and Kingdom of the Lord and*
Savior Jesus Christ. London: W. H. Broom, n.d.

-----*Lectures on the Second Coming of the Lord Jesus Christ.* London:
G. Morrish, n.d.; London: W. H. Broom, n.d.

-----*The Lord's Prophecy on Olivet in Matthew 24 and 25.* London: T.
Weston, 1903.

-----*Notes on Daniel.* New York: Loizeaux Brothers, n.d.

-----*Notes on Ezekiel.* London: G. Morrish, n.d.

-----*The Prospects of the World According to the Scriptures* (new ed.). London: Hammond, 1946.

-----*The Revelation Expounded.* London: F. E. Race, n.d.

-----*The So-Called Apostolic Fathers on the Lord's Second Coming.* London: T. Weston, 1904.

-----*Three Prophetic Gems.* Charlotte, NC: Books for Christians, 1970. [combines in one volume: *The Lord's Prophecy on Olivet*; *The Coming and the Day of the Lord* ; and *The Heavenly Hope*]

Ladd, George E. (1911-1982) A Baptist minister and educator. Ladd took degrees from Gordon College, Gordon Divinity School, and Harvard. From 1950 until his death in 1982, Ladd was a professor of New Testament at Fuller Seminary. He is best known for his critical scholarship on the Kingdom of God and his post-tribulation rapture premillennial views.

-----*The Blessed Hope.* Grand Rapids, MI: Eerdmans, 1956.

-----*A Commentary on the Revelation of John.* Grand Rapids, MI: Eerdmans, 1972.

-----*Crucial Questions about the Kingdom of God.* Grand Rapids, MI: Wm B. Eerdmans Publishing Co., 1952.

-----*The Gospel of the Kingdom.* Grand Rapids, MI: Eerdmans, 1959.

-----*The Last Things: An Eschatology for Laymen.* Grand Rapids, MI: Eerdmans, 1978.

-----*The Presence of the Future.* Grand Rapids, MI: William B. Eerdmans Publishing Co., n.d.

LaHaye, Tim F. (b. 1926) A Baptist minister and conference speaker. After serving in the U. S. Air Force at the end of the Second World War, LaHaye attended Bob Jones University. In 1956, LaHaye moved to El Cajon, CA, where he served for twenty-five years as minister of

Scott Memorial Baptist Church. Soon after they arrival in El Cajon, LaHaye and his wife, Beverly, began a short-lived Christian television program. In 1965, the LaHayes founded the Christian High School of San Diego, which later grew to become the Christian Unified School District. With Henry Morris, LaHaye founded Heritage College, 1970, and was its president until 1976. LaHaye has written perhaps a dozen books, many of which blend Biblical injunction with popular psychology. In his *The Battle for the Mind* (1980), LaHaye popularized the term "secular humanism," a catch-phrase describing those humanistic (i.e., satanic) cultural forces that he believes have directly contributed to the moral decline of the United States.

-----*The Beginning of the End*. Wheaton, IL: Tyndale House Publisher, 1972.

-----*Revelation Illustrated and Made Plain*. Family Life Seminars Publications, n.d.; (rev. ed.). Grand Rapids, MI: Zondervan Publishing House, 1975.

Larkin, Clarence L. (1850-1924) A Baptist minister, engineer, and an ardent student of dispensationalism. During the First World War, Larkin designed a number of elaborate hand-drawn charts that presented the prophetic portions of the Bible as an unfolding drama of the last days. His charts quickly became popular for their great detail and stunning illustrations of the visionary beasts in Daniel and the Revelation. All four of his books listed below are currently in print.

-----*The Book of Daniel*. Philadelphia: Pub. by author, 1929.

-----*The Book of Revelation*. Philadelphia: Pub. by author, 1919.

-----*Dispensational Truth: or God's Plan and Purpose in the Ages* (rev. and enlarged ed.). Philadelphia: Pub. by author, 1920.

-----*The Second Coming of Christ* (3rd ed.). Philadelphia: Pub. by author, 1918; Philadelphia: Pub. by author, 1922.

Lindberg, Milton B. (1894-1986) Conference Speaker and Director of the Chicago Hebrew Mission. Lindberg was born in Grove City, MN. He earned degrees from Columbia University and the University of

Wisconsin, after which he spent some years teaching high school and college in Wisconsin, Minnesota, and Chicago. From 1926 to 1930, Lindberg served as a missionary to Lebanon. After returning to the United States, Lindberg spent the next eight years as a Bible conference speaker. In 1938, he became the assistant superintendent of the Chicago Hebrew Mission (later American Messianic Fellowship), an organization whose purpose is to convert Jews to Christianity. Lindberg became director of the Mission in 1940, serving in that position until 1959, when his wife's ill health made it necessary for Lindberg to retire.

-----*Gog all Agog "in the Latter Days": News From Russia and Palestine in the Light of Ezekiel 38 & 39.* Chicago: Hebrew Mission, 1938; Findlay, OH: Fundamental Truth Publishers, 1939.

-----*Is Ours the Closing Generation of the Age?* Chicago: Chicago Hebrew Mission (Faithful Word Publishing, St. Louis), 1938.

-----*Jacob's Trouble; A Nation in Distress: The Jewish Nation's Past, Present, and Future Foreshadowed in the Life Story of the Patriarch Jacob.* Chicago: American Messianic Fellowship, 1967, (1st ed., 1941).

-----*The Jews and Armageddon: All Nations to Gather Against Jerusalem.* Chicago: Chicago Hebrew Mission, 1940.

-----*The Jew and Modern Israel.* Chicago: Moody Press, 1969.

-----*A Modern Jonah on the Ship of Tarshish: Amazing Parallelism Between the Story of Jonah and the Prophetic Picture of End-time Events.* Chicago: Chicago Hebrew Mission, 1942.

-----*Palestine and the Jew Today in the Light of Prophecy.* Los Angeles, CA: A. J. Johnson, 1935.

-----*The State of Israel and the Jew Today in the Light of Prophecy.* Chicago: American Messianic Fellowship, 1968 (1st ed., 1930; previously titled *Palestine and the Jew*).

Lindsay, J. Gordon (1906-1973) An itinerant preacher, radio evangelist, and faith healer. Lindsay began his ministry at the age of eighteen, holding revival meetings in the Assemblies of God and other pentecostal churches. During the Second World War, Lindsay served as a pastor in Ashland, OR, resigning in 1947 to manage William Branham's revival meetings. In 1948, Lindsay published *The Voice of Healing* magazine to publicize the successes of Branham's meetings. When Branham retired in 1949, Lindsay stepped in. Later that year in Dallas, Lindsay's organization sponsored the first convention of faith healers, a forum which has been popular among pentecostal evangelists ever since. To reflect Lindsay's growing interest in foreign missions, The *Voice of Healing* magazine became *World-Wide Revival* in 1968, and then later, *Christ for the Nations* .

-----*The Antichrist and His Forerunner.* Dallas: Christ for the Nations, 1973

-----*The Antichrists Have Come!* Dallas: The Voice of Healing Publishing Co., 1958.

-----*Forty-eight Signs in the Land of Israel of the Soon Coming of Christ.* Dallas: The Voice of Healing Publishing Co., 1968.

-----*Forty Signs of the Soon Coming of Christ.* Dallas: World Wide Revival.

-----*The Great Tribulation.* Dallas: World Wide Revival.

-----*Present World Events in the Light of Prophecy.* Dallas: World Wide Revival.

-----*Thunder Over Palestine or The Holy Land in Prophecy.* Dallas: World Wide Revival., n.d.

-----*The World Today in Prophecy.* Dallas: World Wide Revival., n.d.

Lindsey, Hal (b. 1930) Popular author and conference speaker. After a failed marriage and thoughts of suicide, Lindsey was converted to Christianity through the reading of a Gideon New Testament. For some time afterwards, he studied the Bible on his own, refusing to associate with other Christians. In 1956, however, Lindsey attended a Bible Study group where he became convinced of the centrality of prophecy. He later enrolled for graduate study at Dallas Theological Seminary,

1958-1962. After graduation, Lindsey worked with Campus Crusade for Christ, 1962-1972, and then on his own at UCLA. In 1970, Lindsey published his bestselling work, *The Late Great Planet Earth*, an updated version of Scofield dispensationalism. By some estimates, *The Late Great Planet Earth* has sold over 15 million copies since its publication. A string of endtimes bestsellers followed as well as national appearances on radio and television. Currently, Lindsey hosts his own radio talk-show, oversees a Christian ministries foundation, and pastors the Palos Verdes Community Church in Los Angeles's Rolling Hills Estates.

-----*Combat Faith*. New York: Bantam Books, 1986.

-----*Homo Sapiens: Extinction or Evacuation?* Grand Rapids, MI: Zondervan Publishing House, 1971.

-----*The Late Great Planet Earth*. Grand Rapids, MI: Zondervan, 1970.

-----*The Liberation of Planet Earth*. Grand Rapids, MI: Zondervan, 1974.

-----*The 1980's: Countdown to Armageddon*. King of Prussia, PA: Westgate Press, Inc., 1980.

-----*The Promise*. Irvine, CA: Harvest House Publishers, 1974; Eugene, OR: Harvest House Publishers, 1982.

-----*A Prophetic Walk Through the Holy Land*. Eugene, OR: Harvest House Publishers, 1983.

-----*The Rapture: Truth or Consequences*. New York: Bantam Books, 1983.

-----*The Road to Holocaust*. New York: Bantam Books, 1989.

-----*Satan is Alive and Well on Planet Earth*. Grand Rapids, MI: Zondervan Publishing House, 1972.

-----*The Terminal Generation*. Old Tappan, NJ: Fleming H. Revell, 1976; New York: Bantam Books, 1976.

-----*There's a New World Coming: "A Prophetic Odyssey".* Santa Ana, CA: Vision House Publishers, 1973; (updated ed.). Eugene, OR: Harvest House Publishers, 1984.

-----*The World's Final Hour: Evacuation or Extinction?* Grand Rapids, MI: Zondervan, 1976.

Lockyer, Herbert (1886-?) Lockyer was an English minister who emigrated to the United States to lecture at the Moody Bible Institute. He authored over 50 books, many on endtimes themes.

-----*Cameos of Prophecy: Are These the Last Days?* Grand Rapids, MI: Zondervan Publishing House, 1942.

-----*The Church's Hope.* Eastbourne, England: Prophetic Witness Publishing House, 1971.

-----*The Future of the Gentile Nations.* Eastbourne, England: Prophetic Witness Publishing House, 1971.

-----*The Immortality of Saints: A Handbook on the Hereafter for Christian Workers.* London: Pickering & Inglis, n.d.

-----*Our Lord's Return.* Chicago: Bible Institute Colportage Association, 1935.

-----*The Rapture of Saints.* London: Pickering & Inglis, n.d.

Mauro, Philip (1859-?) A lawyer and erstwhile writer on dispensational premillennial themes. After his conversion to Christianity, Mauro became an ardent exponent of dispensationalism. By the late 1920s, however, Mauro had become dissatisfied with dispensationalism and soon became an even more ardent opponent of it. His book, *The Gospel of the Kingdom* is Mauro's diatribe against dispensationalism. I. M. Haldeman wrote a stinging reply to Mauro in *A Review of Mr. Philip Mauro's Book "The Gospel of the Kingdom": A Defence of Dispensational Truth and the Scofield Bible* (1931) in which Haldeman branded Mauro's critique of dispensational premillennial theology as unscholarly.

-----*"After This" or the Church, the Kingdom, and the Glory.* New York: Fleming H. Revell, 1918.

-----*Bringing Back the King.* New York: Fleming H. Revell, 1920.

-----*Dispensationalism Justifies the Crucifixion.* Swengel, PA: Reiner Publications, n.d.

-----*Dr. Shailer Mathews on the Christ's Return.* Swengel, PA: Bible Truth Depot, 1918.

-----*The Gospel of the Kingdom: With an Examination of Modern Dispensationalism.* Boston: Hamilton Brothers, 1928.

-----*The Hope of Israel -- What is It?* Boston: Hamilton Brothers, 1929 [reprinted by Reiner Publications, Swengel, PA, n.d.].

-----*How Long to the End?* Boston: Hamilton Brothers, 1927.

-----*The Last Call to the Godly Remnant.* Swengel, PA: Reiner Publications, n.d.

-----*More Than a Prophet.* Swengel, PA: Reiner Publications, n.d.

-----*The Number of Man — The Climax of Civilization.* New York: Fleming H. Revell, 1909.

-----*Of The Things Which Soon Must Come to Pass.* Swengel, PA: Reiner Publications, 1933.

-----*The Seventy Weeks and the Great Tribulation: A Study of the Last Two Visions of Daniel, and of the Olivet Discourse of the Lord Jesus Christ.* Boston: Hamilton Brothers, Scripture Truth Depot, 1923; (rev. ed.). Swengel, PA: Reiner, 1975.

-----*Watch. Be Ready: The Parable of the Ten Virgins* (new and rev. ed.). New York: Christian Alliance Publishing Co., 1919.

-----*The Wonders of Bible Chronology.* Swengel, PA: Reiner Publications, n.d.

-----*The World War: How it is Fulfilling Prophecy.* Boston: Hamilton Brothers, 1918.

McBirnie, W. S. (1922-) A Southern Baptist minister. McBirnie is a much traveled speaker and teacher of prophecy. He has been the minister of the United Community Church in Glendale, Cal., since 1961 and has been a professor of Middle Eastern studies at the California Graduate School since the early 1970s.

-----*The Antichrist.* Dallas: Acclaimed Books, 1978.

-----*The Coming Decline and Fall of the Soviet Union.* Glendale, CA: Center for American Research and Education, n.d.

McClain, Alva J. (1888-1968) A Brethren minister. While a Brethren pastor in Philadelphia, 1918-1925, McClain was also a professor at the Philadelphia School of the Bible, 1919-1923. He later taught at Ashland College, 1925-1927, at the Bible Institute of Los Angeles, 1927-1929, and then at Ashland Theological Seminary, 1930-1937. McClain was the founder and president of Grace Theological Seminary, 1937-1962, and helped found the National Fellowship of Grace Brethren Churches in 1939.

-----*Daniel's Prophecy of the Seventy Weeks* (3rd ed.). Grand Rapids, MI: Zondervan Publishing House, 1940.

-----*The Four Great Powers of the End Time and Their Final Conflict.* Los Angeles: American Prophetic League, 1938.

-----*The Greatness of the Kingdom: An Inductive Study of the Kingdom of God as Set Forth in the Scriptures.* Grand Rapids, MI: Zondervan Publishing House, 1959; Chicago: Moody Press, 1968.

-----*The Jewish Problem and Its Divine Solution.* Winona Lake, IN: BMH Books, 1972 , (1st ed., 1944).

McGee, J. Vernon (1904-1991?) A Presbyterian minister. McGee was pastor of the Church of the Open Door in Los Angeles, 1949-1970. He was also a popular radio teacher on prophetic themes for nearly forty years.

-----*The Best of J. Vernon McGee* (vol 1). Nashville: Thomas Nelson Publishers, 1988.

-----*He Is Coming Again*. Pasadena, CA: Thru the Bible Books, 1988.

-----*Reasoning Through Romans* (2 vols; 2nd ed.). Pasadena, CA: Thru the Bible Books, 1973.

-----*Reveling Through Revelation, part 1*. Pasadena, CA: Thru the Bible Books, 1962.

-----*Reveling Through Revelation, part 2*. Los Angeles: The Church of the Open Door, 1950.

-----*World Dominion: Whose Will It Be? (The Time of the Gentiles)*, *Daniel 2*. Pasadena, CA: Thru the Bible Books, n.d.

McPherson, Aimee Semple (1890-1944) A Pentecostal evangelist. McPherson began her career as an itinerant evangelist in 1916. She founded the International Church of the Four Square Gospel in 1923, with headquarters at the Angelus Temple in Los Angeles. She also founded Lighthouse (LIFE) College in 1926. McPherson was a flamboyant and sometimes controversial exponent of the latter-day gifts of the Holy Spirit.

-----*The Second Coming of Christ*. Los Angeles: Pub. by Author, 1921.

Miller, William (1782-1849) A Baptist minister. Through his studies of the Bible, Miller, a New England farmer turned preacher, concluded that Christ would return sometime between October 1843 and October 1844. With the enthusiastic support of Joshua V. Himes, Miller gained a sizable following. When October 1844 passed, Miller's adventist movement collapsed in disappointment. However, not long after the "Great Disappointment," some of Miller's followers formed themselves into various Adventist groups. The most successful of these splinter groups was the Seventh Day Adventist, led by the visions of Ellen G. White.

-----*Remarks on Revelations* [sic] *Thirteenth, Seventeenth and Eighteenth.* Boston: Joshus V. Himes, 1844.

-----*Views of the Prophecies and Prophetic Chronology: Selected from Manuscripts of William Miller, with a Memoir of His Life by Joshua V. Himes* [and] *The Kingdom of God* [and] *A Familiar Exposition of the Twenty-fourth Chapter of Matthew.* Boston: Joshus V. Himes, 1842.

Moody, Dwight L. (1837-1899) A Congregationalist evangelist and revival preacher. Moody is perhaps the most renowned revivalist preacher of the post-Civil War period in America. From 1891 until his death in 1899, Moody travelled throughout the United States and England holding tent meetings and revivals.

-----*Our Lord's Return: A Sermon, 2 Timothy 3:16.* Erie, PA: Free Tract League, n.d.

-----*The Second Coming of Christ.* London: R.W. Simpson & Co., n.d.; (rev. ed.). Chicago: Fleming H. Revell, 1877; Chicago: Bible Institute Colportage Association, 1896.

Morgan, G. Campbell (1863-1945) An English Congregationalist minister. Morgan was associated with D. L. Moody during the latter's several evangelistic visits to England. During an extended stay in North America, Campbell became a lecturer at the Northfield Bible Conference, 1901-1904. During his second long-term visit to the United States, 1919-1932, Campbell was a professor at both the Bible Institute of Los Angeles and Gordon College. A prolific author of both popular books and Bible commentaries, he wrote close to 60 books in his lifetime.

-----*"Behold, He Cometh!": An Introduction to a Study of the Second Advent.* New York: Fleming H. Revell, 1912.

-----*A First Century Message to Twentieth Century Christians: Addresses Based Upon the Letters to the Seven Churches of Asia.* New York: Fleming H. Revell, 1902.

-----*God's Methods with Man, In Time: Past, Present & Future.* New York: Fleming H. Revell, 1898.

-----*The Letters of Our Lord: A First Century Message to Twentieth Century Christians.* London: Pickering & Inglis, n.d.

-----*Sunrise; "Behold, He Cometh!": An Introduction to a Study of the Second Advent.* London: Hodder and Stoughton, 1912.

Morrison, Henry Clay (1857-1942) A Methodist minister and tent revivalist. Morrison was born in Kentucky, educated at the Ewing Institute and Vanderbilt University. He was licensed to preach in 1878, spending the next decades as a circuit rider and itinerant mass evangelist. Morrison became an elder in the Methodist Episcopal Church in 1887. He twice served as president of Asbury College, 1910-1925 and 1933-1938, founding Asbury Theological Seminary in 1923. Morrison was a key figure in the holiness and sanctification movement in the Methodist and Wesleyan Churches of the South.

-----*Lectures on Prophecy.* Louisville: Pentecostal Publishing Co., 1915.

-----*The Second Coming of Christ.* Louisville: Pentecostal Publishing Co., 1914.

-----*The World War in Prophecy.* Louisville: Pentecostal Publishing Co., 1917.

Munhall, Leander W. (1843-1934) A Methodist evangelist. Munhall was a chief participant in the Niagara Conferences as well the Bible and Prophecy conferences. Munhall was also one of the contributors to *The Fundamentals* (1910-1915), the multi-volume statement on Protestant fundamentalism. He was best known for his strong belief in the pre-tribulation rapture position within premillennialism.

-----*The Lord's Return* (8th ed.). Grand Rapids, MI: Kregel Publications, 1962.

-----*The Lord's Return & Kindred Truth.* Chicago: Fleming H. Revell, 1885; (7th ed.). Philadelphia: E. & R. Munhall, 1895; New York: Eaton & Mains, 1898.

Needham, George C. (1840-1902) An Irish evangelist. After spending some time as an independent evangelist in the company of H. Grattan Guinness, Needham emigrated to Boston in 1867 or 1868. He spent the remainder of his life as an itinerant preacher and conference speaker. He was a founder of the Niagara Conference and served as secretary of the International Prophetic Conferences in 1878 and 1886.

-----(ed). *Primitive Paths to Prophecy: Prophetic Addresses Given at the Brooklyn Conference to the Baptist Society for Bible Study (Nov. 18-21, 1890).* Chicago: Gospel Publishing Co., 1891.

Newton, Benjamin Wills (1807-1899) A minister and sometime leader of the Plymouth Brethren. Newton opposed Darby's "secret rapture" teaching and strong separatist ecclesiology. Their disagreement eventually resulted in a split within the Plymouth Brethren Church in 1845. Shortly thereafter, Newton lost his influence among those Brethren who had stayed with him. He left the Brethren Church altogether in 1847. He continued to teach and write until his death some fifty years later.

-----*Aids to Prophetic Enquiry* (3rd ed., considerably enlarged). London: The Sovereign Grace Advent Testimony, 1881, (1st ed., 1848).

-----*The Antichrist Future* [and] *The 1260 Days of Antichrist's Reign Future* (2nd ed.). London: Houlston and Sons; London: The Sovereign Grace Advent Testimony, 1900.

-----*Babylon: Its Future History and Doom: With Remarks on the Future of Egypt and Other Eastern Countries* (3rd ed,). London: Houlston and Sons, 1890.

-----*Elementary Studies on the Facts of Prophetic Scripture in the Book of Daniel and the Book of Revelation* [and] *Studies in 1 John*. Aylesbury: Hunt, Barnard & Co., n.d.

-----*Europe and the East: Final Predominance of Russia Inconsistent With the Declaration of Scripture* (2nd ed.). London: Houlston & Sons, 1878.

-----*Expository Teaching on the Millennium and Israel's Future*. London: The Sovereign Grace Advent Testimony, 1913.

-----*The First Resurrection and the Reign of Righteousness*. London: The Sovereign Grace Advent Testimony, n.d.

-----*How B. W. Newton Learned Prophetic Truth: Reprinted From Watching and Waiting*. London: The Sovereign Grace Advent Testimony, n.d.

-----*Israel and Jerusalem*. London: Houlston & Wright, 1867.

-----*Jerusalem: Its Future History*. London: L. Collins, 1908.

-----*The Judgment of the Court of Arches and of the Judicial Committee of the Privy Council in the Case of Rowland Williams*. London: The Sovereign Grace Advent Testimony, 1866.

-----*The New World Order, or The Pre-Millennial Truth Demonstrated: An Answer to the Post-Millennial, A-Millennial, and Anti-Millennial Theories*. London: The Sovereign Grace Advent Testimony, n.d.

-----*Prophecies Respecting the Jews and Jerusalem Considered: In the Form of a Catechism* (4th ed.). London: C. M. Tucker, 1888.

-----*The Prophecy of the Lord Jesus as Contained in Matthew XXIV and XXV Considered*. London: Houlston and Sons, 1879; (5th ed.). n.p.: E. J. Burnett, 1930.

-----*The Prospects of the Ten Kingdoms of the Roman Empire*. London: Houlston & Wright, 1863; (2nd ed., rev.). London: Houlston and Sons, 1873.

-----*The World to Come* [and] *Ancient Truths Respecting the Deity and True Humanity of the Lord Jesus* (6th ed.). London: Houlston and Sons, 1897.

Pember, George H. (1837?-1910) Educated at Cambridge, Pember was one of the most respected dispensationalists and prophecy scholars of the Victorian era.

-----*The Antichrist, Babylon, and the Coming of the Kingdom* (2nd ed.). London: Hodder & Stoughton, 1888.

-----*The Great Prophecies Concerning the Gentiles, the Jews and the Church of God* (2nd ed., rev. and enlarged). London: Holder and Stoughton, 1885; (3rd ed., rev. and enlarged). New York: Christian Herald, 1887 .

-----*The Great Prophecies of the Centuries: Concerning Israel and the Gentiles* (3rd ed., rev. and enlarged). New York: Christian Herald Office, 1887; London: Hodder and Stoughton,1895; (4th ed.). London: Hodder and Stoughton, 1909; (5th ed.). London: Hodder 1902 and 1911.

Pentecost, J. Dwight (b. 1915) A Presbyterian Minister. A graduate of Dallas Theological Seminary, 1941, Pentecost ministered to churches in Pennsylvania before being invited to join the faculty at Philadelphia College of the Bible in 1948. Pentecost taught there until 1955, when he enrolled for graduate work at Dallas Theological Seminary. He completed the Th.D. in 1956 and joined the Dallas faculty that same year. From 1962 to 1980, Pentecost was chairman of the department of Biblical Exposition, thereafter remaining active as a member of its faculty.

-----*Prophecy for Today: A Discussion of Major Themes of Prophecy.* Grand Rapids, MI: Zondervan Publishing House, 1961.

-----*Prophecy for Today: God's Purpose and Plan for Our Future* (rev. ed.). Grand Rapids, MI: Discovery House Publishers, 1989.

-----*Things to Come: A Study in Biblical Eschatology.* Findlay, OH: Dunham Publishing Co., 1958 and 1965; Grand Rapids, MI: Zondervan Publishing House, 1976.

-----*Thy Kingdom Come.* Wheaton, IL: Victor Books, 1990.

-----*Will Man Survive? Prophecy You Can Understand.* Chicago: Moody Press, 1971.

Pettingill, William L. (1866-1950) A Baptist minister. Pettingill was minister of the North Church in Wilmington, Delaware, 1903-1914. He was one of the consulting editors of *The Scofield Reference Bible* (1909). With C. I. Scofield, Pettingill was co-founder of the Philadelphia School of the Bible and served as its dean from 1914 until his retirement in 1928. He joined the Independent Fundamental Churches of America after its founding in 1930, serving for a short period as its vice president.

-----*Brief Prophetic Messages.* Waterloo, IA: The Cedar Book Store, n.d.

-----*The Coming One According to Scripture.* New York: Charles C. Cook, 1916.

-----*God's Prophecies for Plain People.* Philadelphia: The Philadelphia School of the Bible, 1905 [reprinted 1923].

-----*Israel: Jehovah's Covenant People.* Harrisburg, PA: F. Kelker, 1905.

-----*Light in Darkness: Simple Studies in God's Revealed Plan of the Ages.* Findlay, OH: Fundamental Truth Publishers, 1941.

-----*Loving His Appearing and Other Prophetic Studies.* Findlay, OH: Fundamental Truth Publishers, 1943.

-----*Nearing the End: Simple Studies Concerning the Second Coming of Christ and Related Events.* Chicago: Van Kampen Press, 1948.

-----*Simple Studies in Daniel.* Philadelphia: The Philadelphia School of the Bible, 1909.

-----*Simple Studies in Matthew* (6th ed.). Philadelphia: The Philadelphia School of the Bible, 1910.

-----*Simple Studies in Revelation*. Philadelphia: The Philadelphia School of the Bible, 1916.

Pierson, Arthur T. (1837-1911) A Presbyterian minister, 1860-1891, a Baptist minister, and then an itinerant evangelist. Pierson was a popular speaker at missionary conferences and an occasional associate of D. L. Moody. He helped launch the Student Volunteer Movement out of the Y.M.C.A. in 1886. After ministering briefly at Charles H. Spurgeon's Metropolitan Tabernacle (Baptist) in London, Pierson adopted the Baptist position on adult immersion and was himself immersed a Baptist in 1896. An ardent premillennialist, Pierson regularly lectured at Niagara Bible Conferences and Bible Institutes and authored several books on various millennialist themes. He was listed as a consulting editor of *The Scofield Reference Bible* (1909).

-----*The Coming of the Lord*. London: Passmore & Alabaster, 1896; Chicago: Fleming H. Revell, 1896.

-----*The Second Coming of Our Lord*. Altemus, 1896.

Rader, D. Paul (1879-1938) A Congregationalist minister and evangelist. From 1909 to 1924 Rader was associated with the Christian and Missionary Alliance, becoming its president, 1919-1924. He was minister of the Moody Church in Chicago from 1915 to 1921 and an independent evangelist and radio preacher thereafter.

-----*The Coming World Dictator*. Chicago: World Wide Gospel Couriers, 1934 and 1943.

-----*The Midnight Cry*. Chicago: Chicago Gospel Tabernacles, 1938.

Rice, John R. (1896-1980) A Baptist minister, revivalist, and radio preacher. Rice was a tireless "soul-winner," popular conference speaker, and prolific writer. His books and pamphlets number well over a hundred titles. In 1934, Rice founded The Sword of the Lord in the Chicago area, later moving its headquarters to Murfreesboro, Tennessee.

Under Rice's leadership, The Sword of the Lord gained a reputation as a staunchly fundamentalist organization.

-----*Christ's Literal Reign on Earth from David's Throne at Jerusalem.* Wheaton, IL: Sword of the Lord, 1947, 1950, and 1953.

-----*The Coming Kingdom of Christ.* Dallas, TX: John R. Rice, n.d. [Wheaton, IL: Sword of the Lord, 1945].

-----*Five Parables Illustrating Christ's Second Coming.* Murfreesboro, TN: Sword of the Lord Publishers, 1975.

-----*Jewish Persecutions and Bible Prophecies.* Wheaton, IL: Sword of the Lord, n.d.

-----*The Second Coming of Christ in Daniel.* Dallas: Pub. by author, n.d.

-----*World-wide War and the Bible.* Wheaton, IL: Sword of the Lord, 1940.

Riley, William Bell (1861-1947) A Baptist minister. Staunchly conservative, Riley gained a reputation early on for his attacks against liberal clergymen, urban crime, and liquor consumption. During the 1920s, Riley derided liberal Christianity and crusaded against evolution. He was pastor of the First Baptist Church of Minneapolis from 1897 to 1943 and the founder and president of Northwestern Schools, 1902-1947. Riley was also a leading figure in both the World's Christian Fundamentalist Association and the Baptist Bible Union. From 1891 to 1933, he edited the *The Christian Fundamentals* and was also one of the contributors to *The Fundamentals* (1910-1915), the renowned multi-volume statement on the Protestant fundamentalist position.

-----*The Coming and the Kingdom.* Kansas City, MO: The Western Baptist Publishing Co., n.d.

-----*Daniel and the Doom of World Governments: Is There Any Redemption?* Minneapolis: L.W. Camp, 1935.

-----*The Evolution of the Kingdom.* Chicago: Charles C. Cook, 1913 [enlarged version of *The Coming and the Kingdom*].

-----*Is Christ Coming Again?* (4th ed.). Grand Rapids, MI: Zondervan, n.d.

-----*The Only Hope of Church and World: What Is It?* London: Pickering & Inglis, n.d.

-----*The Seven Churches of Asia.* New York: Christian Alliance Publishing Co., 1900.

-----*Wanted -- A World Leader!* Pub. by author, 1939.

Rimmer, Harry (1890-1952) A Friends minister, 1916-1919, who became a Presbyterian in 1919. Rimmer was principal of the Research Science Bureau from 1920 until his death in 1952. He served as minister of the First Presbyterian Church in Duluth, MN, 1934-1939. Rimmer was the author of over forty books, most attempting to reconcile science and the Bible. His final flurry of literary activity came during the period just before and after the Second World War when he was overcome by enthusiasm for the second coming of Christ. In these works, Rimmer attempted to link current events in Europe and the Middle East with the prophecies of the Bible, at times letting his imagination get away from him. Many of his boldest predictions did not come to pass, an embarrassment that overshadowed the thoroughness and characteristic balance of his earlier works.

-----*The Coming King.* Grand Rapids, MI: Wm B. Eerdmans Publishing Co., 1941.

-----*The Coming League and the Roman Dream.* Grand Rapids, MI: Wm B. Eerdmans Publishing Co., 1941.

-----*The Coming War and the Rise of Russia.* Grand Rapids, MI: Wm B. Eerdmans Publishing Co., 1940.

-----*Palestine, the Coming Storm Center.* Grand Rapids, MI: Wm B. Eerdmans Publishing Co., 1943.

-----*The Shadow of Coming Events*. Grand Rapids, MI: Wm B. Eerdmans Publishing Co., 1950.

Roberts, Oral (b. 1918) A Pentecostal minister and faith healer. Roberts began his ministry career after he was cured of tuberculosis and a speech impediment at a faith healing service in 1935. From 1936 to 1947, Roberts served small Pentecostal Holiness churches in Oklahoma and the South. Upon hearing the voice of God in 1947, Roberts embarked upon his healing ministry. In 1948, Roberts held large tent healing services in Tulsa, Okla. By 1952, he had already begun his ventures into radio broadcasting and films. By 1954 Roberts had added television broadcasts, and with these, wider appeal. In 1965, Roberts attended the World Congress on Evangelism, gaining greater acceptance among mainstream churches as well as the close friendship of Billy Graham. In 1967, the Oral Roberts University was founded, with Graham participating in its dedication ceremonies. Though an independent evangelist and successful Christian media star, Roberts has remained linked to the pentecostal movement. For instance, he supported the founding of the Full Gospel Business Men's Fellowship International. Roberts's long public ministry has not been without personal strain, however. When his new medical center was in dire need of funds in 1987, Roberts once more heard the voice of God. This time, however, God threatened to take Roberts's life unless Roberts raised 8 to 10 million dollars. The money was raised and Roberts's ministry continues, though somewhat discredited among many evangelical Protestants.

-----*The Drama of the End Time*. Franklin Springs, GA: Pentecostal Holiness Publishing House, 1941.

-----*God's Timetable for the End of Time*. Tulsa, OK: Heliotrope Publishers, 1969.

Robertson, Pat (b. 1930) A Southern Baptist televangelist and Christian businessman. The son of a U. S. Senator, Robertson graduated from Washington and Lee University and attended Yale Law School. After failing to pass the New York State bar exam, Robertson decided to enter the ministry. In 1956, Robertson enrolled at New York Theological Seminary, graduating in 1959 and receiving his ordination from the

Southern Baptist Church in 1961. During his seminary years, Robertson served as an associate minister at the First Reformed Church in Mount Vernon under Harold Bredesen, an early figure in the charismatic movement. In 1959, Robertson resurrected a defunct radio station in Portsmouth, VA, and began broadcasting in October of that year as the Christian Broadcasting Network (CBN). In 1963, Robertson gained the financial commitment of 700 "faith partners", giving birth to his "700 Club." The program itself debuted in 1966, becoming nationally syndicated in 1972. The "700 Club" remains one of the most financially successful television evangelistic programs in America. Robertson founded the CBN University in 1978, with schools of business, education, communication, journalism, biblical studies, and law. In 1988, Robertson made an unsuccessful bid for the Republican presidential nomination; Robertson plans to run again in 1996.

-----*The New Millennium.* Dallas, TX: Word Books, 1990.

-----*The New World Order.* Dallas, TX: Word Books, 1991.

-----*The Secret Kingdom.* New York: Bantam Books, 1984.

Ryrie, Charles C. (b. 1925) A professor at various colleges and dispensational premillennialist centers, including: Westmont College, 1948-1953; Philadelphia College of the Bible, 1958-1962; and Dallas Theological Seminary, 1954-1958, and since 1962.

-----*The Basis of the Premillennial Faith.* New York: Loizeaux Bros., 1953.

-----*The Bible and Tomorrow's News: A New Look at Prophecy.* Wheaton, IL: Scripture Press Publications, 1969; Wheaton, IL: Victor Books, 1973.

-----*Dispensationalism Today.* Chicago: Moody Press, 1965.

-----*The Final Countdown.* Wheaton, IL: Victor Books, 1982 [rev. & updated version of *The Bible and Tomorrow's News*].

-----*The Living End.* Old Tappan, NJ: Fleming H. Revell, 1976.

-----(ed.). *The Ryrie Study Bible.* Chicago: Moody Press, 1978.

-----*Warnings to the Churches*. London: The Banner of Truth Trust, 1967.

-----*What You Should Know About the Rapture*. Chicago: Moody Press, 1981.

Scofield, C. I. (1843-1921) A Congregationalist minister. After serving as a private in the Confederate Army, Scofield moved West to study law. In 1879, Scofield converted to Christianity and joined a Bible study group led by dispensationalist James H. Brookes, the devoted follower of John Nelson Darby. A popular teacher and conference speaker, Scofield developed and popularized Darby's dispensational thinking throughout evangelical circles in the United States and Canada. Scofield's most enduring influence has been through *The Scofield Reference Bible* (1909), a cross-referencing Bible connecting Old and New Testaments and casting a dispensationalist gloss over the Christian Bible. Scofield was also founder and president of the Philadelphia School of the Bible, 1914-1921.

-----*Addresses on Prophecy*. Los Angeles: Bible House of Los Angeles, n.d.; Swengel, PA: Bible Truth Depot, 1910 [reprinted in 1914 by Charles C. Cook Publishers of New York].

-----*Dr. C. I. Scofield's Question Box* (compiled by Ella E. Pohe). Chicago: Bible Institute Colportage Association, 1917.

-----*Prophecy Made Plain: Addresses on Prophecy*. Glasgow: Pickering & Inglis; London: Alfred Holness, n.d. [British edition of *Addresses on Prophecy*].

-----*Rightly Dividing the Word of Truth: Being Ten Outline Studies of the More Important Divisions of Scripture*. New York: Loizeaux Bros., 1896 [1888].

-----(ed.). *The Scofield Reference Bible*. New York: Oxford University Press, 1909.

-----*Things New and Old* (compiled and edited by Arno Gaebelein). New York: Publication Office of Our Hope, 1920.

-----*What Do the Prophets Say?* Philadelphia: The Sunday School Times Co., 1916.

-----*Will the Church Pass Through the Great Tribulation?; Eighteen Reasons Which Prove that It Will Not.* Philadelphia: Philadelphia School of the Bible, 1917.

-----*The World's Approaching Crisis.* New York: Our Hope, n.d.; Philadelphia: Philadelphia School of the Bible, 1913.

-----, and Arno Gaebelein. *The Jewish Question.* New York: Our Hope, 1912.

Seiss, Joseph A. (1823-1904) A Lutheran minister. After only two years at Pennsylvania College, Seiss was licensed to preach in 1842 and held ministry positions at churches in Virginia and Maryland. From 1858 to 1874, Seiss was pastor of St. John's Lutheran Church in Philadelphia. During this period he helped found Lutheran Theological Seminary, 1865. Seiss was also editor of *The Lutheran,* 1867-1879. In 1874 Seiss begin the Church of the Holy Communion in Philadelphia, remaining there until his death in 1904. He was active in the early Prophecy conferences and wrote several works on prophetic themes.

-----*The Apocalypse: A Series of Special Lectures on the Revelation of Jesus Christ with Revised Text.* New York: Charles C. Cook, 1900 [1865].

-----*The Last Times and the Great Consummation: An Earnest Discussion of Momentous Themes* (6th ed. rev. & enlarged). Philadelphia: Smith; London: Wertheim, McIntosh & Hunt, 1866.

-----*The Letters of Jesus* (Lenten Lectures). New York: Charles C. Cook, 1903.

-----*Millennialism and the Second Advent.* Louisville, KY: Pickett Publishing Co., n.d.; Louisville, KY: Pentecostal Publishing Co., n.d.

-----(ed.). *Our Blessed Hope; or Select Tracts on the Advent.* H. B. Garner, 1884.

Simpson, A. B. (1844-1919) A Presbyterian minister. Simpson founded the Christian Alliance in 1889. In 1897, the Christian Alliance and Interdenominational Missionary Alliance were joined to form the Christian and Missionary Alliance. Simpson was also instrumental in the founding of Nyack College, 1882.

-----*Back to Patmos: Prophetic Outlooks on Present Conditions.* New York: Christian Alliance Publishing Co., 1914.

-----*The Coming One.* New York: Christian Alliance Publishing Co., 1912.

-----*The Gospel of the Kingdom: A Series of Discourses on the Lord's Coming.* New York: Christian Alliance Publishing Co., 1890.

-----*The Midnight Cry.* Pub. by author, 1914.

Smith, Chuck (b. 1927) A Four Square Gospel minister. Smith graduated from LIFE Bible College and was ordained a minister of the International Church of the Four Square Gospel, holding pastorates in Arizona and Southern California. In 1965, Smith was called as minister to Calvary Chapel in Costa Mesa, CA, where he has served ever since. In the early 1970s, Smith became a leader of the Jesus People movement and caught the nation's eye with his mass baptismal services held at local California beaches. The highly dynamic growth of Calvary Chapel membership and its many ministries has led to the founding of satellite churches throughout Southern California.

-----*End Times: A Report on Future Survival.* Costa Mesa: Maranatha House Publishers, 1978; Costa Mesa, CA: The Word for Today, 1980.

-----*The Final Curtain.* Costa Mesa, CA: The Word for Today, 1984.

-----*Future Survival.* Costa Mesa, CA: The Word for Today, 1980.

-----(with Dave Wimbash). *Dateline Earth: Countdown to Eternity.* Old Tappan, NJ: Chosen Books, 1989.

-----*Snatched Away!* Costa Mesa: Maranatha House Publishers, 1976; Costa Mesa, CA: The Word for Today, 1980.

-----*The Soon to be Revealed Antichrist.* Costa Mesa: Maranatha House Publishers, 1976; Costa Mesa, CA: The Word for Today, 1979.

-----*The Tribulation and the Church.* Costa Mesa, CA: The Word for Today, 1980.

-----*What the World is Coming To.* Costa Mesa, CA: The Word for Today, 1980.

Smith, Oswald J. (1889-1986) A Presbyterian minister. Smith graduated from Toronto Bible College and McCormick Theological Seminary. He founded the People's Temple in Toronto, 1930, serving as its minister until 1959. Smith's primary interests were in supporting foreign missions. During his long life, Smith authored 35 popular books and wrote over 1,000 hymns.

-----*Antichrist and the Future* (2nd ed.). Toronto: The People's Church, 1932.

-----*The Clouds are Lifting* (2 pts). London: Marshall, Morgan & Scott, 1937 (pt 1: *Studies in Prophecy* ; pt 2: *The Visions of Daniel*).

-----*The Dawn is Breaking.* London: Marshall, Morgan & Scott [Grand Rapids, MI: Zondervan Publishing House], 1937.

-----*Is the Antichrist at Hand?* (5th ed.). Toronto: The Tabernacle Publishing Co., 1926.

-----*Prophecies of the End Times.* Toronto: Toronto Tabernacle Publishers, 1932.

-----*Prophecy: What Lies Ahead?* London: Marshall, Morgan & Scott, LTD, 1955 [1943].

-----*The Rider on the Red Horse.* Toronto: The People's Church, 1934.

-----*Signs of His Coming* [and] *What Will Happen Next?* Toronto: The People's Church, 1933.

-----*The Visions of Daniel* (3rd ed.). Toronto: People's Church, 1932.

-----*The Voice of Prophecy.* London: Marshall, Morgan & Scott, 1954.

-----*When Antichrist Reigns.* New York: The Christian Alliance Publishng Co., 1927.

-----*When He Is Come.* Chicago: World-wide Christian Couriers, 1929.

-----*When the King Comes Back.* Wheaton, IL: Sword of the Lord Publishers, n.d.

-----*World Problems in the Light of Prophecy.* London: Marshall, Morgan & Scott, n.d.

Smith, Wilbur M. (1894-1976) A Presbyterian minister. After twenty years serving pastorates in churches in the middle Atlantic states, Smith became a professor at the Moody Bible Institute, 1938-1947. In 1947, he became professor of English Bible at Fuller Seminary, remaining there until disagreement over Fuller's doctrinal stance caused him to resign in 1963. From 1963 to 1971, Smith was professor at Trinity Evangelical Divinity School. Smith also served on the committee which revised the reference notes to the *The Scofield Reference Bible.* A respected fundamentalist writer and an avid bibliophile, Smith's books were typically centered around prophetic subjects and endtime themes.

-----*The Atomic Age and the Word of God.* Chicago: Moody Press, 1945; Boston: W. A. Wilde, 1948.

-----*The Bible History of World Government, and a Forecast of its Future From Bible Prophecy.* Westfield, IN: Union Bible Seminary, Inc., 1955.

----- *Egypt and Israel Coming Together?* Wheaton, IL: Tyndale House, 1978.

-----*Egypt in Biblical Prophecy.* Boston: W. A. Wilde Co., 1957.

-----*55 Best Books on Prophecy.* Chicago: Moody Bible Institute, 1940.

-----*Israel, the Bible, and the Middle East.* Glendale, CA: G/L Publications, 1967.

-----*Israeli/Arab Conflict and the Bible.* Glendale, CA: G/L Publications, 1967.

-----*A Preliminary Bibliography for the Study of Biblical Prophecy.* Boston: W. A. Wilde Co., 1952.

-----*The Second Advent of Christ.* Washington, D.C.: Christianity Today, n.d.

-----*Studies in Bible Prophecy.* Westfield, IN: Union Bible Seminary, n.d.

-----*World Crises and the Prophetic Scriptures.* Chicago: Moody Press, 1950.

-----*You Can Know the Future.* Glendale, CA: G/L Publications, 1971.

Strauss, Lehman (b. 1911) A Baptist minister and conference speaker. For some years, Strauss was host of a popular religious radio program. He has authored over 14 books on various subjects, mostly prophecy and the endtimes.

-----*Armageddon.* Findlay, OH: Dunham Publishing Co., n.d.

-----*Christ's Literal Reign on Earth.* Findlay, OH: Dunham Publishing Co., n.d.

-----*Communism and Russia in Bible Prophecy.* Findlay, OH: Dunham Publishing Co., 1959.

-----*Daniel.* Neptune, NJ: Loizeaux Brothers, 1969.

-----*The End of the Present World.* Grand Rapids, MI: Zondervan Publishing House, 1969 .

-----*God's Plan for the Future.* Grand Rapids, MI: Zondervan Publishing House, 1965.

-----*God's Prophetic Calendar.* Neptune, NJ: Loizeaux Brothers, 1987.

Sunday, Billy (1862-1935) A Presbyterian minister and itinerant tent evangelist. Sunday played professional baseball for the Chicago White Stockings, Pittsburgh, and Philadelphia. It was while playing for Chicago that Sunday attended the Pacific Garden Mission and was converted to Christianity. He began full time work for the Y.M.C.A. in 1891. Sunday then worked with J. Wilbur Chapman, 1893-1895, before striking out on his own in 1896. Though his major concern was mass evangelism, Sunday preached against modernism, moral laxity, and "booze." During the First World War, Sunday vigorously crusaded for the American war effort. After 1920, Sunday's popularity dropped precipitously. His last crusade was against the Catholic Democratic presidential candidate, Alfred E. Smith, in 1928.

-----*The Second Coming.* Fort Wayne, IN: E.A.K. Hackett, 1913.

Swaggart, Jimmy (b. 1935) A televangelist and sometime minister of the Assemblies of God. In 1957, Swaggart began his work as an itinerant evangelist, preaching judgment on America for its moral corruption. His blood relationship to popular rock singer Jerry Lee Lewis lifted Swaggart out of obscurity and helped fill his meeting halls. Swaggart began his radio ministry in 1969. In 1973, he began his switch to television, becoming exclusively a televangelist by 1981. Scandal has followed Swaggart throughout his ministry, however. The 1987 revelations that Swaggart had been frequenting prostitutes caused great shock among his followers. The Assemblies of God defrocked Swaggart in 1988 for insubordination. Despite such negative publicity, Swaggart has remained a popular televangelist and revival speaker.

-----*Armageddon: The Future of Planet Earth.* Baton Rouge, LA: Jimmy Swaggart Ministries, 1987.

-----*Four Conditions for Being Included in the Rapture.* Baton Rouge, LA: Jimmy Swaggart Ministries, 1981.

-----*The Future of Planet Earth.* Baton Rouge, LA: Jimmy Swaggart Ministries, 1982.

-----*The Great White Throne Judgment.* Baton Rouge, LA: Jimmy Swaggart Ministries, 1979.

-----*Will the Church Go Through the Great Tribulation Period?* Baton Rouge, LA: Jimmy Swaggart Ministries, 1981.

Talbot, Louis T. (1889-1976) A Presbyterian minister. Talbot moved to the United States from Australia in 1911 to attend the Moody Bible Institute, graduating in 1913. After brief ministerial service in Texas and ordination as a Congregationalist minister, Talbot returned to Chicago in 1915 for study at McCormick Theological Seminary. Beginning in 1917, Talbot served several parishes throughout the Midwest, starting a radio ministry while in Minneapolis. Talbot moved to Los Angeles in 1931 to begin his long tenure as pastor of the Church of the Open Door, 1931-1948. He was twice president of BIOLA College, 1931-1935 and 1948-1952, remaining on its board of directors in the interim. In 1952, Talbot was named chancellor of BIOLA's seminary, named for him. At Talbot's urging, both BIOLA College and Talbot seminary moved to the Los Angeles suburbs, relocating in La Mirada in 1957.

-----*The Army of the Two Hundred Million and the Lord's Return.* Los Angeles: Livingstone Press, 1931.

-----*The Book of Revelation.* Grand Rapids, MI: Eerdmans Publishing Co.

-----*The Coming World Dictator: the Second in a Series of Addresses on Bible Prophecy.* Los Angeles: The Church of the Open Door, n.d.

-----*The Feasts of Jehovah: Foreshadowing God's Plan of the Ages from the Past Eternity to the Future Eternity.* Los Angeles: The Church of the Open Door, n.d.

-----*God's Plan of the Ages: A Comprehensive View of God's Great Plan from Eternity to Eternity illustrated with Chart.* Los Angeles: Pub. by author, 1936; Grand Rapids, MI: Eerdmans 1936.

-----*The Great Prophecies of Daniel.* Los Angeles: Pub. by author, 1934.

-----*Is It Possible for Christ to Return in This Generation?* Glendale, CA: Church Press, 1942.

-----*The Prophecies of Daniel.* Los Angeles: The Church of the Open Door, 1940.

-----*The Prophecies of Daniel in the Light of Past, Present, and Future Events* (3rd ed.). Wheaton, IL: Van Kampen Press, 1954 [1940].

-----*The Revelation of Jesus Christ: An Exposition on the Book of Revelation.* Los Angeles: The Church of the Open Door, 1937.

-----*Russia: Her Invasion of Palestine in the Last Days and Her Final Destruction at the Return of Christ.* Los Angeles: Pub. by author, n.d.

-----*The Thousand Years' Reign of Christ on the Earth: The Characteristics of that Reign.* The Livingstone Press, 1931.

-----and William W. Orr. *The New Nation of Israel and the Word of God: A Discussion Between Louis T. Talbot and William W. Orr Conducted Over the Bible Institute Radio Hour.* Los Angeles: Bible Institute of Los Angeles, 1948.

-----and Samuel H. Sutherland. *The Shape of Things to Come: Questions and Answers on Prophecy, as Given Over the Bible Institute Hour.* Los Angeles: Bible Institute of Los Angeles, n.d.

Torrey, Reuben A. (1856-1928) A Yale-educated Presbyterian evangelist. Torrey's evangelistic interests were piqued by the mass appeal of D. L. Moody, whom Torrey came to respect and admire. At its founding, Torrey became head of the Moody Bible Institute in 1889 and served in that post for almost twenty years. In 1908, Torrey moved to Los Angeles to become dean of the Bible Institute of Los Angeles, a position he also held for nearly twenty years. During this period, Torrey assisted A. C. Dixon in compiling *The Fundamentals* (1910-1915). A popular lecturer and conference speaker, Torrey was also the founding minister of the Church of the Open Door in Los Angeles.

-----*The Personal Return of Christ.* London: James E. Hawkins, n.d.

-----*The Return of the Lord Jesus: The Key to the Scripture and Solution of All Our Political and Social Problems; or The Golden Age That is Soon Coming to the Earth.* Los Angeles: The Bible Institute of Los Angeles, 1913.

-----*What War Teaches: The Greatest Lesson of the Year 1917.* Los Angeles: The Bible Institute of Los Angeles, 1918.

Tregelles, Samuel P. (1813-1875) A Plymouth Brethren and an accomplished Greek New Testament scholar.

-----*The Hope of Christ's Second Coming.* London: Samuel Bagster & Sons, 1864; (2nd ed.). Aylesbury: Hunt, Barnard & Co., n.d.; London: Samuel Bagster & Sons, 1886.

-----*The Man of Sin.* London: The Sovereign Grace Advent Testimony, 1850.

-----*Remarks on the Prophetic Visions in the Book of Daniel (A new edition revised and greatly enlarged): With Notes on Prophetic Interpretation in Connection with Popery, and a Defence of the Authenticity of the Book of Daniel.* London: Samuel Bagster & Sons, 1852.

-----*Remarks on the Prophetic Visions of the Book of Daniel.* London: Samuel Bagster & Sons, 1883.

Trumbull, Charles G. (1872-1941) A Presbyterian and leader of the American Keswick Movement. After completing studies at Yale, 1893, Trumbull became assistant editor of *The Sunday School Times* under his father. At the death of his father in 1903, Trumbull took over the editorship, serving in that position until his own death in 1941. A leader in the fundamentalist movement and protegé of C. I. Scofield, Trumbull authored and edited several books on prophetic subjects, including a biography on the life of Scofield.

-----(ed.). *How I Came to Believe in Our Lord's Return and Why I Believe the Lord's Return is Near.* Chicago: Bible Institute Colportage Association, 1934.

-----*Prophecy's Light on Today.* New York: Fleming H. Revell, 1938.

Tulga, Chester E. (b. 1896) A Baptist minister. For twenty-five years Tulga served churches throughout the middle United States. After that, he was for twelve years executive secretary of the Conservative Baptist Fellowship.

-----*The Case for the Second Coming of Christ.* Chicago: Conservative Baptist Fellowship, 1951.

-----*Premillennialists and Their Critics.* Somerset, KY: Eastern Baptist Institute, 1961.

Unger, Merrill F. (1909-1980) An Old Testament scholar. Unger received doctoral degrees from both Dallas Theological Seminary, 1945, and Johns Hopkins, 1947. He served as a professor of Old Testament at Dallas Seminary, 1948-1967, and thereafter at Gordon College. He was also an assistant editor of *Bibliotheca Sacra* from 1956 until his retirement, regularly contributing articles on prophetic themes.

-----*Beyond the Crystal Ball.* Chicago: Moody Press, 1973.

-----*Great Neglected Bible Prophecies.* Chicago: Scripture Press Foundation, 1955.

Van Impe, Jack (b. 1931) An independent Baptist evangelist and radio preacher. Van Impe has been a popular conference speaker, crusade leader, and radio evangelist among fundamentalists for nearly forty years. His sermons typically center around the second coming of Christ. Van Impe has been dubbed "The Walking Bible" by fundamentalists because of his keen memory and his amazing ability to quote Bible passages verbatim. He is a master of the art of the "Bible Reading," first developed at the early Bible and Prophecy conferences.

-----*America, Israel, Russia, and World War III.* Royal Oak, MI: Jack Van Impe Ministries, 1984.

-----*11:59...And Counting!* Nashville: Thomas Nelson Publishers, 1987.

-----*Israel's Final Holocaust.* Nashville: Thomas Nelson Publishers, 1979; Royal Oak, MI: Jack Van Impe Ministries, 1983.

-----*Revelation Revealed: Verse By Verse.* Royal Oak, MI: Jack Van Impe Ministries, 1982.

-----*Signs of the Times.* Royal Oak, MI: Jack Van Impe Ministries, 1979.

Walvoord, John F. (b. 1910) A Presbyterian minister, author, and educator. Walvoord was Professor of Theology and the president of Dallas Theological Seminary from 1952 to 1986. He has authored a dozen books and scores of articles on dispensational themes. He was a member of the committee that revised *The Scofield Reference Bible*, 1967. Even in retirement, Walvoord remains active and influential in dispensational circles, an influence that cannot be overstated.

-----*Armageddon: Oil and the Middle East Crisis* (rev. ed.). Grand Rapids, MI: Zondervan Publishing House, 1990.

-----*The Blessed Hope and the Tribulation: A Biblical and Historical Study of Posttribulationism.* Grand Rapids, MI: Zondervan Publishing House, 1976.

-----*The Church in Prophecy.* Grand Rapids, MI: Zondervan Publishing House, 1964.

-----*Fifty Arguments for Pretribulation.* Minneapolis: Central Conservative Baptist Seminary, n.d.

-----*Israel in Prophecy.* Grand Rapids, MI: Zondervan Publishing House, 1962.

-----*Major Bible Prophecies: 37 Crucial Prophecies that Affect You Today.* Grand Rapids, MI: Zondervan Publishing House, 1991.

-----*Matthew: Thy Kingdom Come.* Chicago: Moody Press, 1974.

-----*The Millennial Kingdom.* Findlay, OH: Dunham Publishing Co., 1959.

-----*The Nations in Prophecy.* Grand Rapids, MI: Zondervan Publishing House, 1967.

-----*Prophecy Knowledge Handbook.* Wheaton, IL: Victor Books, 1990.

-----*The Prophetic Word in Crisis Days.* Findlay, OH: Dunham Publishing Co., 1961.

-----*The Rapture Question.* Findlay, OH: Dunham Publishing Co., 1957; (rev. and enlarged ed.). Grand Rapids, MI: Zondervan Publishing House, 1979.

-----*The Return of the Lord.* Findlay, OH: Dunham Publishing Co., 1955; Grand Rapids, MI: Zondervan Publishing House, 1977.

-----*The Revelation of Jesus Christ.* Findlay, OH: Dunham Publishing Co., 1957; Chicago: Moody Press, 1966.

-----*The Thessalonian Epistle.* Findlay, OH: Dunham Publishing Co., 1955.

West, Nathaniel (1826-1906) A Presbyterian minister. West studied at the University of Michigan, graduating in 1846. He served a number of pastorates and taught for a time at Danville Theological Seminary in Kentucky, 1869-1875, and briefly at the Moody Bible Institute. West was one of the founders of the Niagara Conferences. A major participant in the Prophecy conferences, West later adopted a posttribulational premillennialist view of the rapture which does not expect the rapture of the saints to occur until *after* the seven-year Tribulation period.

-----*The Apostle Paul and the Any-Moment Rapture Theory.* Philadelphia: J.H. Armstrong, 1893.

-----*The Coming of the Lord in the "Teaching of the Twelve Apostles."* Philadelphia: J.H. Armstrong, 1892.

-----*Daniel's Great Prophecy: Its Twelve Chapters Explained.* Salisbury Square, London: Prophetic News Office, n.d.; New York: The Hope of Israel, 1898.

-----*John Wesley and Premillennialism.* Louisville: Pentecostal Publishing Co., 1894.

-----*The Present Condition and Future Glory of Believers and the Earth.* St. Louis: Gospel Book and Tract Depository, n.d.

-----*The Thousand Years in Both Testaments: Studies in Eschatology; With Supplementary discussions Upon Symbolical Numbers, the Development of Prophecy, and its Interpretation Concerning Israel, the Nations, the Church, and the Kingdom, as Seen in the Apocalypses of Isaiah, Ezekiel, Daniel, Christ, and John.* New York: Fleming H. Revell, 1880 and 1889. [reprinted as *The Thousand Years: Studies in Eschatology in Both Testaments* by Scripture Truth Book Co., Fincastle, VA, 1967].

White, John Wesley (b. 1928) An author and evangelist with the Billy Graham Ministries. White was graduated from the Moody Bible Institute, 1950, and Wheaton College, 1952. He later studied at Oxford University and was awarded the DPhil degree in 1963. In 1964 White became an associate evangelist with Billy Graham Ministries, a position he still holds. Since 1967 has also been chancellor of Richmond College in Ontario and associated with the People's Church in Toronto.

-----*Arming for Armageddon.* Milford, MI: Mott Media, Inc., 1983.

-----*Re-entry: Striking Parallels Between Today's News Events and Christ's Second Coming.* Grand Rapids, MI: Zondervan Publishing House, 1970; Minneapolis: World Wide Publications, 1971.

-----*Thinking the Unthinkable: Are All the Pieces in Place?* Lake Mary, FL: Creation House, 1992.

-----*W W III.* Grand Rapids, MI: Zondervan Publishing House, 1977.

Wilkerson, David (b. 1931) A Pentecostal minister and evangelist. After briefly attending Central Bible Institute, 1951-1952, Wilkerson pastored a small Assemblies of God church in Philipsburg, PA. He soon became interested in television and began broadcasting programs from his church. In 1958, Wilkerson was inspired to move to New York City to minister to seven teenagers on trial for murder. Though thwarted, Wilkerson soon began Teen Challenge in order to evangelize urban street gangs. In 1966, Wilkerson established Teen Challenge Bible Institute to train reformed gang members for Christian ministry. In 1972, Wilkerson founded World Challenge. His book, *The Vision* (1974), recounts the "spirit-led" vision of the endtimes Wilkerson claims to have received from an angelic emissary of God.

-----(ed.). *David Wilkerson Presents the End Times New Testament.* Chappaqua, NY: Chosen Books; Old Tappan, NJ: Revell, 1975.

-----*The Vision.* New York: Pillar Books, 1974; New York: Spire Books, 1975.

Winrod, Gerald Burton (1900-1957) A fundamentalist minister, writer, and lecturer. Winrod founded Defenders of the Faith during the 1920s to combat the teaching of evolutionary theory in the public schools. His *Defenders Magazine* sought to combat anti-Christian teachings and the spread of Communism in the United States and the world. His interest in the role of the Jews in the Last Days led him to believe in a worldwide Jewish conspiracy. His 1933 book, *The Hidden Hand: The Protocols and the Coming Superman,* charged that Jewish conspiracy was directly responsible for the First World War, the Bolshevik Revolution, and even the Great Depression. Winrod's praise of Hitler in the 1930s and his own anti-Semitic views created a stir. In 1944, Winrod was brought to trial before the federal grand jury under charges of sedition. After eight months of testimony, a mistrial was declared and Winrod was released. Undeterred by criticism, Winrod tenaciously held to his conspiracy theories until his death in 1957.

-----*Antichrist and the Atomic Bomb.* Wichita, KS: Defender Publishers, 1945.

-----*The Hidden Hand: The Protocols and the Coming Superman.* Wichita, KS: Defender Publishers, 1933.

-----*Hitler in Prophecy*. Wichita, KS: Defender Publishers, 1933.

-----*Mussolini and the Second Coming of Christ* (9th ed.). Wichita, KS: Defender Publishers, n.d.

Young, Edward J. (1907-1968) An Orthodox Presbyterian. Young was professor of Old Testament at Westminster Seminary, 1936-1968. From 1950 until his death, Young also taught at Winona Lake School of Theology. In 1956, he was moderator of the Orthodox Presbyterian Church.

-----*The Messianic Prophecies of Daniel*. Grand Rapids, MI: Eerdmans, 1954.

-----*The Prophecy of Daniel*. Grand Rapids, MI: Wm B. Eerdmans Publishing Co., 1949.

SUMMARY AND CONCLUSIONS

The primary focus of this book has been on the literature of popular eschatology in America within the mainstream evangelical tradition. Taken as a whole, this body of literature is not only vast, but theologically and eschatologically diverse. Such a broad spectrum of views on the endtimes makes inferences difficult, if not impossible, to draw.

But one common aspect of this literature that makes generalization possible is the interpretive assumptions made by the authors, that is, their common frame of reference. To millennialists, both sections of the Bible -- "Old" and "New" Testaments -- are two halves of the same sacred story that together point to the same ending. To millennialists, then, the Bible as a whole is not only a collection of sacred writings that document the developing religious consciousness of the Hebrews (Old Testament), nor is it holy scripture meant simply to teach people how to live a life of love (New Testament). Rather, the Bible is a blueprint of history, a history made significant by the life and death of Jesus Christ and a history that will culminate in the second coming and personal reign of Christ on Earth.

For premillennialists, the key to history, and the prophetic reading of it, is the Jewish people and the salvation of Israel as a nation. As Samuel Kellogg argued over a century ago, the prophecies of the Bible "make all else to culminate and terminate in the return of the scattered nation to the land of their fathers, and their conversion to the faith in the Pierced One as their promised Messiah" (1883:218-219). Nearly a hundred years later, John Wesley White put it more succinctly: "The *sine qua non* of scriptural prophecy is the people of Israel" (1971:133).

With this interpretive assumption in mind, I have divided the literature of popular eschatology into several classes, separating out the largest and most prevalent and pervasive grouping for consideration, namely premillennial. In turn, I have divided premillennial literature into ten periods, from roughly the time of Napoleon to the present, each period reflecting the premillennial interest in world events as they relate to Israel.

As this literature shows, millenarians believe that current events shed light on the future, a future prophesied in the Bible. In each section, I have emphasized both the events of the respective periods along with the concomitant developments within the premillennial subculture.

In this concluding section, I intend to address a final question that begs consideration: How does the conviction that Christ may return "today" remain convincing in spite of persistent disappointment? My answer will appear to beg the question slightly but it is meant to preface three possible reasons why premillennialists hold on to their views in the face of continual disconfirmation.

Perhaps one way to explain why premillennialists hold tenaciously to the conviction that Christ will return "soon, perhaps today," has little to do with the future and everything to do with the "here and now," that is, with present circumstances and current concerns. Perhaps the question might better be framed this way: What need does the literature of popular eschatology seek to fill or what problems does this literature attempt to address?

After a closer reading of these works, what we find is that "prophecy" and its fulfillment are not actually the primary concerns of the premillennialists; that is, the fulfillment of prophecy is not in itself the major concern. True, "prophecy" is a major preoccupation of these millennialists but only as it relates to issues of greater concern for them. These central concerns include the historical reliability of the Bible, the virgin birth and atoning death of Christ, the supremacy of the Christian religion, and, more broadly, the survival of Western civilization or Christian culture in the face of modern secular society. As tensions with modern society heightened, these concerns became increasingly central to the evangelical premillennial subculture -- concerns that later shaped the fundamentalist movement, as witnessed by the publication of *The Fundamentals* (1910-1915). "Prophecy," might then be thought of as millennialism's weapon against modern science and secularism in that it became a means, in fact, the chief means by which premillennialists of all stripes fought, and still fight, against the erosion of confidence in Biblical authority. Indeed, it is upon the reliability of the Bible that the whole system hangs.

We might chart the rise of prophetic speculation and "proof-texting" beginning from the time of Napoleon and the first archaeological discoveries that began to cast doubt on the historical reliability of Bible history. Viewed this way, one might make the case that the emergence of millennial expectation among British and American Protestants in the nineteenth century and its growing popularity among conservative Protestants in the twentieth century were largely the results of the uneasiness evangelicals and fundamentalists experienced in the face of critical scientific work, the results of which cut to the heart of Biblical reliability (cf., Sandeen 1970:103-114). The turn, then, to prophecy and an apocalyptic vision of the "immediate" future is not an indication of millenarian disinterest in the modern world, as some have suggested, but a very real attempt to parry challenges to their traditional Biblical worldview. The hope for an apocalyptic tomorrow and predictions of its imminence are perhaps an attempt to mitigate the deleterious effects of scientific naturalism on their supernatural cosmology. Put differently, the turn to a prophetic reading of history is a way to make credible a worldview -- the Christian worldview -- that had increasingly been losing both its credibility and relevance in an ever more secular and scientific world. In short, prophetic speculation is the attempt to make the Bible relevant to the modern world without accepting the findings of the natural sciences and without adopting the methods of the social sciences.

One reason for premillennialism's problem with modern science is its own literal reading of the Bible, to the point of taking even the most obvious figures of speech literally. John Walvoord's comment in his book, *The Nations in Prophecy*, exemplifies this literalistic misreading of apocalyptic imagery: "Prophecy must be fulfilled and we don't know of an event in History which corresponds to these utterances of Ezekiel [in chapters 38 and 39]" (1967:52). The assumption Walvoord and other millennialists have made is that if an apocalyptic symbol or Biblical imagery does not match history, it thus becomes a literal historical event to be fulfilled sometime in the near future.

This overly literalistic approach to the Bible has proven quite treacherous to the cognitive consonance of millennialists throughout the past century. It is difficult to hold a firm position in the face of disconfirmation without eventually giving in to reason, or without becoming a thoroughgoing fideist. The hazard of a literalistic reading of the Bible to millennialists, both past and present, observes Sandeen, is that it "tied the future of millenarianism to the maintenance of an inerrant and infallible text." Far from adapting their views to modern scholarship so as to avoid the hazards of overliteralism, the millennialist position grew more and more rigid over time. As a result, they found themselves caught in a cognitive bind. As Sandeen relates their quandary: "The millenarians could not give up belief in the single-level, totally divine document postulated in their theory of interpretation without sacrificing their faith" (1970:112). Interestingly, millenarians have been able to navigate the reefs and shallows of prophetic disconfirmation with remarkable facility and finesse, to such an extent, to change the metaphor, that their central refrain -- history and prophecy prove the Bible -- has been the carillon call for premillennialists since the late nineteenth century.

Several references from their writings should suffice to illustrate the millenarian argument that the link of human history with divine prophecy is the touchstone of the Bible. Reflecting on the precarious history of the Jews, Samuel Kellogg concluded that "we may, therefore, truly say that the Jews present an argument for the supernatural inspiration of the Christian Scripture" (1883:ix-x). In his book, *The Wonders of Prophecy*, John Urquhart (1906) compiled what he called a "book of Christian evidences." Prophecy's fulfillment, he told his readers, points inevitably to the certainty of future fulfillments. Urquhart looked to prophecy to support the threefold purpose of his book: to prove the Bible, God, and the testimony of Jesus.

In his commentary on the Seventy Weeks of Daniel, Alva McClain remarked that "the prophecy of the Seventy Weeks has *an immense evidential value as a witness to the truth of Scripture*," for in its fulfillment, "we have an unanswerable argument for the divine inspiration of the Bible." McClain then took aim at science and critical thought: "This great prophecy is *the impregnable rock upon which all naturalistic theories of prophecy are shattered*" (1940:5-6). Several decades later, C. M. Ward asserted that "fulfilled prophecy encourages us to believe that the same God will fulfill unfulfilled prophecy" (1975:22). Later, Ward offered a challenge: "If you doubt the accuracy of Bible prophecy, read the history of the Jews. *Could it have been fulfilled any more expressly?*," he asked rhetorically (1975:56).

In *The Late Great Planet Earth*, Hal Lindsey takes his readers on a tour of fulfilled prophecies in human history as they relate to the nation of Israel, the "paramount prophetic sign" (1970:43). To Lindsey, however, the veracity of the Bible is of utmost importance, modern Jewish history forming the basis for his argument. Writes Lindsey, in his typically matter-of-fact style: "Some theologians of the liberal school still insist that prophecy has no literal meaning for today and that it cannot be taken seriously. It is difficult to understand this view if one carefully weighs the case of Israel's rebirth as a nation" (1970:48-50). Lastly, Tim LaHaye, author of *The Beginning of the End*, likewise explores the prophetic implications of the reestablishment of Israel as a nation. Pointing to the Jewish state, LaHaye confidently proclaims that "what skeptics classify as a coincidence is in reality an infallible sign of divine authorship of the Scriptures" (1972:43). As before, history proves prophecy and prophecy, in turn, proves the Bible.

But the original question still remains: Why this enduring conviction in the face of renewed disconfirmation? With the above discussion in mind, I will now attempt an answer. First, much of the impetus and drive exhibited by premillennialists comes from the ambiguity of history, an ambiguity that leaves a lot of room for a supernatural interpretation of it. The problem comes, however, in the way premillennialists link prophecy and history. Prophecy, they believe, gives history a supernatural meaning and thus, they argue, supports a supernatural view of history. This type of circular reasoning does not seem to bother premillennialists, but then it should not. History, they believe, is made significant only in its connection to Israel and its covenant relationship to God. The logic of the premillennial system, though circular, follows from their basic assumptions about the meaning of history. Let me explain.

To a great extent, "History" is an invention of the reflective mind in search of meaningful patterns to explain the course of certain events -- natural and human -- as well as the importance of those events to individuals and societies or their relation to other events both past and future. "History" is a concept, therefore, not a concrete entity or thing. As a result, some scholars would argue, "History" can be constructed, reconstructed, deconstructed, and even preconstructed to suit the agenda or views of those writing it.

In the case of premillennialism, "History" proves them right; but it is a "History" largely constructed through the selection of events that confirm their assumptions about history generally. The "Bible Reading," for example, is a way to construct history by stringing together Bible verses with little or no regard for their contexts or their authors's intentions. Bible verses, historical incidences, and current events are jigsawed together by millennialists into a pattern that seems to defy and often does defy common sense. The logic of the premillennial hermeneutic, however, is within the system itself, not outside of it. Thus, one becomes quite baffled, to put it mildly, by an interpretive system that allows egregious hermeneutical flights of fancy, such as the belief that *Meshech* and *Gomer* in Ezekiel 38:1-6 are modern day *Moscow* and *Germany*, and the assumption that "birds hovering over Jerusalem to protect it" in Isaiah 31:5 is an allusion to British biplanes liberating Palestine during the First World War, and the belief that Jesus' comment that in the Last Days "great signs shall there be from heaven" (Luke 21:11), means just that, literal letters in the sky warning humanity: "Repent, or Else!" Their fellow premillennialists might also marvel at these fascinating interpretations, but for altogether different reasons. As before, these are the more colorful examples of premillennial excesses, excesses that tend to overshadow the more scholarly and balanced eschatological works within the evangelical tradition.[1]

A second explanation for why premillennialism persists stems from its conviction that before Christ returns the world will grow increasingly worse -- socially, politically, economically, environmentally, and so on. On this score, premillennialists have been quite successful. World events have tended to confirm their belief in the inevitable decline and destruction of civilization. Indeed, wars, social upheavals, economic depressions, and the "greenhouse effect" have become key components of their apocalyptic vision of the endtimes.

The last and perhaps the most plausible reason of the three is millennialism's correct reading of historical currents that resulted in the return of Jews to Palestine and the creation of a Jewish state in their ancient homeland. These two events have given credence to the premillennial interpretation of the Bible for a host of conservative Protestants, and many others. In sum, though all other predictions fail, millenarians can point to these two fulfillments to reassure themselves and to buttress their faith in the literal future fulfillment of the Bible's prophetic and apocalyptic passages.

---

1. Perhaps one reason why scholars tend to focus on the "lunatic fringe" of popular millennialism might be to avoid asking the inevitable and nagging question: What if the premillennialists are right? In this text, I have attempted to present premillennial views as evenhandedly as possible, though not at the expense of critical analysis. Even so, if it should turn out that the premillennialists are right, I, for my part, have read a sufficient amount of their literature to know when to plead for mercy, hoping that God will be magnanimous and overlook my amillennial upbringing.

INDEX

A

Adams, Jay E., 2041
Adams, John Q., 670-671
Adkins, E., 259
Alderman, Paul R., Jr., 1198,
1375
Allis, Oswald T., 2042-2043
Allwood, Philip, 73
Alnor, William M., 1
An American Layman, 74
Andersen, Loren E., 1497
Anderson, John A., 672
Anderson, Robert, 260, 381-383,
1498
Andrews, Samuel J., 384
Angley, Ernest W., 1199
Ankerberg, John, 1804
Anstey, B., 1805-1806
Appelman, Hyman J., 1046-
1047, 1200-1201
Armerding, Carl, 1376-1377,
1499
Arnaud, R. K., 385
Ash, Edward, 75
Askwith, Charles, 1202
Atkinson, B.F., 1048
Auchincloss, William S., 386-
387
Austin, E. L. C., 1807
Austin, John S., 388-389

B

Bacchiocchi, Samuele, 2044

Baillie, William, 390
Baines, T. B., 263
Baker, Caleb J., 391
Baker, Charles F., 1500
Baker, Ernest, 673-674
Baker, Nelson B., 2045
Baker, William A., 147
Baker, William W., 1808
Baldinger, Albert H., 2046
Ball, C. T., 675-676
Banki, Judith, 2
Baring-Gold, Sabine, 392
Barkun, Michael, 4-5
Barndollar, Walter, 1378
Barnhart, David R., 1809
Barnhouse, Donald Grey, 1501,
2128
Baron, David, 393-395, 677
Barsoum, F., 1810
Barton, G. A., 396
Barton, Harold E., 678-679
Bartz, Ulysses S., 397
Bass, Clarence B., 3
Bates, Leon, 1811
Bates, William H., 398
Baughman, Ray E., 1379
Bauman, Louis S., 680-682,
1049-1050
Bauman, Paul, 1380
Baxter, Michael P., 148-151,
264-266, 2129
Baxter, Trvin, Jr., 1812
Beale, 152
Becker, Abraham A., 1203-1204
Beckwith, George D., 1051
Bedell, Gregory T., 76